Eric

9. v. 07

OLD MEN OUGHT TO BE EXPLORERS

The Journal of a Journey

A catalogue record of this book is available from the British Library

First Edition: November 2006

ISBN: 1-84375-277-8

To order additional copies of this book please visit:
http://www.upso.co.uk/ericjames

Published by: UPSO Ltd
5 Stirling Road, Castleham Business Park,
St Leonards-on-Sea, East Sussex TN38 9NW United Kingdom
Tel: 01424 853349 Fax: 0870 191 3991
Email: info@upso.co.uk Web: http://www.upso.co.uk

OLD MEN OUGHT TO BE EXPLORERS

The Journal of a Journey

Eric James

UPSO

BY THE SAME AUTHOR

The Double Cure (1957)
Odd Man Out? (1962)
A life of Bishop John A T Robinson - Scholar, Pastor, Prophet
(Collins 1987)
Judge Not - A Selection of Sermons preached in Gray's Inn
Chapel 1978-1988 (Christian Action 1989)
Collected Thoughts: Fifty Scripts for BBC's *Thought for the Day*
(Christian Action 1990)
A Last Eccentric. A Symposium concerning the Reverend
Canon F A Simpson - Historian, Preacher and
Eccentric (Christian Action 1991)
Word Over All: Forty Sermons (SPCK 1992)
The Voice Said, Cry: Forty Sermons (SPCK 1994)
A Time to Speak: Forty Sermons (SPCK 1997)
In Season, Out of Season: Forty Sermons 1996-1997
(SCM Press 1999)
Who is This?: Holy Week Meditations and Other Sermons
(Continuum 2001)
Collected Thoughts: BBC Radio 4 *Thought for the Day*
Broadcasts (Continuum 2002)
The House of My Friends: Memories and Reflections
(Continuum 2003)
The Voice of This Calling (Continuum 2005)

To Geoffrey Court
and all the friends who have helped me recover from the
health problems which beset me in March 2006.

CONTENTS

Postscript after my Fall
Two Sermons preached by Eric James

ACKNOWLEDGEMENTS

My thanks are due to Roger Tamplin for the cover photograph; to Jane Spurr for typing my manuscript and to Gwen Rymer who typed my journal in 1972 when it arrived from foreign parts, and despatched it to my friends. The conch shell that illustrates the cover was presented to me by the boys of the Litogohira Senior Primary School, on the island of Santa Isobel in the Solomon Islands, when I visited them on my 1972 journey.

The extracts from Bertrand Russell's *Autobiography* are reprinted with permission of the copyright holders, the Bertrand Russell Peace Foundation Ltd as well as the Publishers, Taylor and Francis.

PREFACE

In 1971, I was forty-six. A friend called it 'the year of your mid-life crisis'. But the crisis wasn't primarily mine. I was standing by someone else, and couldn't retain my integrity and not do so. Several of the others involved in that sad situation are now dead, so it would not be right to go into detail.

It was my good friend David Sheppard, then Bishop of Woolwich, who said to me: "You need to get right away". So I did.

I kept a journal of my six months away, and headed it *Old Men Ought to be Explorers* - from Eliot's *East Coker*. I felt strangely old when I set out, and that I was on a journey of exploration.

It wasn't only that I was visiting foreign parts, where I had not been before. As Eliot continues:

> Here or there does not matter
> We must be still and still moving.

When I was away, I thought little about what was happening in England. Wherever I was - Nigeria, Uganda, Zambia, South Africa, Australia, New Zealand, Fiji, Vanuatu, the Solomon Islands, New Guinea, Singapore, Hong Kong, India, Sri Lanka - were all so engrossing.

When I returned, Robert Runcie - by then Bishop of St Albans

- asked me to be Canon Missioner there. In fact, I had twenty more years of unretired existence ahead of me - in St Albans; as Director of the charity, Christian Action; as Preacher to Gray's Inn; and involved in the Archbishop's Commission on Urban Priority Areas - which produced - twenty years ago! - the Report *Faith in the City*.

Whenever - infrequently - I have taken the journal from the shelves, I have been reminded that what I had written in 1972 is now history - 'time past' - for 'time marches on'! But it is also biography. And I have found myself thinking "There may be something here which I should perhaps share - maybe, indeed, publish."

It was obvious immediately that another dozen or so chapters could be added - but not by me! - to show how the situation in each country that I had visited had changed - in most cases, dramatically.

I decided I should leave what I had written as history - and publish it - now I have reached four score years - before it is too late!

The original journal was despatched to many friends, and I treasure the letters I received in response. Bishop John Robinson, for instance, then Dean of Trinity College, Cambridge, wrote on April 19 1972: "Both Ruth and I have enormously appreciated your marvellous letters, and the impressions they have conveyed have been extremely vivid".

So I publish this journal in the hope that it may encourage others - in quite different situations - to be 'explorers' - and I do so in thankfulness for John Robinson, David Sheppard, Robert Runcie and others - several of whom are named in the journal - 'whom we love but see no longer'.

Preface

I have simply added this Preface and, as an Epilogue, the letter I wrote recently in thanks to my sixteen year-old great nephew, Charlie Rowland, just returned from China.

I am grateful to my erstwhile secretary, Mrs. Jane Spurr, who has again prepared another manuscript of mine for the press with her continuing skill and application.

Eric James 2005

An explanatory note from Jane Spurr

It is necessary to add a word of explanation at this point. Because of the health problems which beset him in early 2006 and to which he refers in the sermon which ends this volume, Eric James asked me to oversee the publication of this book on his behalf. I have endeavoured to carry out his wishes 'to the letter' but if there are any errors or omissions, I trust I will be forgiven!

Jane Spurr 2006

Stage 1: Nigeria

December 28th 1971

I've wanted lately to add one more definition to the list of definitions of man: "Man is a good-bye saying animal." Not only tonight but for several weeks the shadow of this good-bye to my friends in England for six months has coloured everything a dark grey-blue. Now the parting has been made. (I suppose it's just because Tolstoy and Dostoievsky are writing about what is central to human beings that so often they write of farewells at railway stations, and just because what is central to human beings is so painful, that, so often, to make the pain bearable, we prefer to have stories told us of animals endowed with what is uniquely human - "'O Rat' said Mole, his eyes shining with unutterable love.")

The farewell at Victoria foreshadowed the chaos of the next hours (and was all of a piece with the chaos there had been in getting a visa into Nigeria). The instruction to report at 8.00 pm was an hour and a half early; but it provided time for a final happy meal with friends. The British Caledonian VC 10 was delayed leaving Gatwick for half an hour while a window was replaced, but we were airborne by 11.30 pm, and I was toying with a now superfluous supper (salmon and steak) at midnight. The vodka and lime was not superfluous!

December 29th 1971

Most of the night I read a remarkable biography of Albert

Schweitzer by George Marshall and David Poling. It was entirely the right book for the moment. Indeed, as we touched down, I was reading the chapter headed 'Arrival in Africa'.

It had become clear that the estimated time of arrival I had been given - 7.40 am - was nonsense, and that I should miss the connection from Lagos to Port Harcourt scheduled to leave at 9.30 am. When we landed, the chaos was complete. The dust-carrying wind from the Sahara, the Harmattan, had closed down Lagos airport for a while; but I was told the so-called 9.30 am Lagos-Port Harcourt 'plane in any case did not depart until 12.30 pm. There was only one slight difficulty: I wasn't on the passenger list! - and the 'plane was completely full. It had in fact been overbooked by about a dozen places. My first experience of the effects of bribery and corruption. (No doubt I shall learn!) It was curious to find oneself in Lagos, one of a group of haggling passengers of different nationalities - American, Arab, Nigerian, Danish, British, etc. - in a sweltering and crowded booking office, violently demanding a seat on the 'plane. Two people failed to turn up for their booked seats, and I eventually got one of them. (But where are the ten?)

Schweitzer had helped me to keep some of my composure whilst I waited to see whether there was a ticket. I particularly liked this paragraph:

> "Goethe became even more personally meaningful to him in other ways. The mind of Schweitzer - penetrating, all-encompassing, constantly wrestling with great issues - functioned best when it could personalise intellectual concerns. It was through people that such concerns came alive and acquired vitality for him. Goethe had asked the question in the Sorrows of Werther. 'Must those things that make a man happy necessarily become the source of his misery?' Schweitzer's entire life offered an affirmative

answer to this question. It was true of Schweitzer as a pensive, introspective boy; as a student.... The renunciation of Europe that helped to bring him to Africa as a mature man also was a partially affirmative answer to that same question.....Further, the joys of accomplishment in scholarship led to Schweitzer's estrangement from the Christian Church he dearly loved. Finally, his love for his wife, Helene, faithful to the end, however fulfilling or unfulfilling, brought with it years of misery as they were separated by his mission and her broken health."

I hadn't realised before that, after the first World War, Schweitzer had a breakdown and depression that took several years - and the help of a Swiss psychoanalyst, Oscar Pfister - to recover from.

I eventually arrived at Port Harcourt at 2.25 pm. The Revd Martin Wright, Dean of Port Harcourt Christian Council Project - about which more later - came to meet me and take me to his home, for my time in Nigeria. I had never met him before, so his hospitality was a tremendous act of generosity. (He and Roger Royle are great friends and Roger had commended me to him. Martin was Industrial Chaplain in Peterborough, and had been out here only since last August.)

There was time before dusk only for a quick visit to the town and a walk in the garden. In the town we called on an electrician in his home - a three storey slum by English standards; but it was marvellous to be amongst immediately friendly Africans with innumerable near-naked children. We also called at the prison. How much one learns - and receives - simply by looking at people's faces: and exchanging smiles as a fellow human being. The garden around Martin's house has towering oil, coconut and raffia palms, mango trees, banana, lemon, lime, grapefruit, orange, balsam, acacia, rubber, hibiscus, frangi-pani, bougainvillea and paw-paw. It is like a dark green sultry Rousseau painting, penetrated by shafts of sunlight that make the blossom and the flowers - the canna lilies, for instance - bright against the darkness. The garden is absolutely still, but lizards abound - some green, some red-headed.

The first birds I saw in W Africa were white egrets - like herons, with golden bills and golden plumes on their crowns - and vultures, which sit hunched up on the roofs, and then soar on motionless wings until they make a sudden evil dive.

In the evening, Martin and I baptised my travel Scrabble and played the tape recording of *Cosi fan tutte* I had brought with me. And so to bed in W Africa, at midnight, to sleep under mosquito nets, an uninterrupted eight hours.

December 30th 1971
Shortly after breakfast (there is nothing to touch fresh limes, fresh grapefruit, fresh pineapple!) three Ibos appeared in the garden, seeking work. They had finished school, and were qualified, but were unemployed - because they were the defeated Ibos. Although there had been a great deal of reconciliation since the war, the hostility towards the Ibo remains. Much Ibo property, for instance, is still in the hands of others. A little later, we went into the market, a vast concourse of stalls packed with buyers and sellers, with all sorts of goods for sale. I took my first photographs in W Africa.

Martin then took me to look at various bits of property belonging to the Christian Council Project. The first was - once - the Seamen's Mission, on the dock side. The swimming pool was empty, but alive with lizards. The library, billiards room, bar, restaurant and chapel were also derelict, waiting to be 'reconditioned', and for Martin to open them up after post-war repair - with the aid of the Missions to Seamen.

Then we went to some property of the Project now occupied by squatters, which also has a chicken rearing project of the Christian Council of Nigeria based on it - to encourage people to keep their own chickens and rear them well. This property also has considerable possibilities.

Nearby was Diobu, a slum suburb of 100,000 people or so. The people live one family to a room, for the most part, with no main drainage or sewerage, and no running water. It was almost impossible to take a car down the streets, the potholes and craters were too bad. The open drains were covered with an evil green slime, but again, wherever we went there were smiles to welcome us. It was here that the Project ran a Community Centre particularly concerned with health work for mothers and children and infants, with home-making and family planning advice. This will soon be opened.

We had a look at some property of the Project which Michelin have temporarily rented after paying for their post-war repair, and then at property which the army has temporarily requisitioned. There was also a girls trade school connected with the Project.

Clearly in its first years - 1963-1967 - the Project was a great piece of Christian initiative. (Ian Taylor from South London Industrial Mission - and Peter Duncan, who had been in Battersea - were associated with it - and Robert Gibson was going to it from SLIM when the war broke out. The moving spirit was Michael Mann, now Industrial Adviser in Norwich, and Bishop Afonya.) What was a booming oil port, with many new industries - Michelin, United Africa, Shell-BP, Heineken Beers, etc etc - was a specially appropriate place for Industrial Mission, seminars between management and labour, orientation courses for Europeans coming to W Africa etc. But the Project was not only concerned with Industry, there was the Social

Welfare at Diobu and elsewhere, and an equal involvement in education, (forty evening classes drawing on the skills of the wives of Europeans, who found thereby an acceptable way of passing on their skills to W Africa.). The Project ran a primary school, but now the Government has taken over all schools. There was also a research committee, seeking openings for people in industry. (A walk through Diobu gives a clear indication of how few of the unskilled are employed.)

I have the impression that what has been done here in the name of Christ is magnificent. (It was supported by the World Council of Churches, by several Anglican Dioceses - Manchester, Winchester, W Massachusetts - and by several other Christian bodies.) Martin Wright has come here to set to rights property damaged, looted and occupied in three years of war and to present a scheme for the future development of the Project - in terms of work, scope, staff, manpower, buildings, equipment and finance.

It may be worth while summarising how Martin envisages the work developing.

The work could be divided into that which will require the direct involvement of the Project (which in the present financial and skilled labour situation of Nigeria will be much more often appropriate than in England today) and that of only indirect involvement.

Direct:
(1) Diobu Day Care Centre for fifty pre-school children - referrals by Government. There are many war orphans and war widows. School fees have to be paid after three years of schooling. There would be the kind of person who could never afford school fees. (There are many such who do not get any education.) Could there be some kind of 'adoption'

of children by people in England? The staff needed would be three Social Workers, Cook, Domestic Staff, a Nurse. Above all, someone to be willing to live in the slums of Diobu. *Who?* The problems of living there would be huge - of health, theft etc. Even the work of visiting raises problems. Could anyone married do it?

(2) The 'Anchor Inn' Missions to Seamen project has real possibilities. The ships that call here are mostly regular callers. Port Harcourt has so little otherwise to offer sailors - except prostitutes galore, which is inevitable in a city of poverty and unemployment.

(3) A youth work centre at St Andrew's - which could *train* people for youth work. (St Andrew's is the property near Diobu which the squatters have at the moment.)

(4) There is such an absence of skilled workers that a pre-apprenticeship training centre in craft skills is vital. (£100,000?!) It would need skilled instructors. It would work by short courses of 2-3 weeks. This would be to train an elite. The Church should also therefore try and set up!

(5) A vocational training centre for the disabled. If the able-bodied find it so difficult to get work, how much more the disabled. The Centre could be concerned with every aspect of what it means to be a disabled person in this kind of society.

(6) The need for evening classes in this country is tremendous - and a library for the insatiable thirst of those willing to read and educate themselves (in a land in which humidity soon ruins books and in which the facilities for home study are often negligible).

(7) There needs to be Clergy and Student Training in Industrial Relations and Industrial Mission.

(8) The prison - at which at the moment there is no work for prisoners - needs to be a Project concern. There is no place to keep boys on remand, or any Borstal. The Project could begin a scheme of prison visiting and counselling, and care for prisoners' families. Again: the Project could be concerned with every aspect of 'prison' in this kind of society.

(9) A Psychiatric Social Worker is urgently needed to be concerned with the mentally ill - there is no separate provision for them in Port Harcourt. Those certified go to prison!

All these come under the heading of *direct* concerns of the Project - as yet just Martin's vision. Without cash, it will all remain a vision. But the *indirect* concerns, though they can be summarised more briefly, will be increasingly important. Turning Christ Church, Port Harcourt, into a Centre from which there will emerge a continuing informed debate about the standards, values and goals of this society, and how they can be changed, achieved etc. From Christ Church there could be a creative chaplaincy of (a) Industry (b) Educational establishments (c) the major institutions of Port Harcourt (d) the systems and organisations on which the institutions depend (e) civic and political life.

This is how Martin's commission to spend six months carefully reviewing what should be the second stage, the post-war stage of the Project, is taking shape at the moment.

In the early evening, a young Scottish farmer from Perthshire suddenly walked in. He had been to his sister's wedding in

Northern Nigeria and was spending some weeks traversing Nigeria as best he could. I admired his courage and his simple goodness, and equally admired the way Martin immediately received him, gave him a drink, and supper, and a bed for the night.

December 31st 1971

After we had taken the Scottish farmer to where he could get a 'bus out of Port Harcourt, (a mini-bus crammed tight with Africans and merchandise), and had been to the bank and the bookshop, Martin and I had a quiet day, spending some time talking over the Project.

As New Year's Eve drew on I found my spirits lowering for the first time since I had left England - as thoughts of one's friends in England spending their New Year took hold of me. I went into the garden and tried to photograph a palm tree against the bright moonlight. I doubt if it will come out! At midnight, all the ships' sirens in port sounded, and we gathered with neighbouring African families in the garden. It was an hour ahead of England's New Year, so that, when we came in from the garden, we were able to get fairly clearly the Watch Night Service from Westminster Abbey on the BBC Overseas Service. Edward Carpenter gave a very moving message on Nicodemus ("Can a man be born again when he is *old?*") Martin and I might have become very nostalgic and morose, had not the Africans begun dancing in the garden, using a plastic washing-up bowl as a drum. They improvised words and harmonies as they - we! - danced and sang "Happy New Year"!

January 1st 1972

The Minister of Health of the State (Rivers State - Nigeria was divided into twelve States in 1967) had invited us to lunch. It was a fascinating occasion. The Minister, an Oxford graduate, formerly a barrister, has a wife who has an English father (born in Salford - Manchester Grammar School - now Professor of Mathematics Singapore University: Professor Oppenheimer) who was present at the party, and an American mother. The Minister's children and his brother and sisters - beautiful Nigerians, beautifully dressed - were there; a Yoruba police officer; several oil people of different nationalities; a bank manager and his wife; a young woman social worker, straight out of Somerset Maugham; former civil servants back here on holiday, etc. I learnt a lot. I had time to, as the party began at one and broke up at five!

January 2nd 1972

This first Sunday in W Africa has been memorable beyond words. (It is difficult to believe that last Sunday was the day after Christmas and that I was in London.)

At 10.00 am, I preached at Christ Church, Port Harcourt. It is a joint Anglican, Methodist and Presbyterian Church. Martin thought it a good idea to use the Methodist Covenant Service - in the context of Holy Communion - for this first Sunday of the New Year. It was very moving indeed. The Church is fairly new, and is set amongst flowering jacaranda trees, loaded at the moment with purple blossom. (Opposite the Church is the shell of the Kingsway supermarket, destroyed during the war.) There were about 300 people present, 100 of them children. The colours of Nigerian 'Sunday best' made the congregation look like a black Ascot, ablaze with glorious colour, fabrics and designs. The organist didn't turn up, so at the last moment I was pressed into service. If you want to sweat, pedal a harmonium on a boiling hot Sunday morning in W Africa, so as to produce enough noise to lead 300 people!

At the heart of the Covenant Service is that astonishing prayer of Wesley's - which I found particularly powerful here:

I am no longer my own, but Thine.
Put me to what Thou wilt,
Rank me with whom Thou wilt;
Put me to doing,
Put me to suffering;
Let me be employed for Thee or laid aside for Thee;
Let me be full, let me be empty;
Let me have all things, let me have nothing.
I freely and heartily yield all things to Thy pleasure and
     disposal....

In the afternoon, we - Martin, Sarah (the Somerset Maugham
Social Worker) and I - drove out to Okrika, an island which is
about five miles as the crow flies, but fifteen by road and water.
On the way, Sarah took me into a village - where we picked up
a little girl now restored to a community, who had been living
in Port Harcourt orphanage - and an old lady took me into her
one room mud hut. The poverty and simplicity of the village
was extreme, but we were received with joy by the children
and grown-ups. The island of Okrika is reached from the
mainland by travelling in a dug-out canoe. A teenage Nigerian,
sitting high up at one end of the boat, paddling furiously with
one paddle, gets you across for a shilling. It all seemed very
precarious! The water is half a mile or so wide. On the other
side is a poverty stricken fishing village. We arrived just as a
good many people were going to their various churches for
Evensong. The main church had been badly damaged in the War.
We went to the Archdeacon's house - he is also the baker. His
wife was a woman of great dignity, charm and joy, who was
fostering several children. Our visit provided quite an 'occasion'
for the crowds of village children. We were paddled back across
the water just as the evening sun was sinking like a red ball
behind the palm trees. Martin thinks the Project should do
some work on this island.

In the evening, we visited the home of two Nigerians in the Shell compound. She had been a nurse in Southampton. He had done a degree in Southampton University. He is Secretary to the Project. Again: quiet dignity, warmth and charm - and highly intelligent. We discussed Nigeria's problems all the evening. Miraculously, as a family, they had come through the war, but from their lips, and from others, one gradually builds up a picture of the terrible ordeal of civil war, of the three years nightmare through which they have passed.

January 3rd 1972
Another ever memorable day.

Martin and I drove to see Benjamin Nwankiti, the young Bishop of Owerri with whom I had made friends at the Lambeth Conference in 1968. When I met him then he was in great distress. He was separated from his wife and family, and Owerri, in Biafra, was in imminent danger of capture. I saw him most days at the Conference, and I had promised to visit him in Nigeria as soon as I could. But all my letters to him when he went back to Biafra, until the end of the War, were returned to me. Seeing Benjamin again was really my first objective in coming to Nigeria.

We drove to him - about 100 miles away - along pot-holed roads, with the effects of the War still only too plain. The drive was very beautiful, through tropical woodland. It is still territory virtually occupied by the army. But, all the way, the people, when they catch sight of a white man in a car, wave, and the children smile and shout out their welcome - naked children carrying huge loads on their heads.

It was marvellous to see Benjamin again. He has been ill, but he was full of love and joy today; and it was so good to meet his wife and children, and his brother and his wife - married on

New Year's Day. It is odd how much of a natural 'brother' to you some people are, though colour, race and nation may separate you. (The nonsense of apartheid!) When we all sat down to lunch, Benjamin said a very loving grace, gathering us all in. He then said suddenly: "It is good to see your mischievous grin again!" I said: "That makes two of us, my Lord!" Everyone laughed. They know only too well that *he* is mischievous.

In the afternoon, we talked over the problems of the Diocese in the aftermath of war. Some had felt in the war God was on their side, and defeat in the war had reduced them to despair. But Benjamin thinks that the suffering of defeat has enabled them to learn things that could never have been learnt in victory. The 'Bishop Cockin Church Centre', for clergy and laity training, has just been opened. The diocese has been divided into twelve zones to work as twelve teams. It was clear that Benjamin was giving the theological and pastoral lead that the situation requires - pressing the Church to participate in the works of compassion and rehabilitation that needy area requires; thinking out afresh the relation between Church and State; thinking out the role of the Christian teacher when all schools have been taken away by the Government (and £176,000 in the bank at the end of the war commandeered); preparing to meet the challenge of an increasingly urban ministry; making sure that a Christian word is said publicly and powerfully on things like Public Execution as Punishment for Armed Robberies. The theological college has just re-opened - combined Anglican, Methodist and Presbyterian - and young men are coming forward in good numbers as well as there being a new scheme for training older men.

I felt - as I felt when I met Benjamin at Lambeth - that here was a spiritual leader of outstanding quality. Love, and light, and humanity, and humour, shine out of him.

When we got back, Martin and I were exhausted; but Michael, Martin's Nigerian cook and 'steward', had prepared us a lovely meal of steak, cooked in palm oil, with yams and okra and fresh fruit salad; and we were soon refreshed. I found that Michael - a really lovely person - had done all my washing, and pressed my suit, while we were away.

Martin and I sat talking till the small hours on this last evening in Nigeria (with Fauré's *Requiem* in the background!)

I could never have come to a better place for this first stop from London. I shall always be deeply grateful for Martin's friendship here.

January 4th 1972
I had thought this last day before going to the airport at 3.45 pm would be unplanned. Sarah Lazenby (Somerset Maugham girl!) had other plans. She called by at 9.30 am and suggested we go to the Imo River, forty five miles away.

It was a wonderful excursion. Again, the tropical woodland - rubber, cassava, palms; and soon we came to a bridge over the wide and deep green river, where families were washing themselves and their washing. Then, walking a quarter of a mile, we found a kind of beach, from which Martin and Sarah could swim. I paddled! - amongst hordes of tadpoles, and fish; and the most beautiful water lilies at the water's edge. A cluster of naked children came to watch us, and we made friends with them. Then the older members of the family came along from their mud huts, and some fishermen brought their dug-out canoe up to 'our' beach. It was an idyllic scene.

We were home in good time; and then there was for me my first very sad farewell since Victoria a week ago. It is unbelievable how involved in Nigeria one can get in a week - and in those who look after you!

But the end was not yet! Port Harcourt to Lagos was alright. But, at Lagos, I discovered that the 'plane to Entebbe was not going from Lagos after all! and that there was only one from Accra, in Ghana; that there would not be one from Lagos for twenty four hours - yet in Port Harcourt my booking had been confirmed! I had expected to leave Lagos at 11.30 pm. But Lagos airport was closing down at 7.00 pm, and the last flight to Accra was just leaving, and was fully booked! Again I had to fight (a) with the man behind the desk (b) with the head of the airways who had booked me. Then I ran out across the tarmac to the 'plane that was just about to leave and pleaded with the captain to take me. He agreed - all the time there was one empty seat! - and I subsided into the vacant seat in a bath of sweat. The man I sat next to was a Nigerian lawyer in the Federal Government, who was at King's College, London in 1961! - an Ibo, yet in the Government. A marvellous sign of peace.

So here I am at Ghana airport at 8.50 pm - still sweating - waiting for the 'plane that will come in two hours to take me to Entebbe, via Addis Ababa. I had dinner in the airport restaurant with (i) a student from Mauritania (ii) a Nepalese (iii) a coloured American girl going back from Lagos to school in Kenya.

One world! And from here I think of my friends in England.

Stage 2: Uganda

January 5th 1972

The Ethiopian Air Lines 'plane took off at 10.00 pm from Accra - with the most beautiful Ethiopian air hostess. We were very few on the 'plane perhaps twenty in all in the vast Boeing. The small number in the large 'plane; a window seat by myself, from which to look out on the dark world five and a half miles below; the strangeness of the territory over which we were passing - Douala in the Cameroons; then the Northern Congo; the fact that I had just left friends in Nigeria, and was in a kind of no-man's-land between meeting friends in Uganda - and fitfully reading a magnificent new novel of V S Naipaul's - *In a Free State* - in the main, about British expatriates living in a world which is not theirs, in Africa, seeking, but not finding, their home there any longer - all this created a feeling of belonging only very tenuously anywhere.

Having put my watch back an hour in Ghana (Lagos was an hour forward) - I was expecting quite a long flight. But when my watch said 2.20 am, it was suddenly announced we were landing at Entebbe in fifteen minutes. (We were due there at 6.05 am!) In fact, we were nearly an hour early; but I still couldn't work out why time was so haywire!

The 'plane's early arrival defeated the carefully planned kindness of Peter Nkambo-Mugerwa, who had hoped to be at the airport to meet me. Nkambo is now Attorney-General of

Uganda. He was an undergraduate at Trinity College, Cambridge, in my days as Chaplain, and I married him to his wife, Ada, from Holland in St George's, Camberwell. Nkambo and two of his children, Michael and Mirembe, ten and eight, had got up at 4.30 am, and, in the government Mercedes, with the flag of Uganda flying on the bonnet, had come to meet me. Nkambo was really sad to be late - "You made me welcome in your country. I wanted to be the first to welcome you to my country." We drove the twenty miles from Entebbe to Kampala watching a storm circling Lake Victoria (which is the size of England) - blinding flashes of lightning in the darkness. Dawn had come by the time we reached Nkambo's house in Kampala, and there was a joyful reunion with Ada, and with a Trinity undergraduate friend of mine, now a barrister in London, Eben Hamilton, who had also come to stay for a few days - and the delight of seeing Nkambo's youngest two children. Nkambo is one of my dearest friends, and I greatly looked forward to sharing his home - and his country - for a week.

East Africa is so different from West Africa. Kampala is a beautiful city, clean and relatively new - compared with Lagos and Port Harcourt - and far less densely populated. Although it is on the equator, it is not humid. It is 4,000 feet above sea level. I had realised in West Africa that I needed a more spectacular shirt than the subdued ones I had brought with me. This was good reason for exploring the shops of Kampala. I hadn't realised the strength of the Asian/African problem till it was clear that almost all the shops of Kampala were run by Asians. Yet there are less than 100,000 Asians (and less than 10,000 Europeans) in a country of six million Africans.

I went to the two Cathedrals, Anglican and Roman Catholic, overlooking the city from splendid sites, and also visited the Kasubi tombs - the cane-roofed vast native huts that contain the bodies of the Kabakas for centuries (including the last

Kabaka, who died in Rotherhithe not long ago). The Kasubi tombs are as much mausoleums and temples as palaces. We had to take our shoes off before entering, and, in the shrine, old ladies - relatives of the Kabaka - were sitting in continuous vigil.

Nkambo had laid on a very good celebration for my first evening in Uganda. Prince Stephen Karamaji - who was at Cambridge with him, and who was his best man in St George's - came round for drinks, with his wife Margaret. Then we all went to a Chinese restaurant, and at 11.30 pm went on to a night club - until 2.00 am. (Darkness, red lights and a Congolese band). I particularly enjoyed meeting Margaret, Stephen's Rwanda wife - who had nursed in Woolwich, at the Mother and Baby Home. She and Stephen have this marvellously tall race-horse-like beauty (like the Ethiopian air hostess). Nkambo is Bugandan - black, small, kind and - except when he chooses *not* to be! - mischievous. The evening revealed that high office had not spoilt him. He is still basically loving and mischievous - and stubborn!

January 6th 1972

A quiet day. Eben and I visited the Ba'hai Temple in the morning, on another beautiful site overlooking the city. (The hills really do 'stand about' Kampala.) We also went to the great University of Uganda, Makerere. I am to baptise three of the children of Nkambo on Sunday in Makerere Chapel.

Nkambo was kept at work in the Parliament Buildings until midnight. His tradition of 'open house' meant that I had helped to entertain at least a dozen intelligent Ugandans, friends of his, in the Government or the professions, by the end of the evening. One learns a lot by this slow talking with individuals. The four children are very vital. I have taught them liar dice! Michael, nearly 11, is going to be a fine lad - fairly Europeanised; but with Nkambo's hair, and fairly black; Mirembe, about 8,

Nalule, about 6, and Jan, a most attractive little devil, of 4, who wants to be in everything. "Where's your game?" he asks. "Me lie!" Much of life takes place on the large step between the open sitting room and the garden - flowering acacia trees, jacarandas, a moonflower tree - large white trumpets like arum lilies.... gardenia and so on. Birds wheel around, mostly kites, with 'delta' tails. Beyond the garden lie the hills outside Kampala, and an unbroken view of the country, red earth and tropical woodland.

I have been trying hard in travelling round and talking with individuals, white and coloured, both here and in Nigeria, to evaluate as best I can the political issues - particularly as they relate to what Britain has done and still might do. I have been helped greatly by a quite magnificent book, recently published by Margery Perham: *Colonial Sequence*. The dominance - and relatively advanced state - of the Baganda, one tribe amongst several - most of whom are relatively immature - and highly jealous of the Baganda - plus the problem of the white and Asian minorities - makes the English parliamentary system inappropriate here without huge modification. In England, it is easy enough to condemn 'imperialism' and 'colonialism', and as easy to want to wash our hands and forget - because we have now so little direct power. Travelling around, one meets a good many whites - in Nigeria and Uganda - who are bewildered, distressed that so much of what they achieved is apparently ignored, and, maybe, condemned. Here they had power and status, in a way they might not have had at home; and when they return here, they are nostalgic for the old days.

"Was the impetus to civilisation in Africa supplied by Britain (a) superfluous? (b) injurious?" asks Margery Perham. Most African leaders at the moment say - perhaps have to - that it was both. 'Perhaps have to' to give confidence to their own people, and to 'explain' their own political and economic weakness. What is clear is the undoubted culture of pre-colonial Africa, and the huge and tragic miscalculation about inherent negro inferiority (still maintained in Rhodesia and South Africa). What is also clear - even today - is the poverty and disease of many millions of Africans, living in scattered huts of sticks and mud, divided into fairly separate and often mutually hostile groups. What would have happened without the peace and order which Britain brought to large areas; organised with, often, arbitrary frontiers; if they had not been given the basic administrative structure of a modern state, and the mastery, or near mastery, over disease? The Africans couldn't have done this themselves. Of course, we did it with a material interest as well as with a desire to serve. But could this risky and expensive work have been done *only* from motives of pure altruism? The chief valid accusation is undoubtedly the slowness of the pace of independence. But, of course, to train people for independence is to do yourself out of a career. Out here one sees with one's own eyes the immense contribution of Britain - and the Church - to the education of the African. Yet the failure to train a sufficient number of Africans to take over the senior posts is also abundantly clear. Britain has also given to Africa - to accept, modify, or reject - (i) the Westminster model of parliament (ii) an independent judiciary (iii) independent universities and academic freedom. Then there are the lives of countless individuals spent out here in love and service. But, again, there are as many individuals who found here a semi-feudal life. They had money, servants, a pleasant country. There are still many such around, who are now petrified. They are preoccupied with the laziness of the servants and the fear of violence. They see little wrong with the servants living on a pittance, in housing conditions immeasurably below their own. It is right for 'them'. It is easy acceptance of this class distinction which I find the most pernicious legacy. But, given the fundamental acceptance of class distinction in Britain, what else could one expect the legacy to be?

January 7th 1972

After an early lunch, we set out in two cars, to drive two hundred miles to the north of Uganda. I knew how much Nkambo wanted to show me this part of his country. It was a fascinating drive. Rural simplicity and poverty begin not far out of Kampala, the villages consisting of small groups of round rondavels (not square or rectangular huts as in Nigeria). The road was a magnificent new road, built fairly recently by Italian labour from British money.

On the journey I had some good conversations with Nkambo. The road was not just a new road to him. It was something which would join the nation together, the tribes and lands which had been separate, and often hostile, for so long. He would wave his hand and say: "You see that land? It must be developed. We need tractors. We need people trained to drive them. And there must be co-operation. The people have their small plots. How do you get them to come together so that more can be produced?" I suddenly saw what it means to have the pressure and responsibility of government upon you - and the excitement. Here is all this poverty around you, waiting for someone to come along and grapple with it. And you have the chance to do something about it for your people. Nkambo has the dynamism of a leader now. He always had a certain charisma. Now he is 'a prophet new inspired'. When we got to Chiobe, by the Nile - a vast reserve - we saw our first elephants. Then we went on to a small hotel in Gulu, the last important town before the frontiers of the Sudan. Students from a local college were acting four plays in the courtyard of the hotel, It was fun to see their natural acting ability.

Nkambo is alarmingly exhausted. He fell asleep over supper this evening, and we packed him off to bed.

January 8th 1972

We were all breakfasting by 7.30 am. Then we drove back to Chiobe, to a Lodge by the Nile. The river is a mile wide at this point, dotted with small islands covered with bushes and trees. It is fast flowing, and rushes over the rocks; a continuous series of falls for several miles. The children wanted to swim in the swimming pool first. They had great fun. Eben, Nkambo and I then went for a walk along the river's edge. The noses and ears of hippos were sticking out of the water. Sometimes they would rise a bit more - half a hippo back showing. There was a small crocodile on the rocks at the water's edge. In the afternoon we all got into a Land Rover and drove for twenty five miles, along sand paths beside the Nile. There were elephants galore, and buffalo, baboons, warthogs, rhinoceros, Uganda Kob and Water Buck, and birds of many colours - red, green, blue, yellow - small and great. I have never been so entranced by the world of nature.

When we came back, we sat and drank beer, watching the sun set across the Nile. Nkambo managed to survive until supper, but fell fast asleep - profusely apologetic! - over coffee.

Nkambo really is a remarkable fellow. A man of action, but also a philosopher. I am told that he is greatly looked up to in the Government. We can talk on Albert Camus, but he is just as interested in cattle production.

In the car this morning, we had a marvellous talk on the social pressures that are needed to help a nation reach high standards - of hygiene, of education, of public morality, to outlaw corruption, and so on. But Nkambo, who had clearly been thinking a great deal about all this, also understood 'Justification by Faith' - "We must also teach a man that when he fails, and however much he fails, he is still a valuable man; and we must teach people to stand by people when they fail."

Suddenly he burst out singing 'Lead kindly light' - to the old J B Dykes tune. "I believe in that" he said, with quiet conviction, and he went through every verse, as we travelled at nearly a hundred miles an hour on the new road, flying past villagers carrying water on their heads.

"Lead kindly light, amidst the encircling gloom....."

He had learnt it first as a boy at King's School, Budo. He punctured his solo with his own comments:

"'One step enough for me' - I *believe* that!" he said again, passionately. And:

"Pride ruled my will"

I reminded him that this was Gandhi's favourite hymn, and that he often asked C F Andrews (who came to Uganda to see the Indians were being cared for) to sing it for him. (There is a moving description of it being sung for Gandhi in Durban.)

I am thankful for Nkambo's heartfelt sincerity.

January 9th 1972

At half past five this morning, while it was still dark, I crept out of the room in the Lodge where Michael, Eben and I were sleeping, and sat on the balcony overlooking the Nile. At first, trees on the shore, over against the Nile, and islands in the river, were all just patches of dark against the water, catching the moonlight. Between the clouds, the stars shone. The perpetual rushing of the waterfalls filled the air with sound, and the noise of the cicadas. There was an occasional snort from a hippo lying near the shore. I sat in silence for nearly an hour. There was a curious peace - the river flowing all those miles through the rest of Uganda, then the Sudan, then Egypt, to its mouth in the Mediterranean, two thousand miles away. There was not only a unity of land through the river but a unity of time. This age-old river, the Nile.

And then, the birds began to sing, and all the animals in the river began to grunt, and snort, and hoot. It was like ships in port. And, as dawn came, the shapes of the animals that had dared to approach the land between the Lodge and the river could be made out. A giraffe was calmly munching the branches of a tree not a hundred yards away; baboons were frolicking around; a 'school' of guinea-fowl suddenly decided to walk in single file in front of the Lodge in a most determined fashion - to God knows where; great stork-like and pelican-like birds began to take up their perches on the shore and in the trees, spreading their wings as though it was time for a good morning stretch.

We had to leave the Nile after an early breakfast, and drive at break-neck speed back to Kampala. We *averaged* 70 mph, and were indoors in Kampala by 11.30 am. Nkambo and I spent most of the time (accompanied by *The Marriage of Figaro* on cassettes) talking about the necessity - or otherwise - of military government, in an African state like Uganda. Nkambo has been made a Lieutenant-Colonel, and believes in the inevitability and necessity of military power, in such an undeveloped territory, *at the present time*. He refuses to waste his time vote-catching. "I want to serve my people. You cannot do more than do your very best to serve them, taking everything you can into consideration, keeping your ears to the situation." I raised the obvious questions - "benevolent dictatorship?"; the fallibility of human beings who are given power; *when* do you appeal to the *people*, or do you wait until you are overthrown by a coup? - which could destroy so much you have achieved - and so much good leadership. How do you stimulate 'grass roots' leadership in a benevolent dictatorship?

Isn't opposition *essential?* Nkambo was alive to all these questions. The difficulty here is that Obote's administration was so awful that perhaps Amin's military rule is inevitable *for the moment.* Amin has promised it will cease in five years. Nkambo speaks to me like a man tackling giant problems, almost submerged by them. I felt he was glad to have someone with whom to talk on the *fundamentals* of Government, hideously aware that he has to grapple with the hour by hour decisions of the immediate situation. He has asked that we spend an afternoon together on all this. I have given him Lord Butler's - Master of Trinity - *The Art of the Possible* for his birthday.

In the afternoon, I baptised Mirembe, Nalule and Jan in St Francis' Chapel, Makerere University. Nkambo surprised me with the strength of his desire that the three children should be baptised, (Michael had been baptised in Holland ten years ago), seeing that they hadn't been baptised earlier. But his dealings with the Muslims, and, for that matter, with the RCs, have recently led him to see much more the point of the Christian's God, and of one that really respects the individual. I put all the objections to children being baptised at eight, six and four, but he said he wanted them to have all the advantages of 'formation' that the Christian community can provide. Ada had wanted them baptised ages ago. So it seemed absolutely right to baptise them.

The party afterwards was as marvellous as the service. More than fifty people came to the house, and it was fascinating to meet them all - some professional and Government, like the judge - but most of them family and extended family, who obviously have a great love and admiration for Nkambo. For me, the supreme pleasure was to meet Nkambo's mother, a woman of well over seventy, of great grace and dignity, in her native clothes. I spent a long while talking with her through Edward, Nkambo's brother, as interpreter. She put her hands together and put them in mine and bowed her head when we met. I was able to say to her much that I feel about Nkambo, and tell her how he was loved and respected in Cambridge. Finding simple phrases for Edward to translate helped me in some way say what was in my heart, and the simple replies she gave moved me very much. I am going to see her again if I can; it was such a privilege to meet her. She told me of the days of Bishop Tucker of Uganda at the turn of the century. (Since Tucker there has been Willis, then Stuart, then Leslie Brown, then the African bishops.)

Although Nkambo has enormous drive, it is his simplicity that counts, and his humility in most things, in spite of his firmness. For instance, he used the flag on the car to be kind to *me*, but he deliberately doesn't use it most of the time. "I do not want my authority to depend on a flag" he said "or even on being a Minister. That can all be taken away in a moment. My authority must be that people know I want to serve them."

After the party was over, I was utterly exhausted - we were in the garden out in the sun from 4.00 pm until 7.00 pm - Nkambo took twenty of us off to a Chinese restaurant.

January 10th 1972
Nkambo's birthday. I saw Eben off to London from Entebbe airport - the sign said '4,000 miles to London'. When I got back, my first mail from England had arrived.

In the evening, Nkambo and Ada and I had the delayed conversation on the state of affairs here. Nkambo said he did not *believe* military government is inevitable, but that, since it had come it must be used - for a limited time. The coup which brought Amin to power is one of the *facts* which have to be taken into consideration - 'the art of the possible'. We even talked about the possibility of Nkambo's death in a counter coup. "I have one small wish - that, when the histories come to be written, you should say 'He was doing the best he could'." He went on: "What I'm being allowed to do is so important to me that I must forget the possibility of death. I must go on trying to do the best I can do." He gave some examples of his everyday life - seeing whether he could do anything about the hanging of an Obote supporter. (Nkambo is personally against capital punishment). His examples weighed on me. They represented such a continuing burden of frightful responsibility.

I took a photograph in the darkness of the lights of Kampala stretched our below the hillside where Nkambo lives.

January 11th 1972
The inevitable diarrhoea has hit me! But in the last fortnight I have been so bitten by mosquitoes, midges, ants and flies of all sorts that something was bound to happen - as well as the problem of always only using filtered water. A rather sleepless night (with another storm raging) gave me a chance to read a splendid book on Ganda Art, a book that was as much social and religious history of the Buganda, as art history. In the late morning, I went to see, in his workshop, Brother Joseph, a Dutch RC monk, who has been out here most of his life, an expert in making stained glass. It was good to meet such a person - and to look at his work - just after reading the book. The book enabled me to have a fascinating discussion with one of Uganda's top architects later in the day.

I spent all the afternoon with the Organising Secretary of the Uganda Council of Social Service. A couple of hours pressured questioning of such a person - against the background of one's own experience of the London Council of Social Service, and, last week, of Nigeria's social problems - enables one to have a fairly clear idea of the gaps in social work - amongst babies, children, youth, families, those in need of medical help, prisoners and ex-prisoners, in urban and rural areas etc.etc. - and where help from, say, England is still urgently needed, and in what form it can be given.

Nkambo, the architect, Nkambo's brother and I talked - mainly about politics - for another couple of hours; until Nkambo, Ada and I went off to the Speke Hotel for a final dinner. Nkambo, who has had a Cabinet Meeting all day, has to produce an urgent document tomorrow, my last day, on "What I have done as a Minister in the first year of the Second Republic" and see the President with it. Everything is now being geared towards the first anniversary of President Amin's coup on January 25th - the flags are being put up in the streets.

January 12th 1972

In a book *The Mind of the Bugandan* by Professor D A Low, I came across, surprisingly, a quotation from Dietrich Bonhoeffer, which I was able to hand on to Nkambo; "Some seek refuge from the rough and tumble of public life in the sanctuary of their own private virtue.....Only at the cost of self-deception can they keep themselves pure from the defilement incurred by responsible action....Who stands his ground? Only the man whose criteria is not his reason, his principles, his conscience, his freedom or his virtue, but who is ready to sacrifice all these things when he is called to obedient and responsible action in faith and exclusive allegiance to God. The responsible man seeks to make his whole life a response to the question and call of God."

In the morning, Ada took me to the Child Welfare & Adoption Home - for orphans and abandoned babies. We spent an hour with the forty babies and those looking after them. Few things have tugged my heart strings more for a long while than these babies. Nkambo has adopted a baby - as an example - and has made himself responsible for the garden of the place.

We then went on to the Kitwe Community Centre - in the heart of the worst slum in Kampala. Janet Lacey had laid the foundation stone in 1963. I have rarely been so impressed with a Centre - a primary school, a clinic, adult education, youth work, trades teaching, community development, etc.etc. It is financed by the Uganda Christian Council and Oxfam, Christian Aid etc.

It is good to be able to report this positive piece of work by the Church of Uganda, for the tragic fact is that as a Church it is at the moment trapped in the history of the nation, making it an example not of reconciliation but of squabbling. It is a complex story, but to the populace, by the headlines of the daily papers, it is simply that there is a public disagreement whether there should be an archbishop with his residence and his headquarters in Kampala, who would also be *ex-officio* bishop of the capital, or be without a diocese, simply having his archiepiscopal throne in Namirembe Cathedral. The latter would deprive the archbishop of a diocese. The first way would as often as not mean the Buganda sacrificing the chance of having one of their people as their diocesan bishop. Even the Moslem President (with four wives) has tried his hand at reconciling the parties. There is now some hope of peace but much damage to the public image of the Church has been done.

I spent my last afternoon in Uganda in a wonderful way. Nkambo has recently bought a 400 acre farm, twenty miles out of Kampala, to have some place to relax, but also to learn and teach how the land should be used. We all went there for lunch, which was very much of foods grown on the farm, most of them strange to me. Nkambo's mother was there and cooked it all. The vegetables and the chicken from the farm were all cooked in banana leaves. To be quite honest, I wondered whether it would all stay down. Mercifully, it did! Nkambo is very much a 'son of the soil'. He was absolutely at home getting on with the farm workers, and they and the villagers clearly love having him about. He gives orders, but it is clear that he is also asserting that he is one of the people.

Nkambo was busy with his Government work until midnight, so, when the children had gone to bed, the evening was spent quietly with Ada, listening to a recording of the *St Matthew Passion,* and with Nkambo's brother, Edward and his Norwegian wife.

I can only find myself very thankful at the end of these few days, for a multiplicity of things, and such a variety. Today - those babies' faces; the tropical countryside at the farm; the shining black naked muscular back of one of the farm workers, and his handsome face and smile when he turned round; Nkambo's mother; the *St Matthew Passion,* and so on. And Nkambo himself - his face, at one moment dark, frowning, intense, serious: at the next, alive with laughter and friendship. It is a particular privilege to be a friend of such a person at such a time.

January 13th 1972
My 'plane was due to leave Entebbe for Lusaka at 6.35 am so we had to be up at 4.30 am. Nkambo and I drove to the airport - he still philosophising all the way. ("I wonder whether contentment is not a more important concept than freedom. Most often you have to be free in order to be content - free from fear of arrest, free to express your opinion, and so on..... The purpose of government must always be the contentment of *that* man." He waved a hand at someone we happened to be passing.

Contentment was soon to be more than an abstract subject. My 'plane had an accident with its undercarriage, on landing, and eventually was taken out of service. Nkambo stayed with me until 10.30 am, but I had to wait around until another 'plane was provided. We made our getaway at 1.30 pm - seven hours late. I was content. In fact it was quite welcome to have the opportunity to sit peacefully by oneself in a sunlit, air-conditioned VIP lounge! - looking out on Lake Victoria and the runway, interrupted only by the welcome of the odd US Senator, honeymooning with his fourth wife; by the arrival and departure of other aircraft but one's own; and by Humphrey Berkeley and Edward du Cann MP, coming to join me in the lounge at midday. They had spent the evening with the President of Uganda and were flying on to Lusaka to interview President Kaunda.

Stage 3: Zambia

January 14th 1972

The flight from Kampala to Lusaka was extremely beautiful - across, first of all, Lake Victoria, two hundred of the thousand or so miles, then across Tanzania and Lake Tanganyika. The sky was full of scudding clouds, some of them a separate and unbroken column of cloud and rain to the earth itself. Between the clouds, one looked down on the densely covered land or on the water of the lakes.

At the airport, it was marvellous to see Patrick and Ann Appleford and their eight year-old son, Mark, waving from the balcony of the new air terminal. They had been waiting for me there almost from early morning. Patrick has been Dean of the magnificent new Anglican Cathedral of Lusaka since 1966, and is due to come home some time this year. (He is the composer of the *Appleford Mass*. I have known him since he was Curate at All Saints', Poplar, in the 1950's.)

I was too exhausted to do much more than look at the inside of the Cathedral - central altar, large panes of good, many-coloured, glass, almost from floor to ceiling - and have a leisurely drive round the city of 250,000, and so to bed.

The next day - today - it has poured with rain all day - I have hit the rainy season here - and, after going round the shops - to the airlines (I have learnt now to check up on the next stage

- 33 -

early!), and the post office - I worked on the sermon for the Cathedral on Sunday. "When it rains, it rains, it rains...." I have never seen rain like it. The day ended with a very successful evening of Scrabble with the Head of the Health Education Department, and Ann Appleford.

January 15th 1972

We drove out today, fifty miles, to a 21,000 acre farm owned by a farmer who has taken out Zambia citizenship - John Harvey, the son-in-law of the last High Commissioner, Sir Stewart Gore-Browne. They were, of course, an extremely wealthy English family - children at school in England, as is the custom of many, but very kind and hospitable, and I learnt a great deal about the problems and possibilities of agriculture in Zambia. There were some extraordinarily odd shaped bulls, with a large dewlap and a hump on the neck. The flowers in the garden were beautiful beyond words, especially the violet Morning Glory.

We drove back in time to go out to a Chinese restaurant with Theodore Bull. Theodore is really my other reason for coming to Zambia - in the sense of meeting up with friends again. A contemporary of Nkambo Mugerwa at Trinity, he often visited me at St George's, Camberwell, until he came out to Africa - buying up and editing the *Central African Examiner* - which he sold after Smith came to power in Rhodesia. (Theodore took on the Smith government in a law suit.) He is, of course, extremely rich - a near millionaire - and is doing all he can to build houses for Zambians. He has married Mutumba, a Zambia girl (and a London University PhD). Theo knows almost all there is to know about Zambia and Rhodesian politics, and so I learnt a great deal. He is also playing a large part, as a layman, in the affairs of the Cathedral and Diocese. He has really committed himself to Zambia.

The news today is bleak - that Busia has been deposed in Ghana, and that Simon Kapepwe, erstwhile Vice-President to Kenneth Kaunda, has been beaten up here.

January 16th 1972

It was a real joy to preach at the Parish Communion, and at Mattins, in the Cathedral. There were not large congregations, but people were extremely receptive and appreciative.

Theo has driven me round his various building projects, and we lunched on the terrace of the top hotel, the Inter-Continental. I stirred up a heated discussion by querying the whole 'feudal' basis of society out here - which still persists as far as most white people are concerned. Every white has one or more servants, who live in one or perhaps two, rooms, with their family, usually in a small house, detached from the main house. Quite apart from anything else, this is extremely wasteful of land. The servant here will get £10 to £15 a *month*. If food is provided this wage is reduced.

The people at lunch got very angry with my remark that no European would dream of taking such wages or living in such housing conditions, nor could they study in such conditions; so it's not only a question of finance but of education, etc. Theo Bull said I was asking the right questions, but everyone else was furious. One lady told me that she knew for a fact that in Dundee, where she came from back home, "people kept coals in the baths of the new flats" and that "they were slums again after two years". It is quite amazing how long that kind of remark goes on being made. But it unmistakably reveals the connection between class distinction in Britain and 'colonialism' in Africa.

I called this evening on the Bishop of Lusaka, Filemon Mataka, who is goodness itself. He had to take over suddenly when

Archbishop Green-Wilkinson was killed recently in a car crash. (I had met them both first of all at Richard Moberly's vicarage in Kennington, just before the 1968 Lambeth Conference began.)

January 17th 1972
Today was fascinating.

In the morning, I went out to the new University, marvellously architected - concrete, but a very skilful use of local shrubs, cacti, trees and flowers. It was a thrilling place to visit - so *young* all through, buildings and people. Here is the hope of East Africa. The new library was wonderful. I sat in the Senior Common Room by myself for about three quarters of an hour, simply savouring the beauty of faces and bodies: while I had coffee, and eavesdropped on conversations, the scholarly excited exchange of young Zambia dons. In fact, there were, when I counted, sixteen black and fourteen white in the Common Room. Hardly anyone seemed over thirty. They wondered who the 'odd bod' was in the corner, till I broke my silence and introduced myself. (I was waiting for my host to drive me back into Lusaka.) It was so good to hear their pride in the place. There is a kind of 'Open University' side to it all - further education by correspondence - as well as the normal university.

After lunching with Theo, and a priest from the town - a very wise person - I went on to talk to all the clergy of Lusaka and the Bishop. They were very responsive. I liked them. Zambia now is made up of three dioceses, sixty clergy in all, full time. They are determined to be fully self-supporting by 1980, which will almost certainly mean most of the priests being priest-workmen.

I also had a most exciting evening. Nkambo Mugerwa had asked me to get in touch with Bruce Munyama, a brilliant young lawyer (University College, London), who, at twenty nine, had recently resigned from the Zambia Government. Theo took me along to his lovely house. He - and his wife Charity - were very kind - and as attractive as any people I have met over here. We at once established a 'bond', and talked the whole time of what was important to us. He was particularly interesting about the inevitable goal of *money* in Zambia society - the need to help your extended family; high taxation; the cost of housing and living; the sudden availability and appeal of good things. His resignation marks him out as a man of principle - but he stood out mostly this evening as a friend. It's curious, how, travelling around, people who have the natural gift of friendship do stand out. Meeting them, and receiving their warmth, is like coming to a well.

The equally young chairman of the Council of the University came in while I was with Bruce. He divulged how short of money the University is now. For instance, it cannot pay the wage rates to academics that Makerere University pays. He was appalled at the Government for allowing this to happen.

Theo drove me on to the house of the head of the College of Education, another wonderful Zambian, with an English wife. (He was at the Institute of Education and worked in east London for several years.) I managed to persuade him and his sister to sing some of the village songs of his childhood. They were very beautiful.

It was the beginning of the school year today. Throughout Lusaka mothers waited in vain for places for their children. At Chiboya, 300 children were turned away. At Chitenda, 200 were turned away. Some parents began the round of schools, hoping for a Grade One place, at 5.00 am. At Zambia Primary School the Headmaster said "There are 5,000 parents with children to fill 500 places at my school."

Patrick's 'daily' was lucky enough to get her seven year-old to a place at school for the first time.

January 18th 1972

I celebrated Holy Communion in the Cathedral this morning, and then went to see Laurence Taylor, another Trinity friend, who is now Principal of the National Institute of Public Administration in Zambia. He has a staff of twenty three and is in charge of all the training of Civil Servants for Zambia - Local and Central Government, Magistrates, Foreign Office and Diplomats, etc. I saw a lot of Laurence at Trinity - an ardent Methodist then. He came out here in the Colonial Service as a District Officer, when he left Trinity in 1959, and after five years came to Lusaka to help with the founding of the College. Nkambo Mugerwa had been a great friend of his at Trinity and often went to stay at his home in vacations. It is fascinating to see where all this has led Laurence now. He has had over a thousand Zambia students under him already. No one could be doing a greater Christian service for Zambia, or be in a position of greater ultimate influence. The Government is the greatest single employer in Zambia.

In the evening, we went to dinner with the Professor of Social Medicine and his wife, (relatives of Mark and Priscilla Cornwall-Jones), both involved in research in the environs of Lusaka. I learnt a great deal not only about the central causes of child illness around Lusaka, but about witchcraft, and alcoholism, and the *mothers* of Zambia children. I also learnt about the pros and cons of building a vast new splendid university - with medical school - a good status symbol - over against building (as my hosts would have infinitely preferred) many small local clinics. In fact, the Professor and his wife are going now to Dar-es-

Salaam, because they feel the result of their work falls on deaf government ears. We also had a fascinating discussion on jealousy. Given that 'Zambia is the jealous society'. I asked for a definition of jealousy - which took us a great deal of time and up many fascinating bypaths! It is fairly understandable that in a country emerging from poverty, everyone wants to have what the other fellow has, be it education or a Mercedes. The Editor of the Zambia *Times* has been sacked, (ie given another job!). Opposition and criticism is fairly stifled here - as elsewhere in emerging Africa.

January 19th 1972
The news this morning of the arrest of Garfield Todd and Judith Todd momentarily stirred the breakfast table conversation of the Bishop and clergy of Lusaka in Pat and Ann's house - they meet for Communion together each Wednesday at 6.45 am and then breakfast. (The Bishop plus six clergy equalled almost half the staff of the Diocese.)

I have been astonished how little of what is happening next door in Rhodesia figures in either the newspapers or in conversations. The attitude is "Oh well, it's for them now to make up their minds."

My own impression is that (a) military regimes and frequent coups, (b) the stifling of much of the opposition, (c) widespread corruption at even the highest levels, (d) the inability of whatever is the latest government to cope with overwhelming problems, and the continuous necessity of compromise, (e) the division of *black* people into rich and poor, ie taking on the class divisions that are the legacy of the whites, has taken away much of the moral passion of government which existed in the honeymoon period after Independence - whether one is talking of Nigeria, Uganda or Zambia. That *moral* integrity and passion was and is very necessary if one is really to come to grips with

South Africa, to which I fly at 2.40 pm today. 'Shades of the prison house' begin to close upon me. For here, and in the other places I have so far visited, the freedom of intercourse and friendship with black people - which stops this afternoon - has been so great a privilege. I am now going where, for instance, Nkambo Mugerwa and Bruce Munyama could not be what they are. The tragedy is as simple as that. Put it another way: South Africans are denying themselves the privilege of friendship, beyond words, which I have been allowed in these last weeks to share so fully.

Stage 4: Johannesburg

January 20th 1972

For political reasons, there are at the moment no flights direct from Lusaka to Johannesburg. You have to go via Malawi. This is a blessing in disguise, for the flight to Blantyre, Malawi, is, most of the time, along the Zambesi. I have never seen a more impressive river from the air. Even from five miles up it is a deep and wide mud-coloured, seemingly unbridgeable stream. As one nears Malawi, the country becomes more and more beautiful. It is known, with good reason, as 'the Scotland of Africa'. It was pleasant, after the hour's flight, to change 'planes at the little airport and get into another Malawi Air Lines 'plane for Johannesburg. But we were joined by unpleasant company: rich South African boys and girls returning by air to their top South African public schools. They treated the black air hostesses and host like dirt. At fourteen or fifteen, hardly one of them was not smoking; and when the hostesses refused to serve them with anything but soft drinks, there was nearly trouble.

The two hour flight to Johannesburg, mostly across Mozambique (a very large Portuguese colony, which we in England tend to ignore) was full of interest. I was particularly glad that - for reasons which will be clear later - we flew over the Cabora Bassa dam, in process of construction.

My involvement with several people - like Bishop Edward

Crowther - deported from South Africa - and certain other factors, had made me a little anxious about whether I would be allowed into South Africa; but, in fact, clearance at Jan Smuts airport was swifter than at any place in Africa so far, and, thankfully, there was both Geoff Lowick (who last year looked after the interregnum at St Mary's, Battersea) and 'Chippy' Rathbone (who had been staying with me a good deal in Hankey Place since July, when his marriage - which I had taken at Trinity - came to grief) smiling the other side of the barrier. We went off to a steak house, and then Chippy took me to his lovely home. We sat out in the garden in the darkness, having a drink in the warm night air.

I wanted to stay with Chippy, not only because he would particularly welcome my staying with him at the moment, but because he is now a young executive of one of Harry Oppenheimer's companies, and a number of people contend that any breakthrough in the South African race situation is likely to come, as much, if not more, through the pressure of economics as through ideological pressures - and Harry Oppenheimer is the most powerful man by far in the South African business world.

We were up by 7.00 am. At 7.30 am Chippy drove me to his place of work, immediately suggesting I should read an address by Harry Oppenheimer, given recently to the South African Trades Union Movement.

In brief, Oppenheimer says:"Business requires the development of natural resources, the mobilisation of capital, skilled management and trained and efficient workers. People must want the product and be able to pay for it.

What of South Africa? The total population is only twenty million - a dangerously small market to start with today. But even that small market is artificially restricted by the oppressive social system. Only twenty five per cent of the working population have the standard of life which is needed if South African business is to prosper. Of the remaining seventy five per cent - Coloured, Indian and African - many live at or below the breadline.

Only far-reaching social change can remedy this. Low productivity produces low wages. Low wages are rooted in inadequate education and the refusal to allow workers to cultivate their natural endowments. Apartheid may be *ideological*, but *economically* it suffocates seventy five per cent of the country. The system which reserves education, opportunity, productivity, commensurate wages, to an elite must be brought to an end."

"Trade Unions have feared the African worker. They ought to fear far more the effects of present policies. Let Trade Unions be concerned with fair wages - not cheap labour - for all.

Capital is not coming into South Africa because people overseas see the economic writing on the wall - the result of ideological policies.

In any case, we not only need the 'market' the seventy five per cent could provide, we as desperately need their skilled, trained manpower."

It is encouraging to find so many people now convinced that industrialisation should and must greatly alter the social order - a considerable advance on when I was last here in 1964. Many people nevertheless doubt whether the racial relations embedded in that order will thereby be essentially altered.

Dr Ellen Hellmann (formerly President of the South African

Institute of Race Relations and a well-known anthropologist and sociologist) - with whom I shall be lunching next Tuesday - makes that point in an article in *New Nation*, which I was also put on to, and, for obvious reasons, devoured, entitled 'What Mr Neil Wates forgets'. Dr Hellman maintains that "only an increase in the national output will make it possible to provide the educational and other social services on the scale necessary to raise the general standard of living." "Boycotters" she says "engage in what is a theoretically and practically self-defeating strategy of blind retaliation....if they were to succeed in halting and then reversing economic development in South Africa....the main victims and chief sufferers would be the blacks." Dr Hellmann contrasts Polaroid, who attached conditions to their continuance of work in South Africa, ie improved wages and other terms of employment of black staff, the use of a proportion of profits for social, especially educational, purposes, etc. Her arguments are hard to counter, especially as seventy per cent of the black labour force of 400,000 on the gold mines comes from outside the Republic (and despite the fact that the mining industry pays its black labourers only £8 per month, excluding free accommodation, food, medical care, etc.). In fact, South Africa has to guard its frontiers to hold back the influx of Africans seeking entry into the Republic. Dr Hellman - a strong opponent of Government policy - asks that "indictment lead to *constructive* action."

Geoff Lowick collected me for lunch, and to meet again his wife and family. It was good to see Jonathan, born in London two years ago.

I had to go round to the Community of the Resurrection Priory at Rosettenville with a message for Fr Leo Rakale I had brought from Fr Hugh Bishop. (I had last seen Fr Leo twenty five years ago, when we played tennis at Mirfield, when I was a theological student at King's London and he was a novice CR.)

He told me the news that the Government - regarding the CR as a seditious movement - has appropriated the College at Alice, on the coast, near Grahamstown, (I went there shortly after it was opened, in 1964) on the pretext of needing the land for the expansion of Fort Hare, the university for Africans only. Alice is the exciting ecumenical theological college for Africans only. Of course, it always was for Africans only because the Government commanded it should be so.

The gardener of Geoff's church, a good quiet African of thirty, was beaten up by the police last week. Suddenly asked - outside the church - to produce his Pass, while he fumbled for it in panic, the two policemen set upon him. Geoff managed to get to the scene to make his hopeless protest on the man's behalf. "Fuck off Kaffir" said one of the policemen to the African, in Geoff's presence.

How does one preach *quietly* in a situation like this? I have to prepare a sermon for Sunday evening, for the rich suburb of Bryanston, ie where I am staying.

This evening I attended the Diocesan Mission Committee in the house of the Assistant Bishop, John Carter. (He was at Emmanuel, Streatham in Keith de Berry's time.) I did my piece, and they were grateful. They were a good lot - some of the black priests were friends of Walter Makhulu. (I also met a god-child of his yesterday in Lusaka.) But I came away crushed at the problem of how the Church can be the Church when so often black and white are not allowed to meet to discuss together. The black members of the Committee had to leave early to get back to their locations by the time of curfew.

January 21st 1972
I again travelled in early to Chippy's office. He had prepared some literature for me on the Cabora Bassa Dam - and

photographs. Many of my friends in London are against the building of it (which is mainly in the hands of Chippy's Company), and in Uganda and Zambia there were many people who supported those who are trying to prevent and sabotage its building. I personally cannot possibly see how a £150 million hydro-electric project which will make it possible to use 3,700,000 acres of land for agriculture now unused - and develop mining and industry for the people's employment - can be wrong. It will be much larger than either the Kariba or Aswan dams.

I then went over to Geoff Lowick's parish again - Turfontein - fairly inner-city - and worked on my sermon for Sunday till it was time to go back to Chippy's office. The sermon is causing me a good deal of anxiety. How do you both say what is in your heart and mind, and what you believe to be the Gospel truths in the situation, *and* behave with humility and charity towards your hosts? How do you behave with justice to white *and* black *and* to whites on *both* sides and blacks on *both* sides at one and the same time? How do you bring the blessings from the man from outside and avoid the curses? ie bring perhaps a fresh view, but avoid a naive or impertinent one.

Chippy took me out to dinner with some of his friends. We went back to one of the friend's houses and had a serious and worthwhile discussion on "Can a young business executive do justice to his work, his marriage and himself, at one and the same time?" Which should go? The man whose house we were in, a man of my own age, a top man in platinum mining, said he put his marriage first. He and his wife agreed that the decision had to be made twice in their mining lifetime already - in Borneo and Malaya. They are good friends to Chippy.

January 22nd 1972
The Assistant Bishop had invited me to conduct an all-day

conference on 'The Role of the Clergy in Society Today' at the Community of the Resurrection Priory, Rosettenville, for those recently ordained - eight white priests and eight black. It was a fascinating day, sometimes thrilling, sometimes appalling. Two or three white priests had views which were a sick combination of pietism and right-wing racial views. The black priests were silent most of the day, coming up to me in break time and lunch time and afternoon tea to tell me their views, and why they were silent - they feared that honesty on their part might get them into trouble. They have no trust that they will not be betrayed to the state by some of their white brethren. However, half an hour before the day ended, they threw away any caution and there was a most moving confession of faith from the black priests - and very skilled - a kind of assertion of F D Maurice theology - faith, baptism, communion, inescapably involving political and social action - over against all of the pietism they had heard from some of the white priests. But in actual terms of social and political action, so little can be done by them - or anyone - without trouble.

Geoff and Christine Lowick laid on a very happy party in the evening for me to meet various people.

January 23rd 1972
We drove to Pretoria to see, first, Dr Colin Lang, with whom I had made contact on my last visit. Colin is one of the most intelligent, cultured and politically informed South Africans there could be. He is a physician (and is the son of Matheson Lang, the actor - brother of Archbishop Cosmo Gordon Lang), but has been very active in the racial 'resistance'. His brother, a top lawyer, has had to escape to London. Colin was imprisoned with Mark Nye and Hannah Stanton in the 60's.

I asked Colin how he saw the way ahead. He was *extremely* pessimistic. "Do not be seduced by the economic argument" he said. "Even the enforced repeal of job reservation provisions will not cater for human dignity and relationships; on the contrary, undiluted economic opportunism is what has landed us where we are." He said I must understand the South African power structure. The inner Afrikanner caucus has absolute control. I am glad Colin has given me this caution, but I am not *entirely* convinced. It is true that a 'showdown' is inevitable and anarchy may result. But there seems to me a quite new class of educated Afrikaaner arising who, to preserve his own way of life from damage, will see it as necessary to oppose the Government.

We lunched with Rik Currie, a lad who I had met at the Lee Abbey Student Centre in London and who had come to stay at Hankey Place. He is now married and has a babe. His father is the biggest estate agent in Johannesburg and Pretoria, and he is now in the firm. In London he had given me interesting insights into South Africa - the Curries are one of the oldest South African families.

We drove back to Bryanston for me to preach at Evensong there. I have rarely been so nervous about a sermon. Colin Lang's words have made me even more worried. In my attempt to be positive (and yet be uncompromising!) was I being naively over-optimistic about the situation? There was time to introduce a degree more Colin-type caution into the sermon.

In the event, the sermon was listened to very attentively by the large, wealthy, intelligent, entirely white congregation. I felt I had won a hearing for a viewpoint they are not often exposed to, and a large number stayed behind afterwards to meet me and discuss its implications. There were four Trinity men of my generation in the congregation! - and Dr Gardner, wife of Graham Gardner, Archdeacon in Grahamstown, who was a student at King's with me. I have rarely been quite so relieved to have a sermon behind me.

January 24th 1972
A harrowing day.

Chippy drove me to his office, from which I walked to the flat of the Dean of Johannesburg, Gonville ffrench-Beytagh - a half an hour's walk. I still had an hour before my appointment with him, and sat in the park (on the seats reserved for Europeans only) and then in a cafe. I had been warned that a constant watch was being kept by the police on the Dean's flat, and visitors automatically involved themselves in future suspicion and being kept under police observation. The Dean came to the door but quietly pushed me out on to the balcony before we entered and said that the flat was almost certainly 'bugged' and that we should be careful to avoid reference to other people that might implicate them.

He gave me a verbal message from Helen Joseph, who I was to see at her house at 5.00 pm, re-arranging the interview with her at another place. The police had made their presence felt at her meeting with another visitor to her a few days earlier - arranged on the - tapped - telephone. She saw no reason why the police should interrupt our interview! (Helen has been under house arrest since October 1972. This order remained in force until she had to undergo an operation for cancer in June 1971; but she is still a 'listed' person. Nothing she says or writes may be published in South Africa.)

I gave the Dean the Bishop of Southwark's and the Provost and Cathedral Council's greetings, and passed him what I will call in this journal 'various messages'. He told me a great deal about his trial - which makes one sick - a mockery of justice. Now the Appeal - which will last about a fortnight, with perhaps a reserved judgment for three weeks, is only a few weeks away. He is as prepared as he could be expected to be for the worst - imprisonment. In view of the fact that the state felt they *had* to get a *conviction*, it would be optimistic to think that they will not require the conviction upheld. On the other hand, they may feel embarrassed by having a martyr on their hands, especially if he dies in prison. It might suit them to have given this warning to the Church, and then to be relieved of carrying out the warning. On the other hand, again, the Dean is a British citizen and revoked his South African citizenship some years ago. I believe the Archbishop of Canterbury - and the Bishops - must bring pressure upon the British government to ask for the Dean's deportation if he is convicted. My only reluctance for this is that the Africans may feel again that the whites have deserted them under pressure, as many undoubtedly felt when Bishop Ambrose Reeves, then Bishop of Johannesburg, fled the country. It is very difficult to know what is right. The Dean is not the stuff of which martyrs are made or long time prisoners. He just happens to have done what he saw needed doing and finds himself arrested. He has had some heart trouble, and this year has undoubtedly aged him.

He is, of course, a remarkable man. He should have five years of active ministry left. (He is sixty.) He became Dean of Johannesburg in 1965 after being a considerable success - not least on TV - as Dean of Salisbury. He had gone from Johannesburg to there. He is a kind of Geoffrey Beaumont - brilliant with the upper crust and the rejects of society, alcoholics etc. It is work with ex-prisoners and their families which has got him into trouble here.

If he *wins* his appeal he will resign from being Dean of Johannesburg, and wants to come to England. The Church of England has no 'obligation' to him - he was ordained in South Africa - but I hope we shall feel we owe someone who has served the world church so well all the help we can give. If he is found 'guilty' it will be because he was 'proved' guilty of breaking the 'law' - which forbids people helping the dependents of those in prison who are in need!! Law and Bloody Order!

Since the Dean's case is *sub judice*, it would probably be irresponsible to write down much at this moment in this journal about the case itself.

I came away thankful that with all the faults of the institutional Church - and one sees them here as clearly as in England - the Church has produced in this place Raymond Raynes, CR, Trevor Huddleston, CR, Bishop Ambrose Reeves and Gonville ffrench-Beytagh, and a host of other militants. *Without* the Church - the weak and frail church - the opposition to the Government would have been weak indeed. Yet the witness here is not the witness of a united church. Probably the majority of the white congregations - and even some of the clergy - are lukewarm at most on the race issue.

I saw Helen Joseph at 5.00 pm at the new venue. She *is* the stuff of which martyrs are made. She took very much the position that Colin Lang took - the extreme 'boycott' position. No one can deny the huge witness she has given. But there was something of the temperamental extremist there - she could not take any other position. I do not want to 'psychologise' her witness away. But the *necessity* of aggression raises questions. She was utterly confident she could say what 'the African' thinks of the boycott. But *most* Africans have no opinion. They have not been allowed to have one. Again, it is one thing to want the downfall of a government. It is another to accept that a *country* must collapse before anything can happen.

The unpredictable damage - for Africans as well as whites - that sheer anarchy will bring ought surely to be considered. Though I was not *wholly* with her, it was a huge privilege to see her and talk with her. She was at King's London at one time, and has endured her house-arrest not least by doing extra-mural work with London University by correspondence.

During the day Chippy heard that he must pay an urgent visit to the Orange River where his firm is engaged on the huge construction work of dams, tunnels, canals, etc., so that this would be our last evening together. He took Geoff and Christine and me to a Post Office Tower sort of restaurant. There was a wonderful night view over the whole city of Johannesburg, and glorious food - but, above all, a magnificent band. I shall not forget the singing of *Blowing in the Wind* and *He's got the whole world in his hand*, but I've never heard better played and sung what I requested, *Little green apples in the summer time*.

January 25th 1972
I wrote a long letter to Chippy's wife in England. Then Chippy and I drove in early to the city again and I took leave of him. I shall not see him again until July at the earliest, but probably many months later. That's what's hell about life. May he and his wife and family come together again soon.

I took my things to Geoff's vicarage, and then met the small group of clergy of Geoff's area. We had a good morning - *all* of them disillusioned about the role of the clergy as ordinary parish priests here. I was moved by their painful honesty and their *desire* to 'work through' the situation. Geoff himself is now back at auditing, three days a week, leaving two days and Sundays for the parish.

I then spent five very privileged hours with Dr Ellen Hellmann. She is Gary Runciman's mother-in-law. (Gary was an undergraduate at Trinity in my time. He became a fellow of Trinity, now living and working in London in the family firm and also lecturing and writing on Social and Political Philosophy. He and his wife Ruth are special friends of mine in London.) I went first to her most lovely home - I haven't seen such a magnificent collection of South African works of art - and then lunched with her at the Country Club.

Dr Hellmann is still the Chairman of the Research Committee of the Institute of Race Relations, and I doubt whether there is anyone in South Africa who has a greater command of the subject of Race Relations there - theory and practice. Her brilliant intellect has not simply theorised, but, as an anthropologist and sociologist, she has kept 'stuck in', by visiting, over many many years, the native locations close to Johannesburg.

I wanted first to talk theory with her, and we did. Although she supported the Cricket and Sport's Boycott - because it did no harm to the African - she produced detailed and convincing argument against economic boycott. (It is gratifying to find how many significant people are behind the Sports boycott and greatly appreciate the witness of David Sheppard.)

She produced for me the details of the Polaroid scheme, ie the conditions on which they have agreed to remain in South Africa. (1) Drastic improvement of non-white wages, (2) A scheme for training non-whites for important jobs, (3) Establishment of a Trust giving 679 bursaries in 1971 and in 1972 £13,000 in bursaries and £4,500 for other educational purposes, £250 each year to an association for Black educational and cultural advancement, (4) £3,500 to US/South African leader exchange for two Africans to visit US, (v) Guaranteeing educational expenses, including tuition, transport and books, for the children of non-white employees. This all on a percentage basis of Polaroid's operation in South Africa. I was convinced this was better for the African - and all - than boycott. The scheme is being administered by the South African Institute of Race Relations and Dr Hellmann had spent the weekend selecting people for bursaries.

After lunch we went to Soweto, the area south west of Johannesburg of more than half a million Africans - eight miles from Johannesburg's centre at the nearest point and twenty miles away at its furthest. A lot has happened since I last visited it. When I last saw it people were still trying to escape from the area. Today there is a waiting list of over 13,000 families trying to get in. In this area of several locations, although some people are now well off, with a numerically insignificant group qualifying to be described as affluent, sheer poverty and actual destitution are of frequent occurrence, and the majority of the people, particularly the women, battle throughout their lives to make ends meet. Most of the houses are exactly the same - miles and miles of them.

It is interesting that in this area those in semi-skilled employment have increased from 24.9% since I was last here to 44.8% in 1968/9. Skilled workers have increased by 4%. Unskilled workers have decreased by 24%.

The cost of living spirals, and it remains abundantly clear that for urban Africans, the majority clinging precariously to the breadline, resources cannot meet the basic needs.

Dr Hellmann has written a fascinating booklet on Soweto which yields a great deal of information on it all, eg. the majority of Christians in Soweto still go to witch doctors - and they regard their ancestors as intermediaries between them and God.

The tragedy of Soweto is the so-called 'single' African - 142,469 people, 100,000 of whom are men, who would like to have their wives and children with them, but are prevented from doing so by the Pass Laws. A woman whose husband had died - or who is divorced - cannot rent a house.

Thousands of children leave school before working age. Their respect for the law is nil. But how can you expect them to respect a law which carries criminal sanctions which make one section but not another subject to them? How do you encourage them to differentiate between technical offences and 'real' crimes? How do you get people to respect law when part of it is outright oppression and flagrant injustice?

The Government actively discourages making the area better and more attractive with more facilities. The theory is 'he is only here temporarily: don't discourage him away from his real homeland'. But most of the people have never had any other homeland than Johannesburg, and are never likely to.

Dr Hellmann drove me around Soweto for hours, introducing me to people - the black headmaster of Orlando School, for instance; taking me into houses; showing me the workshop for the handicapped. I was full of admiration for her years of work, for her detailed knowledge - which she shared with me as we drove along; for her unremitting factually based work on behalf of the people of Soweto - providing chapter and verse against the Government - and her marvellous kindness to me. I came out of the location punch-drunk. This bloody country that fences people in like this and so restricts their lives! And yet even around Soweto, a country of such beauty.

It was good - essential - to spend a quiet evening with Geoff and Christine.

In fact, I'm beginning to look forward to a rest somewhere on this 'sabbatical'!

January 26th 1972

After doing an interview for a South African journal, I went to have lunch with the Bishop of Johannesburg, Leslie Stradling - who was one time at St Luke's, Camberwell. He was very calm and friendly. He is probably just the man this situation requires, even though he has been criticised for not being a vocal crusader. He is a patient person, and stands by people quietly - the Dean, the disillusioned clergy, the Africans, etc. There was no despair about him and no false optimism. He has a benign sense of humour, and has no doubt needed it.

I spent an hour in the Institute of Race Relations, and then Christine collected me, and we all went out for an hour in the beautiful country surrounding Johannesburg. Geoff and Christine have been marvellous to me, carting me wherever I needed to go. They really are very special friends. They took me for my last evening to dinner, and to a revue *Hair, Hair*, a remarkable South African satirical production - 'Footlights' type of thing - which has been playing to full houses for three years. This fairly devastating attack on the Government's policies by way of *humour* is, again, one of the hopeful signs in the situation. It could not have happened six years ago.

January 27th 1972

I am really thankful for my month in Africa, and really sad to be leaving it. Even the evil of South Africa's present situation serves only to make the situation tragic and poignant. I feel as I felt when I last left South Africa that this is one place outside England I would love to try and serve. But it is one thing to visit for a week and quite another to stay with it, year in year out. In any case, it is up to this bloody Government whether they let you stay. Maybe the best one can do is to support from outside as best one can those who are struggling within.

> God Bless Africa,
> Guard her people,
> Guide her rulers,
> Give her peace.

Christine drove me with Jonathan to Jan Smuts airport. Geoff met us there, and at 11.30 am the Qantas Boeing 747 was airborne, and we were soon travelling at 35,000 feet and at 600 miles per hour. We left the coastline of Africa at Lourenco Marques. I felt as though I was closing a book that I might never open again.

Stage 5: Australia: Perth, Adelaide, Melbourne

January 28th 1972

The flight from Johannesburg to Perth across the Indian Ocean was long and arduous. You fly over the south of Madagascar, and then, after 1,900 miles, touch down for one hour at the beautiful island of Mauritius. It's dusk when you leave Mauritius, but it's dawn before you arrive at Perth - another 3,000 miles.

A book becomes an indispensable companion through the long night hours.

I read, at midnight, the first lines of the *Autobiography* of Bertrand Russell. The moon, clear and nearly full, shone in the darkness over the cloudless ocean. We were travelling six miles up. Through the window of the Qantas Boeing 747, the wing, stretched out for a hundred feet, was white and incandescent in the moonlight. I tried to photograph it, but the vibrations of the aircraft were almost certainly too great. And perhaps that's right: perhaps that kind of incandescence, seen as one traverses the 'rim of the world', should be left as vision, not trapped and caught.

I never feel nearer my friends, and - the irony of friendship - further away from them - than at such moments. I put the book down for a long while and just looked out of the window into the Abyss, then took it up again, and read:

"What I Have Lived For

Three passions, simple, but overwhelmingly strong, have governed my life: the longing for love, the search for knowledge, and unbearable pity for the suffering of mankind. These passions, like great winds, have blown me hither and thither, in a wayward course, over a deep ocean of anguish, reaching to the very verge of despair.

I have sought love, first, because it brings ecstasy - ecstasy so great that I would have sacrificed all the rest of life for a few hours of this joy. I have sought it, next, because it relieves loneliness - that terrible loneliness in which one shivering consciousness looks over the rim of the world into the cold unfathomable lifeless abyss. I have sought it, finally, because in the union of love, I have seen, in a mystic miniature, the prefiguring vision of the heaven that saints and poets have imagined. This is what I sought, and though it might seem too good for human life, this is what - at last - I have found.

With equal passion, I have sought knowledge. I have wished to understand the hearts of men. I have wished to know why the stars shine. And I have tried to apprehend the Pythagorean power by which number holds sway above the flux. A little of this, but not much, have I achieved.

Love and knowledge, so far as they were possible, led upward toward the heavens. But always pity brought me back to earth. Echoes of cries of pain reverberate in my heart. Children in famine, victims tortured by oppressors, helpless old people a hated burden to their sons; and the world of loneliness, poverty and pain make a mockery of what human life should be. I long to alleviate the evil, but I cannot, and I, too, suffer.

This has been my life. I have found it worth living, and would gladly live it again if the chance were offered me."

I can only say "Amen" to all that. Except that, late in life - and not in his first marriage - Bertrand Russell *found* 'the union of love'. I never quite know whether we are meant to find 'the union of love' in this world. "Now we know in part". "Thou wouldst not be seeking me if thou hadst not already found me".

At the airport at Perth, Howell Witt, the Bishop of N W Australia, was there to greet me, grinning away and waving from a balcony, in an open-necked shirt. Howell was once a curate at St George's, Camberwell. He and Donald Shearman (then Bishop of Rockhampton), stayed with me in S E I for the Lambeth Conference of 1968, and one of the main points of my coming to Perth was to see them again. At this early hour of 5.00 am Howell (who lives in Geraldton, three hundred and more miles to the North) drove me round Perth on the way to the suburb where he had been given a holiday home for ten days. I hadn't been prepared for such a beautiful city. It is magnificently sited, overlooking the wide estuary of the Swan River, close to the Indian Ocean. (The river meets the ocean at Fremantle, a few miles away.) The new buildings that have sprung up in the last ten years are splendid, and so are the surviving Colonial type houses. A good deal of 'bush' has been left to form parks overlooking the sea. I am told there is no better city in all Australia, and I can believe it.

It was good to see Doreen Witt again, and meet the family. After breakfast I went to bed till nearly lunch time. Then beer, and Australia v The Rest of the World on TV. Howell drove me back into town after lunch, to the Archbishop of Perth's house, a lovely Colonial house overlooking the river, where I am staying the weekend. The Archbishop, Geoffrey Sambell, is a specially fine man. He and Donald Shearman (now Chairman of the Australian Board of Missions) and I had a drink before going off to hear Howell Witt give the opening address at the Provincial Conference on Mission at which I am also to speak. Howell, who is in many ways as much unlike a bishop as anyone could imagine, is a raconteur second to none, and his address was a *tour de force*. He is utterly direct, open and warm - a born working-class (Welsh) pastor.

January 29th 1972

After lunch, the Witts drove me down to Fremantle - which was founded before Perth - and we went round the fascinating local museum. There were a great many interesting prints, photographs and newspaper cuttings of the founding era, relating especially to the transportation of convicts there. The museum is, in fact, the old gaol. There were also relics of the ships wrecked on the coast in the 17th century but only recently brought to the surface.

It's an odd thought that Perth is nearer Indonesia than Sydney, two thousand miles away. It was on the direct route to the East Indies via the Cape.

In the evening, Howell and I visited a family whom Howell had known when he was a curate at St George's, Camberwell, and who had called to see me at St George's just before they left the country in 1961 - the Goodys. They were ecstatic at seeing us. We had to call on several families before we traced them, and it was fascinating to learn the problems of a Camberwellian emigrating to Australia and trying to 'make it'. They had moved from several flats and had just moved into their own house.

January 30th 1972
I went to Holy Communion at 8.00 am, in the Cathedral, and came away angry. They were celebrating the Feast of King Charles the Martyr - in Australia! - and most of the congregation were fan-waving old ladies. Later, I did a seminar on 'the Church and the City' at the Conference, and in the evening was one of the panel to answer questions, with Bishop Shearman and the Assistant Bishop, Bishop Macdonald, and Michael Challen, who I had taken to the Mayflower pub, in Rotherhithe, when he visited England. The Archbishop was in the Chair.

Besides a visit to the very beautiful university, the high spot of the day for me was a film shown at the Conference. The film, *This Man*, was produced for the Australian Board of Missions. It won first prize at the Australian Film festival, and was the only Australian film shown at the Moscow Film Festival this year. It is about the impact of Western Culture on the Pacific islanders. It portrays the terrible dilemma - how to take the best of Western civilisation and not also take the worst. It is based on a play written about a Solomon Islander, whom I shall be meeting soon. It speaks of the Melanesian loss of a sense of identity and meaning, and the disappearance of the old ways that gave happiness and security. The part of 'This Man' is played by the Melanesian whom I shall also be meeting - he speaks very simply his inmost thoughts for himself and his people; but the questions come back like a boomerang on those watching the film. 'How to take the best of Western civilisation and not also take the worst' is not simply a Melanesian problem. The film begins:

"I am looking for myself....."

I must try and get it screened on TV in England.

Late in the evening, I returned with the Archbishop, and, before going to bed, had a long talk with him about the Church in Perth, in Australia, in Southwark and in England. It is good to meet a man who is so right as the leader of the Church in this fastest expanding city in Australia, who is full of love, wisdom and strength - though I suspect that the 'strength' can sometimes be used rather powerfully!

It was incredibly lucky that Howell Witt should be on holiday here, and that Donald Shearman should be at the Conference here - 2,000 miles from his base - and that the Archbishop (whom I had never met) should be such an open and generous host to me. In the Archbishop's house, there have also been Peter, the Archbishop's nineteen year-old Melbourne nephew, and Tao, a twenty year-old Laotian, who have both been very kind to me.

Just as Nigeria turned out to be so right a beginning of my time in Africa, so this place has been a marvellous beginning to Australia - and the Pacific. The four bishops have shared with me the problems and hopes of the Church in Australia; the people at the Conference have given me an introduction to the 'ordinary Australian'; and there has been this wonderful city as the background.

The temperature, the first day, was one hundred degrees! It has been cooler since. It needed to be!

January 31st 1972
Some of Howell Witt's clergy were at the Provincial Conference, others were holidaying near Perth. As Monday was a national holiday, he invited all his clergy who would like to, to bring their wives and families - and their lunch - to a spot in one of the 'bush' parks, and to picnic together. The large majority of them did so. It was huge fun, and a great tribute to

Howell that so many came so readily. After lunch I was asked to talk to them and to answer their questions. It was like talking to a group of clergy and their wives on Hampstead Heath! It was not so easy in the extreme heat of the burning sun; but they were so friendly it all went off marvellously. Talking to them individually gave me an insight into and sympathy with their problems - priest and wife and family. The next priest to them is probably over a hundred miles away. The cost of getting even to Perth makes it impossible to get there more than once a year. Further afield is out of the question. N W Australia is an isolated area; and even Perth is somewhat cut off from the rest of Australia. In the North West there is a personal and mental isolation to be faced, and the extreme mobility of the well-paid mining population increases the problems of living there.

The problem of the Aboriginal - which is now on the conscience of all Australians - has to be faced directly by the Church in the North West. I have been reading all I can about it since I arrived in Australia. I have found *The First Australians* by RM and CH Berndt particularly helpful.

In the evening, as it was Mrs Witt's birthday - 'Old Mother Witt' as the Bishop insists on calling her (at fifty-one) - I went out with them for a marvellous family dinner. It was a perfect end to a memorable weekend.

Howell put me on the 'plane taking me to Adelaide, which left Perth at one in the morning. It reached Adelaide at 6.00 am, their time; but we have lost two hours in flight. The flying time (ie sleeping time) was only three hours.

February 1st 1972
I was visiting Adelaide not to see any bishops or archbishops! I simply wanted to see again an Australian school-mistress, Shirley Bates, whom Peggy Taylor (now Headmistress of

Benhilton JM & I School) had met in her year in Australia, and who had come to stay in Camberwell with Peggy for quite a while when I was at St George's. Shirley was up early to meet me at the airport, and took me to her bungalow home to meet her eighty year-old father. He had been a baker in earlier years, and I was not disappointed in thinking I'd learn a good deal about Australia from him.

I retired to bed quickly, after breakfast, not only to catch up on sleep, but because I had interior evidence that I should not have abandoned my daily Entero-Vioform tablets so readily!

Early in the afternoon we drove thirty-five miles, to one of Shirley's colleague's weekend house, overlooking a wonderful sandy cove and beach, as long as any I've ever seen. The breakers were considerable, but I managed to find a quiet spot away from all the intimidating young gentlemen in their twenties, with surfboards or underwater swimming equipment, leaving Shirley and her friend, Barbara, to indulge in more orthodox swimming in the shallows. I simply lay on the beach, covered by the warm breakers when they rolled up the shore, but left like flotsam (or jetsam?) when they receded. A quiet half hour of this erotic pleasure of burning sun and warm water was very heaven. I did venture into the breakers a little, but they were bigger than me and I was told there was an 'under tow'; and I didn't see the sense of ending life in that particular way. In fact, early on, one breaker got hold of me and threw me on the beach, grazing my kneecap, which I thought was quite uncalled for. An evening meal in Barbara's house, while we watched the sun fall into the sea, ended a most marvellous and refreshing day.

February 2nd 1972

In the morning, Shirley and I looked first at the Cathedral, at which an Ordination was about to begin. I had a quick chat with the Bishop, who was having a last minute smoke behind the vestry! At the time, I was trying to find traces of Baroness Burdett-Coutts, who gave the money for the building of St Stephen's, Rochester Row, and I remember, for the founding of the Dioceses of Adelaide, Cape Town and British Columbia.

To my surprise, the Cathedral was just off a main street, 'Montefiore Hill'. Nobody seemed to know who *this* Montefiore was; so, while I was in the Museum, I looked him up in the Australian National Dictionary of Biography. Joseph Barrow Montefiore, of Barbados and London, went to New South Wales in 1828. He did a great deal of merchanting there, but went bankrupt! The Rothschilds, and others, enabled him to begin again in South Australia: viz Adelaide. 'Enterprising, urbane, noted for his wit and prodigious memory.....Being young and enterprising, and with a penchant for large speculative ventures.' He had ten daughters and three sons. I went from the Museum to the Art Gallery; a small but fine Collection. There was a particularly good head of Nehru by Epstein, and a sensitive painting of a boy's head by Lucian Freud.

Adelaide is surrounded by a semi-circle of hills, with marvellous views of the city. Shirley and I drove out - and up - twenty miles, into the glorious country, to Oakbank, where she and Peggy Taylor had both taught.

In the evening, after all too brief a visit to Adelaide, I caught the 'plane to Melbourne.

The Co-adjutor (Assistant) Bishop, Jim Grant, met me at the airport. The Archbishop, Frank Woods, had decided to put me up at Trinity College - which is very much the child of Trinity College, Cambridge (where the Archbishop was also once chaplain), and where the Co-adjutor still lives.

Having left Shirley's house at 5.30 pm, and arrived in Melbourne at 7.55 pm, I imagined there would be an evening meal; but our 'common tongue' failed me. Jim Grant invited me to 'supper'. But, in Australia, 'tea' is not merely tea but tea plus quite a lot - an evening meal, in fact - whereas 'supper' is tea plus nothing, save, perhaps a biscuit. I therefore went empty to bed on 'supper' - with the knowledge that I was neverthless in a land of *promise* where hospitality is concerned! I was showered with food for the mind by the Warden, Dr Sharwood - *The Historic Buildings of Victoria, Australia in Painting*, etc and I had an enjoyable browse before putting my light out.

February 3rd 1972
After a good breakfast in College Hall, Jim Grant drove me to the Cathedral office. I had five minutes with the Archbishop, whose son, Theodore Woods (with whom I shall be staying in New Guinea) was one of my undergraduates at Trinity, Cambridge. I then spent a fascinating morning with Laurie Styles, the Director of the Inter-Church Trade and Industry Mission of Melbourne, (whom Frank Woods brought out with him from Manchester). Laurie had landed himself very nicely with 'consultancy work' (I don't mean to be cynical!) which takes him regularly to New Guinea and the Phillipines - preparing, for instance, the clergy of New Guinea for the Industrial Revolution, which - it may be hard to credit - is already hitting them very hard.

Laurie is also as convinced as I am that Community Development work is the real hope in the inner-city areas of big cities - Melbourne and Port Moresby here. For several years I have been trying to press this as *the* appropriate method for our 'inner-city' areas, having seen it in operation in Chicago. I was interested to see reports of it here from Calcutta and Manila.

The 'inner-city' work in Australasia is bound to involve the migrant question - which is here not only the 'colour' question but the uprooting and resettling of peoples of very many places - Greeks, Papuans, Samoans, Italians, British, etc. etc.

I was interested to note that in Melbourne it was regarded as essential that all Industrial Chaplains should be trained pastoral counsellors - the pressures of technological organisations and social change were so great upon workers. But although the requirement of this training could be partly attributable to the fact that industrialists are less ready than in England to have the parson around in industry - unless he can prove he is doing a specific job, eg. on the personnel side - ITIM was clearly by no means closed to consideration of the vast issues that confront industry and society, as distinct from individuals in industries.

My morning was very valuable in terms of comparing and contrasting the urban and industrial problems of Melbourne and South London, but it was also valuable as an induction course for my visits to Fiji, the Solomons and New Guinea. Most people in England, when I have told them I wanted to visit the Solomon Islands, have chuckled. One of the main reasons I have wanted to visit the area is because it had become clear to me in reading about the Solomons that the Industrial Revolution had burst upon it in the last decade. For instance, the largest mine-working *in the world* is now on Bouganville Island - copper. The 'Bouganvillea' image is being shattered by the realities of politics, finance and technology. Copper was only discovered there in 1964.

Laurie took me to lunch at the headquarters of Melbourne's Electricity Board, in the centre of Melbourne, in a new building sixteen floors high. (He is Chaplain there.) The views of Melbourne, ancient and modern, from his office, were dramatic.

Basically, Melbourne is a Victorian city, like Liverpool; but the new 'high rise', as elsewhere, transform the skyline.

In the afternoon, I was taken to St John's, Camberwell - an affluent suburb (with Camberwell Road and Denmark Hill!) to speak to the Diocesan Team Ministry Commission. I was very direct with them, speaking as honestly and openly as I could about my Southwark - and around England - experience. They were very appreciative. My Chairman, Archdeacon Peter Monie, I had last met at Edward Thompson's induction as Vicar of St Michael's, Camberwell, SE5 - the Archdeacon had been Vicar of St Michael's until 1942, but only revealed this in his closing remarks!

Dinner back at Trinity College was very good and very civilised. At certain times there is little to beat the don's life for the bachelor. Good meals, provided at stated times. Cultured company and conversation in agreeable surroundings. Tonight there were half a dozen young dons in for dinner, all under thirty; an older fellow who was at Pembroke College, Cambridge; and the Bishop and myself. The Australian wines were excellent. Then I could retire to my own room, with obligations to no one. (I have simply loved staying with people in the last five weeks, and without exception they have been marvellous to me; but there have been few times when I could simply go to my own room.) As the evening meal was at 6.30 pm, I was back in my room at 8.00 pm. After an hour's work, I decided to walk into the city, half an hour's walk. It was a wrong decision. I ought to have learnt by now that there is little to be said for walking by oneself - it is different with company - in the centre of big cities at night. All the world's loneliness meets there. I stood looking over a bridge into the river Yarra for ten minutes and decided to catch the first tram back to College! Trams are such friendly things - their noise as they clang and whine their way along; their sudden jovial lurches; their triumphant occupation of the middle of the road; their reminiscence of one's childhood. The Number Nineteen had almost succeeded in making me feel a member of the human race again by the time I was put down outside the College. I went to bed immediately, but pursued sleep with only spasmodic success.

February 4th 1972

I spent the morning working on my address for the afternoon, on 'Planning and Strategy for Inner-city Ministry'. The title had been given me when I arrived by the excellent Archbishop's Chaplain, Barry Martin, who had worked in, and been baffled by, the Melbourne inner-city; and I wanted to produce something worthwhile for the gathering the Archbishop had invited.

I had only time for a bar of chocolate for lunch, near a towering Insurance block in the city. (I took what I hope will be impressive photographs from its sixteenth floor observation balcony.) The ecumenical group who gathered in the Cathedral Council Chamber for my paper, under the Chairmanship of Bishop Robert Dann, were very receptive, and well repaid the work on it.

In the evening, it was good to dine again in College Hall. Being with the young dons is becoming like being part of a family. You don't have to say much to get them to talk excitedly about their particular subjects, and some of them are young enough to try hard to converse well.

The evening's walk, in the immediate area of the College, was a little more successful. It is, in the main, an area built in 1860, with a great deal of cast iron decoration - fences and gates, balustrades, and stucco ornament, parapets and cornices, urns, date plaques, name plaques, verandahs and balconies. The area, having been occupied for some time by Italians, is now becoming a student area surrounding the university. It is very attractive - so attractive that as one walks one forgets one doesn't belong, until a happy gang of students comes along in jeans, and one can only look at them from the outside!

Derek Tasker writes that when Lord Beaverbrook was asked why he paid Godfrey Winn the largest salary of anyone on his staff, he replied, "Y'sse, he shakes hands with people's hearts". There must be millions who want to do that, but very few who do it without invasion. It really takes two to shake hands - that's why wandering around as 'a stranger in a strange land' is rarely all joy!

But Bishop Grant has just called to say that two students want us to go over to have some Australian port with them. How absurdly grateful one is for such spontaneous kindness! 'I was a stranger and ye took me in.'

February 5th 1972

I spent the morning working on my sermon for the Cathedral tomorrow evening. After lunch, the Warden of Trinity asked me if he could show me Melbourne's new National Gallery. I had no idea it was so staggeringly beautiful. It is a building of immense space, with careful use of wood, lighting, fabrics, water, glass, stone, to give glorious patterns and rhythms, and different qualities of light. The Great Hall has a modern stained glass ceiling which is magical: a canopy of coloured glass by Leonard French that reminded me of Rouault. One open court of stone slabs has a Rodin carving of Balzac and a Henry Moore - and a persimmon tree, on which the sun shone brilliantly. It was all thrilling; and the paintings and the glass and china within, are all displayed in stands that are perfect. I think I could only express in music the joy the building gave me.

The Warden and I then went on to the Botanical Gardens,

which are renowned amongst those who know about such things throughout the world. In the brilliant sun they were most lovely. The Union Jack on the white Government House - like Osborne - just behind, fluttered against clear blue sky - 'dominion over palm and pine' - literally that, for the gardens are dense with palms and pines, and golden shafts of light pierce the deep paths between them, until the path opens on to wide lawns and a lake with water lilies.

The Warden, and the Bishop and Dr Max Thomas, the Senior Lecturer in Divinity, took me to dine at an Italian restaurant in the evening. Very kind. The Bishop, Jim Grant, is like Bing Crosby in his *Bells of St Mary's* days, a lovable teddy bear, who was as good at his inner-city parish as he was, more recently, at the other end of things, as Bishop's Chaplain.

February 6th 1972

I preached in the College Chapel this morning. It is still vacation, so it had a congregation of intelligent and upper-middle-class townspeople. I preached on 'That which cometh upon me daily: the care of all the churches. Who is weak and I am not weak? Who is offended and I burn not?' The choir was very good, but the organist was superb. I haven't been so taken to the ramparts of heaven by an organist for years. He made one feel that on a clear day you would be able to see the pearly gates! I talked to him afterwards. He had been trained in France.

Dr Max Thomas celebrated Holy Communion and took me off with his wife and family to a barbecue lunch at their home. The twelve year-old boy, Mark, had marvellous brown eyes and was very kind to me. It was Blanche, in *Streetcar named Desire*, who said "I have always depended on the kindness of strangers". I don't suppose the boy realised he was being kind.

At 5.30 pm, the Dean picked me up, to transport me to the Deanery and then to the Cathedral. It is a large William Butterfield building. There was something very English about Evensong there. I preached on: "But a Samaritan, as he journeyed *came where he was.*"

After Evensong, I had dinner with the Archbishop and Mrs Woods. He is a really good and lovable person, and I think, great. We talked a lot about his recent visit to Melanesia, for the commemoration of the centenary of the martyrdom of the first martyr, John Coleridge Patteson; and his visit afterwards to the copper mine at Bouganville; and to New Guinea; and an earlier visit last year to East Africa. We also talked a good deal about the problems of the Church in Australia, and about his family. The three or four hours went very quickly. Melbourne could not have had a better Archbishop in these last years.

I was delighted to see a photograph of F W Head, Archbishop of Melbourne 1929 - 1941, in the entrance to Bishops House. I remembered him as one of John Robinson's uncles - Forbes Robinson's - proteges, and also as the person who had lived with CFG Masterman and Reggie Bray in one of the flats of 'the Albany', at the junction of Albany Road and Camberwell Road, in St George's parish, at the beginning of the century; 'with a sheet over their heads to prevent the bugs from falling on them'! Later, he was Dean of Emmanuel College, Cambridge, and Vicar of Christ Church, Greenwich.

Before putting the light out, I read a fifty page biographical sketch of Archbishop Head by his wife, which Frank Woods lent me. Head had 'recurrent attacks of unreasonable depression... He could immerse himself in his work, and in helping other people, but for days the burden would be there, waiting for his leisure moments, until release would come, for no apparent reason, and he could say with a sigh of relief to the one person to whom he spoke of it: "Good. The blue devils have gone. Thanks be!" How like CFG Masterman!

February 7th 1972
I was glad to celebrate Holy Communion in the College Chapel before packing my bags for New Zealand. Barry Martin, the Archbishop's Chaplain, drove me round his former inner-city parish; took me to his home for a snack; and transported me to the airport. He has been so kind. He wanted to talk this morning about coming to England to pursue Basil Bernstein's theories on the education of children from deprived backgrounds. It is interesting that David Sheppard and he - from different ends of the globe, and quite different churchmanship - have come to see Bernstein as central to the Church's work in inner-city areas.

Stage 6: New Zealand

February 7th 1972

The flight to New Zealand from Melbourne is a surprise for someone from England. It is much longer than one expects. I left at 1.30 pm and arrived at 7.05 pm in Wellington: and although you lose a couple of hours in travelling, and travel in a Lockheed Electra Jet Prop, (which is a good deal slower than the aircraft I've been travelling in during the last weeks), it is a much greater distance than most English people imagine - 1,490 miles. But the real surprise comes when you eventually reach New Zealand. In the Wellington 'plane, the first land you sight is the most violent and hostile mountain country you can imagine. You cross some of the Southern Alps in the South Island. It is more dramatic, rugged and barren country than I have yet seen anywhere in the world. I knew, of course, that New Zealand had its mountains, but the pastoral image one has of New Zealand (New Zealand butter etc!) tames the mountains in the Englishman's imagination. In reality, they are angry, savage and forbidding. But, before the 'plane reaches Wellington, they give way to country much more like Switzerland - densely wooded alps that rise up out of the lakes, with roads perched precipitously not far from the water's edge: a ribbon girdling the mountains.

You come into Wellington - on the southernmost tip of the North Island - from behind it, between mountains; and the runway stretches nearly to the shore of the harbour. It is a lovely city, like, I imagine, Hong Kong, and Rio, but, of course, much smaller. It is only 120,000 people. The houses cling to the hills rising from the water's edge. The city area itself is fairly confined. Now, inevitably, there are several skyscrapers.

David Swain and Cally, now married two years, met me at the airport. They were at Clapham Parish Church until a year ago. David had just become Anglican Chaplain to Wellington University, and they had only moved in ten days earlier to Ramsey House, the Anglican Chaplaincy Centre. (There is an inter-denominational Chaplain as well, who is also an Anglican, so David's job will not be easy!)

While they drove me up hill and down dale, in a lightning tour of the areas encircling and above the harbour - with wonderful views of the twilight - we caught up on news. Cally is out at work all day as a psychiatric social worker, at a hospital twenty miles away; so time was precious. The Bishop of London and Mrs. Stopford, Cally's parents, had not long left them, after a stay of two months.

The first evening's conversation was important to me, not least because I rather desperately needed to be 'put in the picture' about New Zealand. While I was in Australia, I had reluctantly agreed to broadcast this coming Sunday from one of the Wellington churches, and I was very anxious to get my bearings. In fact, I wrote the first draft of the sermon for the broadcast in bed before I went to sleep, to get it out of my mind a little.

February 8th 1972
Cally went off to work at 8.00 am. At 8.15 am David celebrated Holy Communion downstairs in the Centre Chapel (term had not yet begun). Then we went on foot to look at the University and the city. It really is a very attractive city. A couple of

museums - one with a fine display of Maori culture, the other with interesting prints, paintings and records of the early days of Wellington and New Zealand - and the Art Gallery - were all fascinating. (There were three Brangwyns in the Art Gallery.) I managed to get ten minutes' nap, lying full length on the floor of David and Cally's flat (always the best way to recover, I think) before Hazel Voizey came at 2.45 pm, to take me off ten miles to Lower Hutt, where she is Warden of the Retreat and Conference Centre, Frederick Wallis House. I have been in touch with Hazel ever since she lived in the parish of St Stephen's, Rochester Row, Westminster, where I was a curate. For thirteen years she has been running Wallis House, not least as a lay training centre; and I have always wanted to see where she was working. At 4.30 pm, Hazel took me in her car to the new Dowse Art Gallery in Lower Hutt which is run by David Millar. In his vacations from Westcott House, Cambridge, David used to come and live with us at St George's, Camberwell, and once I holidayed with him. I have corresponded with him over the years, but he was a person I longed to see again and to talk to. We took up exactly where we had left off seven years ago and he told me the splendid news that he had just got engaged. After looking at his fine modern art gallery, and having a rather ecstatic conversation with him, he took me home to meet his fiancée, Susan. I was overjoyed for him.

After a couple of hours with David, I went back to Wallis House, where Hazel was giving a supper party for me. David and Cally, Godfrey Wilson, (from whose church I shall be broadcasting on Sunday), and his wife; William Alington, an architect, and his wife, were there. It was a specially happy evening.

February 9th 1972
After breakfast and Holy Communion in the Centre - David had asked the 'Inter-Denom' Chaplain to celebrate the

Communion - I talked with the Wellington Inner-City Ecumenical Team Ministry from 8.45 am until 10.15 am. Then I was whisked off to the airport to catch a 'plane to Dunedin.

New Zealand had come to mean a great deal to me through one of my curates at St George's, Camberwell, himself a New Zealander, John Latham (who brought David Millar to the Vicarage). He then became Chaplain of Trinity, until he returned here with his wife and children a year ago. A lot of my time in New Zealand will be spent with John, and relations and friends of his, who have come to stay with me either at Camberwell or at Hankey Place, and who have become special friends of mine.

The flight to Dunedin, to the south of the South Island, 400 miles from Wellington, mainly above clouds, revealed what a diverse country New Zealand is. As we passed near Christchurch, there were flat fields as far as the eye could see. As we came down to land at Dunedin, once over the coast - we travelled mostly over the sea - we were over a coastal plain of square fields edged with firs and poplars and gentle hills of the lushest green. No wonder New Zealanders love their country - and are grieved the English so often think of it as a mere postscript to Australia!

John's sister, Ann, married to Leatham Edmond, the director of a hardware firm in Dunedin, came to meet me at Dunedin airport, twenty miles out of Dunedin. Ann and Leatham had stayed with me two years ago, but I had never met the three marvellous children, Neil, Ian and Genevieve. We drove to Dunedin itself through country very like the Tweed valley, and it was no surprise to see a heavy statue of Burns in the centre of Dunedin opposite the Cathedral. I popped into the Cathedral, which has just had a modern East End added on to it, because I knew I would be seeing the Dean, Timothy Raphael, later on, and his wife and family. Timothy was my fellow curate for a while at St Stephen's, Rochester Row, and then became Vicar of St Mary's, Welling, Kent, in Southwark Diocese. We also popped into Leatham's hardware shop - one of several branches in the South Island - which, again, you might find in, say, Melrose or Peebles.

Dunedin is ten miles or so along a beautiful estuary, which looks more like a lake - or a loch. Port Chalmers is at the mouth of the estuary. Ann and Leatham's beautiful wooden house is just above the estuary, twenty minutes' drive along the estuary shore road, and commands most wonderful views. After lunch, Ann drove me back into Dunedin to see Timothy Raphael and Anne and the children. Timothy is a New Zealander and is without doubt one of the most gifted young churchmen in New Zealand. (He writes a column in the local paper and is, at the moment, in the centre of a controversy. He is regarded as far too 'permissive'!) His wife, Anne, is a Lancashire girl, and was a nurse at St Thomas's Hospital. A place like Dunedin is nowadays almost bound to be a curious combination of Victorianism and the rejection of it. A great orchestra will come to it once or twice a year. But all the time television, for instance, breaks into what might be and to some extent is, a fairly enclosed world.

Ann and Leatham had invited Timothy and Anne to dinner. We had a memorable evening, though almost inevitably Tim and I reminisced a little too much of St Stephen's, Rochester Row, and what had gone on there, fifteen to twenty years ago, when George Reindorp was our Vicar. However, it bears repeating - occasionally!

February 10th 1972
The day of a lifetime.

Having said goodbye to Leatham, Ian and Genevieve (we

dropped Neil off at his school), Ann drove me to an airfield - more a field - outside Dunedin - not the airport. With great generosity, John and Ann Latham's mother, 'Da', had arranged to meet me there at 9.10 am with a Cherokee aeroplane! We saw it in the sky just as we approached the airfield. It was a little Piper four-seater. John's brother, Bill, was also in the 'plane, and Keith Wakeman, one of New Zealand's most experienced pilots, was at the controls.

We first flew, taking about an hour, to Wanaka, where the Lathams have a summer house on Lake Wanaka. I didn't realise at the time just what a 'preparatory' flight this was for the afternoon! We rose to five thousand feet, not needing to fly higher, but the snow-covered mountain summits were beginning to appear in the distance. I could hardly believe I was flying in this minute 'plane, seated next to the pilot, learning how to take control of it, and that I was not more scared! The weather was clearing, and we were travelling over increasingly barren country. Lake Wanaka is like a Norwegian fjord. We dropped down on a field at one end of it. There was a heavenly interlude. The Lathams have a jet-boat which we launched on the lake, and for an hour we drove around it - the Lake is so vast, we, even so, only saw a fraction of it. I took the control of the boat for quite a while. (Fascinating for someone who wouldn't dream of driving a car!) Back at the summer house we lunched on crayfish and salad. 'Da' Latham wanted me to taste what she considers New Zealand's best food. It was magnificent. The Visitors' Book revealed that Sir Edmund Hillary and Tenzing had stayed in the house just a little while earlier.

By two o'clock we were taking off again from the airfield. Then began a flight which beggars description. We flew into the course of the Hunter river, mountains following first of all Lake Hawea, the mountains towering either side and around us. As we gradually gained height, the grey jagged slate-like mountains became more and more snow-covered at their summits. We slowly made our way past the summit of Mount Aspiring - 9,959 feet - and the Fox Glacier, and a host of other lesser peaks. Eventually, there was Mount Cook, 12,349 feet, not many yards away, as majestic as the Matterhorn. We kept a safe distance, for, although the sky was now fairly clear, a moving pall of clouds held close to the mountains themselves, and although we were remarkably free from disturbances, every few minutes we would be buffeted sufficiently to remind us how precarious was our existence. A sudden fall of a few feet could make you feel the end was at hand! I took the controls every now and again. It was astonishing to see how the 'plane responded to the slightest pressure, the little right wing on my right or the little left wing on Keith Wakeman's left dipping as you touched either side of the joystick. Just past Mount Cook, a most beautiful valley and then the coastal plain and the sea opened up. The mountains are not ten miles from the sea. We landed on the Franz Joseph Glacier airfield, and had a drink at the hotel there. We had been flying for more than an hour. At four we took off again, and, within, twenty minutes, we had gained ten thousand feet, and were passing close to Mount Arrowsmith, 9,971 feet. (On this mountain Ann Latham had had a climbing accident and her climbing partner had been killed.) The saddles of the mountains had sharp jagged edges like the backs of prehistoric monsters. We then came back to have a look at Mount Hutt. Keith wanted to have a closer look at it, and we turned round in a confined space, near the mountain, banking, of course, very steeply. Only then did I *wish* for the end! The erosion here was frightening. I know no scene of such utter and unrelieved primeval devastation.

Within a very short time, once we had set course for Christchurch, we were over the patchwork of flat fields. Keith said: "You take over now: it's downhill all the way from here", and by half-past five we were on the ground at Christchurch airport. In our little Cherokee I felt that all the jets were 'Big Brother watching us'! The airport itself seemed vast after the landings strips we had used during the day.

After a farewell drink with our good pilot, Keith, Bill Latham drove his mother and me to their home at Little River - twenty miles south east of Christchurch, where her husband, Tom, who had been 'holding the fort' all day, was there to greet us. Tom had come to stay at Hankey Place three years ago and visited us several times at Camberwell. He had been a schoolmaster for many years at Wanganui Collegiate School, where John is now Chaplain; but fifteen years' ago, when 'Da's' father died, Tom and 'Da' returned to where 'Da' was born, to what had always been her family home; a lovely white-boarded house, built at the turn of the century. We sat outside, recalling the day, as the sun went down, and then dined on hogget (lamb!) from the farm. It had been a thrilling day - and exhausting. 'Da' is over sixty and Tom just a little older. Twenty years younger, I was as ready for bed as they were, and I was fast asleep before ten.

February 11th 1972

I was awoken in the early morning by a low-flying aircraft, which was spraying the farm with fertiliser. It was misty and drizzling with rain. (How lucky we were yesterday!) I stayed in bed finishing my sermon for Sunday. At 12.30 pm, John Denny and Jill and two of their children came to lunch. They had lived for a while in the clergy house at Camberwell. Now he is a priest in Christchurch. He is a very fine priest but was sceptical about the future of the Anglican Church in New Zealand.

After lunch, I went for an hour's walk around the farm with 'Da'. The farm stretches each way to the top of the surrounding hills. Having been brought up in towns (and chased as a child by the local dogs - and perhaps too often at the receiving end of remarks like: "Don't go near him: he may bite you.") I am rather pleased with my increasing ability nowadays to walk around a farm happily with half a dozen dogs.

The trees out here are simply wonderful - many trees we never see in England. The country is a cross between the Lake District and parts of the Highlands of Scotland. I spent a long time just looking at five hundred or so sheep in their pens. They just looked at me! I was saying to myself: "Why ever do you exist?" I wondered what *they* were thinking! They were all the same, and all different.

When we got back to the house, there was one of those gatherings from which one learns so much. Tom, 'Da', Bill and their agent, and Del, who works on the farm, shearing and so on, gathered on the step with two men who had come to buy 531 ewes - and their adviser and arbitrator. Over a few drinks, I learnt more about rearing sheep - and the New Zealand economy in general - than I would ever otherwise have learnt. They were all, in their own way, what I would call 'gentlemen': people of honour, with a definite job to do, who are part of the fabric of the world. Mrs Usher, who helps in the house two days a week, and Ann, a girl who looks after the racehorses, also joined the drinking and talking together. It was a marvellous *meeting*.

After lamb chops and Australian wine, and a very good chat with Tom and 'Da', I had another welcome early night.

February 12th 1972
Tom brought up to my room the sermon he had preached in the Chapel of Wanganui School when he was a housemaster, and his collection of sayings which had meant a lot to him in life. A generous thing to do. I then took my leave of the house. I was quite sad to leave a house which combines so well the hard work of the farm world with a good deal of a different

sort of culture. The rooms of the house are full of books - and also of fine water colours done by earlier generations of Montgomery's - 'Da's' family - who lived in the house.

'Da' drove me over for coffee to Bill's house, five miles away, through the hill country close to the sea of Akaroa, much of it Montgomery-owned farm country. Then we drove to Christchurch, via Lyttelton harbour. I lunched again with John and Jill Denny - this time in their vicarage in Christchurch - and Jill drove me with the children to the airport.

David and Cally were waiting for me again at Wellington airport. It had become a windy but sunny afternoon, and we had a very enjoyable tea on the rocks of the harbour. Within the harbour, yachts were busily engaged in a regatta. Outside it, the breakers dashed themselves over the shore. David drove us all round the peninsula - great seas in the sun.

Cally had prepared a marvellous dinner for my last night with them.

February 13th 1972
I preached at St Peter's, Wellington at 11.00 am. The service was broadcast. The Gospel for the day in the New Zealand liturgy was the story of Zaccheus. He seemed the appropriate subject for a sermon broadcast to an affluent society.

Afterwards we called on Harry Baines, the Bishop of Wellington, and acting Archbishop. His mother is a Lyttelton, and he is thus closely related to Mrs CFG Masterman and Hilda Grenfell, the two aged daughters of General Sir Neville Lyttelton, whom I still see from time to time. Hilda is now bedridden in Westminster, but - having seen Lyttelton, the port of Christchurch, on Saturday, and having seen the Bishop, I was able to send her a postcard, in the hope that she will be lucid enough to read it.

David and Cally and I quickly took leave of the Bishop, and drove to Wanganui, 120 miles north of Wellington, almost entirely along the coast road. It was the longest journey by car I had yet made in New Zealand. The sun shone all the way. We were seldom far from the sea and always in beautiful country, again like the Scottish lowlands, but rarely green, more a dun brown. David and Cally had been specially kind to drive me to Wanganui. They had to return immediately. For me, it was a parting from them and a reunion with John Latham and Jill and their five children. They are also just adopting a baby boy who has an Indian mother and a white father.

Wanganui Collegiate School, at which John is Chaplain, is one of the top public schools of New Zealand. His house is immediately opposite the school. It was soon time for evening chapel. The Bishop of Waiapu, Paul Reeves, was the preacher. He was under forty - like a vigorous London slum priest. He has Maori blood in him. He preached well, with a rugged modern style. (He had been curate to Dennis Rutt, in Norwich.) Immediately after chapel, the Bishop, the deputy head and his wife, Tony Latham (who is 'Public Prosecutor') and Sue his wife, (John's aunt and uncle) came to dinner. There was a great deal of fairly serious conversational battling over the role - if any - of such a school as Wanganui today - given to Bishop Selwyn in 1852 in trust for 'the education of our children of all races and of other destitute persons being inheritors of islands in the Pacific Ocean.....' I withdrew from the fray, exhausted, at 1.30 am.

February 14th 1972
I spoke to half the School at Assembly time, and took the Sixth Form Divinity periods in the afternoon, otherwise I intention-

ally did very little except be with the family, which was a huge delight.

February 15th 1972

I spoke to the other half of the School at Assembly time on, again, 'What you see depends on where you stand'. I was going to the school library afterwards, in search of a book that Tom Latham had put me on to - the edition of the Collected Poems of Rupert Brooke which has in it the memoir of him by his mother, which includes his account of his journeys to the South Seas - Samoa, Tahiti, Fiji and New Zealand. I was introduced to the Headmaster, Tom Wells, on the way, who wanted to thank me for what I'd said at Assembly. He said he had a copy of this book in his study, "But", he asked, "have you read what he writes on 'Mysticism'?" I hadn't, but I jumped for joy when I read it. It says what I've been feeling all the way round the world so far:-

Mysticism.....

"consists in just looking at people and things as themselves - neither as useful nor moral nor ugly nor anything else; but just as being. At least, that's a philosophical description of it. What happens is that I suddenly feel the extraordinary value and importance of everybody I meet, and almost everything I see. In *things* I am moved in this way especially by some things; but in people by almost all people. I roam about places - yesterday I did it even in Birmingham! - and sit in trains and see the essential glory and beauty of all the people I meet. I can watch a dirty middle-aged tradesman in a railway carriage for hours, and love every dirty great sulky wrinkle in his weak chin and every button on his spotted unclasped waistcoat....Its the same about the things of ordinary life. Half an hour's roaming about a street or village or railway station shows so much beauty that it's impossible to be anything but wild with suppressed exhilaration. And it's not only beauty and beautiful things. In a flicker of sunlight or a blank wall, or a reach of muddy pavement, or smoke from an engine at night, there's a sudden significance and importance and inspiration that makes the breath stop...."

Jill and I went round the local Museum and Art Gallery this morning. In the Museum there were a great many examples of the ancient Maori arts and crafts. In the Art Gallery - another Brangwyn. John, Jill and I then drove out seventeen miles to someone I had been simply longing to see again for many years - Dougall McIntosh, who stayed with us at Camberwell, and who now owns a farm in the most wonderful highland country, along a twisting road round gullies and crevasses of several hundred feet. Dougall has been married for two years and has a beautiful one year-old, flaxen-haired child, Ewan. His wife is expecting another in the next four days. We all lunched - on venison - in the open, (Amaryllis were growing on the lawn)and then Dougall drove us round the farm. When he was in London he was quickly the man-about-town, but there was always something of the solitary about him. Now he lives the hard-working and often solitary life of the New Zealand farmer, with several thousand sheep and cattle to be looked after by his brother and himself on horseback and motorcycle. It is agonising to think one can only see friends like him once in ten years. But we both knew the bonds of friendship established in Camberwell had in no way been loosened. Rupert Brooke quotes the verse of Hilaire Belloc:

> "From quiet homes and first beginning
>   Out to the undiscovered ends,
> There's nothing worth the wear of winning
> But laughter and the love of friends."

We hurried back to Wanganui, where a Maori woman of great dignity was waiting to show us the Maori church there, decorated a great deal with their skilled designs and materials. It was fascinating to hear her unfold the meaning of the designs.

We then went to a dinner party Tony and Sue Latham had prepared for us with much kindness. Twelve of us sat down. Fairly soon the subject of South Africa came up in conversation, and 'a division arose amongst the people'. The basic insularity, conservatism and paternalism of many New Zealanders was clearly revealed.

February 16th 1972
We set off from Wanganui at eleven. I was quite sad to leave John and Jill's home - they have made it so unmistakably 'theirs' after only a year. At the moment, the town of 30,000 people is ablaze with avenues of flowering gums - vivid vermilion, scarlet, pink, all the unique beauty of Australasia. Eighty miles behind Wanganui, in glorious highlands, at Rarimi, John and Jill have a £200 wooden shack/cottage. From the hill on which it is set there are views; on one side the far distant Mount Egmont (8,260 feet), on the other, of the volcano Ngavruhoe (7,515 feet), still pouring out smoke to the heavens, and the snow-covered Mount Ruapehu (9,175 feet). After lunching outside, we pressed on past the mountains to Rotorua, where I shall catch a 'plane to Auckland tomorrow. As we came into the town, an area famed for its geysers, we made our way through cloudbursts, which had suddenly appeared after blazing sun. But the curious escaping steam from fissures all around still made its way upwards unperturbed.

We put up in a motor camp - one down from a motel! - and 'took the waters' as soon as we arrived: lying in square small swimming baths of sulphurous smelling hot water. The rain - and the thunder and lightning - and the sulphur - and the hot water - made it all a kind of pantomimic prevision of hell rather than an unalloyed pleasure. The only restaurants available in the town had that international anonymity which affects to be all things to all Americans, British, New Zealanders and Hawaiians.

February 17th 1972

Before catching a 'plane from Rotorua to Auckland, we explored some of the fantastic local natural phenomena - a geyser shooting to about seventy feet; a vast area of craters, lakes, rivers, all boiling; other areas of boiling mud! The rocks were richly coloured, reds and sulphuric yellows, and there were glittering silica terraces. And all this 'thermal' display was amidst glorious forests. In another natural spring - cold! - you could feed dozens of trout by hand.

I just about kept a dry eye when I said farewell to John and Jill. But this is John's country, and already, in rather an aristocratic setting, he is being 'a voice for the voiceless' - for instance, the Maori and the delinquent. New Zealand, with all its richness of nature and society, needs such people.

Stage 7: A Weekend in Fiji

February 18th 1972
The aircraft taking me from Auckland, New Zealand to Fiji had trouble with its undercarriage, so we were more than an hour late in taking off. By an extraordinary coincidence, I met Peter Harden - Diocese of Southwark Bishop's Council - in the airport entrance, who was also *en route* for Fiji, just for a day. In getting our seats changed to sit near each other, we were both given vacant First Class seats and received the First Class treatment. (In fact the First Class meal is all you really get if you are unwise enough to pay half as much again for a First Class air fare.)

The Bishop of Polynesia had kindly put me up in a new hotel very near Nadi airport, the International airport of Fiji, which was merciful in view of our late arrival. I went straight to bed at 1.00 am. In the morning, I got up at 6.45 am. A long, black cockroach, as long as my index finger, was looking at me when I came out of the shower. It had antennae almost doubling its length, which it used like mine detectors. I expected it to travel slowly, but when I made a move, it darted in my direction like a goal keeper. It looked the very incarnation of evil. I told myself I was thirty times its size - and laughed when I realised it was making me resort to that weakest of all arguments, the 'argument from size'. But it's odd how certain things seem evil *in themselves*.

At Nadi airport, I caught the 8.15 am 'plane to Suva, the capital, and just had time, before the 'plane took off, for a chat with Jabez Bryce, the young Archdeacon, whom I had last seen at Hankey Place. He is, in fact, my main present contact with Fiji. He was returning from Suva. The hour's flight over the centre of the island was almost all the way over mountainous country, densely wooded, right to the summits of the mountains. The dense woodland continued almost to the shore. There are a host of wooded off-shore islands, some small, some large, and some mountainous. Fiji is, in fact, a constellation of islands.

I was collected at the airport by Peter Wellock, who has had a great deal to do with Christian Education in this part of the Pacific. He drove me first to St Christopher's Home, where a Community of Sisters cares for children in need, about fifty of them. It was rather like being back in Port Harcourt again - the vegetation is also very similar. But as you drive around Suva, where the population is overwhelmingly Indian, you realise that most people are fairly prosperous, and so is their housing.

Peter took me to the Bishop of Polynesia's lovely house where I shall stay one night, and then on to meet the staff of the Pacific Theological College - an ecumenical college with a staff from New Zealand, the USA, Britain, etc. It was an exciting time in an exciting project.

The College is the responsibility of all the Pacific churches, not just of Polynesia. Of course, the problems are immense. The students come from huge distances, at great cost. They are not allowed to get work in Fiji (neither can their wives) though they cannot afford to return home for holidays. It is a multi-racial and multi-lingual community. The supporting island churches cannot begin to pay the costs of a student and his wife and family for three years, hundreds of miles from their home islands. The students are often much older than English students.

The Pacific is going through a quiet revolution - the effects of which are felt in the College. For instance, Fiji - Suva has 90,000 people now. Six years ago it had 45,000. There are children everywhere. There are 3,000 hotel rooms. Already it has all the problems of the City in the 70's, invaded by tourists. Some islands have huge unemployment. Some have natural sources of income. Others have little or none. You may increase the standard of education - only for eventual unemployment. The education at the College is closely related both to the problems of the Pacific islands and to the city in which it is based.

The College is on a marvellous site, a drained marsh close to the ocean. It looks out through palms on to the calm seas within the lagoon and on to the reef in the distance.

It was good to meet Tim Thornton again whom I had last met when he was on the staff at Lincoln Theological College. He is such a wise and loving pastor.

I went back to Bishop's house for lunch, to bread-fruit fritters. Bishop Holland began to share with me some of the problems of the Diocese. There are thirty clergy, twenty two of whom are on the payroll of the diocese. But the diocese is heavily in debt. In a Diocese of 750,000 people, 440,000 of them Christians, but only 12,000 Anglicans, the role of the Anglican Church is obscure! In Polynesia other churches were there before the Anglicans, eg the Methodists in Fiji. The Anglican Church in Polynesia ministers mainly to non-Fijians, eg Solomon Islanders (who are mostly Anglican), Europeans, Indians. The church schools desperately need money - the island authorities most often could not afford to run them. At the moment, there is an 'arranged' voting system, so that the Indian majority population do not have the proportion of votes they would have if there were one man one vote. What would happen if they did get their true share of representation and came to power is 'a matter of concern'. The Bishop's wife has taken a full-time job teaching English in an Indian school. The Sixth Form are often over twenty years old.

After lunch, the Bishop drove me out to a village in the beginnings of the beautiful mountainous country behind Suva. It was so good to be with smiling children again as I went round the classes of the school. Afterwards I walked around the busy dock area in the centre where the largest liners and smallest boats were tied up together. I did some shopping, as it was the last time I would be in touch with crowded 'civilisation', and cheap (?) shopping, for nearly two months.

In the evening, the Bishop gathered a marvellous group together for me to talk with - Tim Thornton and Peter Wellock and about ten Polynesian priests from diverse backgrounds - Solomon Islander, Tongan, Samoan, Indian, Fijian etc. After initial shyness, they all entered into discussion, talking of their problems as priests in their changing world. There was a wonderful warmth and simplicity about them. Each in their own way, young and old, had a stirring beauty - a great basket-ball playing Fijian, who does a lot for the delinquent lads of the dock area of Suva; a small Tongan deacon; and so on. Their faces were bright and direct as they looked at me and I looked at them.

The Bishop - now a New Zealand citizen, originally from English upper crust, like an English Diocesan - was kind to me. I imagine he is the last English gentleman to be Bishop of Polynesia.

February 19th 1972

The Bishop drove me to the airport at Suva. Torrential rain delayed the 'plane's departure. Jabez Price was at the airport at Nadi to meet me. He drove me to his house, where an Indian priest, John Sahayan, was waiting to drive me fifty miles into the country - mostly through sugar cane fields - to where three members of the Melanesian Brotherhood have a house and chapel. They are having to learn Hindi, as most of their neighbours - with whom they work in the fields - are Indians.

There was a touching simplicity about this tiny 'Franciscan' Community who have come from a strange land simply to live together as a Christian Community. We had tea and biscuits, and I chatted with them and with two Indian youths who nodded in. Then I lunched at the Indian priest's vicarage in the nearby town of Ba. His wife had cooked a lovely Indian curry. Jabez collected me at three and drove me back to Nadi to stay the night with an Australian priest and his family, Philip Thelwell.

Philip's academic ability, commitment and wisdom make him an outstanding priest in the diocese. His parish of Nadi is a miniature Suva - including the airport and lots of duty-free shops run by Indians. I cannot believe that continually serving the needs of tourists does not eventually degrade those who serve them. A nation dependent on tourism lives in constant danger. One of the Indian schools in the town, I discovered, was called 'CF Andrews School'. What a tribute to that great Anglican, Cambridge, Walworth priest, beloved friend of Gandhi! He had come to Fiji on two occasions to attempt to do something about indentured Indian labourers.

Philip had some of his PCC in after supper. The young doctor and the agricultural officer were fed up with bureaucracy. We had a very good evening. But I am tired! - longing now for the 'Southern Cross' voyage around Melanesia.

February 20th 1972

I got up at 5.45 am to catch the 7.30 'plane from Fiji for Vila in the New Hebrides. Needless to say, it is going to be two hours late. I can therefore complete my journal, surrounded by American tourists. I am thankful for this stay in Fiji, brief as it has been. It is amazing how quickly and deeply the Church enables one to enter the life of such a place. I suppose I have seen in a weekend a thousand times more of Fiji than most tourists are ever allowed to see. It is a very great privilege. If only the tourists made some attempt to discover the land they are in. They miss so much.

Stage 8: New Hebrides to Honiara

February 21st 1972

I flew yesterday morning from Fiji to Vila, the little New Hebrides port on the island of Epate. John Chisholm, the Bishop of Melanesia, with whom I was curate twenty years ago at St Stephen's, Rochester Row, Westminster, was waiting there patiently (the aircraft was two hours late) with one of his Archdeacons, Derek Rawcliffe. I was very glad to see them, not least because my luggage failed to appear. The Archdeacon and I just managed to rescue it from being carried on by the aircraft to further foreign parts.

The Archdeacon drove us into town, and to the harbour, and then the ship's launch took us out to where the Diocesan ship, the *Southern Cross*, was moored. I settled into my cabin, which I shall share for the moment with the Archdeacon, a very likeable scholarly and saintly person, of my own age, with a very good sense of humour. Then, as soon as I was settled, the ship's launch took us over to the Residency, where, shades of the British Raj, the Bishop, the Archdeacon and I had been asked to lunch.

The New Hebrides Condominium is an extraordinary survival affair. There are two Residences, either side of the harbour, one English, with the Union Jack flying above it, and the other French, with the Tricolour flying! - symbols of this strange joint English-French government.

There were several others at lunch besides the Resident Commissioner and his wife - who were very nice to us - an expert on land tenure out from the Foreign Office; the head of the Agriculture Department and his wife; John Bani, the Melanesian priest who looks after the Anglicans in Vila; a Sister from the Community of the Church, (which has its Mother House at Ham Common), who is returning with us to Honiara. But the chief guest was Lady Metcalfe, out here for a visit on behalf of the *Save the Children* Fund. She is Lord Curzon's daughter and well into her seventies. She was so much like some of the upper-crust 'do-gooders' whom we sometimes used to experience at St Stephen's, Rochester Row, that John Chisholm and I got the giggles, and nearly disgraced ourselves. "Tell me, bishop" said this patrician lady, "do you skin-dive in Honiara?" She knew the Bishop of Southwark well, so I was not lost for pleasantries. The ship's launch carried us back to the *Southern Cross* at 2.30 pm, and we were able to relax on board. The ship is quite small - about seventy feet (a shade too small, perhaps, in view of the hurricanes which have been devastating large areas of the diocese in the last months). There are fourteen Melanesians as crew, besides the Bishop, the Archdeacon and myself, there will be four other Diocesan passengers - Donald, the Bishop's young Polynesian secretary, the aforementioned Sister, and a doctor's wife who has had to come down to Vila from Honiara. We were quickly quite a family. The ship also carries, on a commercial basis, other passengers, not in cabins, who are willing to rough it to get where they want to go.

I was told I had to preach in Vila that evening, so I hurriedly prepared a sermon, and, at six, went ashore with the Bishop and the Archdeacon to preach it. It was rather a moving service - about sixty New Hebridean men sitting on one side, and thirty women on the other, with their children. It was fun to be 'operating' with John Chisholm again. The Archdeacon translated for me into pidgin English.

After drinks with one of the parishioners, we went to a hotel for dinner - preparation for meals on board ship in the next few days! The port was looking idyllic in the moonlight - especially as we stood on the quay side, calling to the ship to send the launch to fetch us.

Vila is a remarkably beautiful little port; the harbour is always busy with little ships like ours and with some much larger old things. The shore, which is only a few hundred yards away from us, is a random collection of corrugated warehouses, customs sheds, the yacht club, cranes on quays, and then rather well-to-do houses fronting on to the water. Tropical palms and other trees sway around them. In the distance are palm covered hills. When the sun shines, the water is a bright turquoise because of the coral and sand beneath it - and absolutely clear. Most of the time the sun shines from cloudless blue skies, but squalls and torrential rains come up suddenly, and all is grey for five minutes - grey water, grey sky, grey trees; but white clouds in blue skies soon follow, and often an absurdly clear rainbow.

On board, there is the unmistakable smell of a ship, and, most of the time, the throb of the pump of the engine. After sleeping very soundly last night there was Holy Communion at 6.00 am, at an open altar in the prow of the ship. All of us, passengers and crew, gathered round. Then breakfast. (The milk with our cornflakes took me back immediately to my tanker trip to Trinidad in 1951.) Then I went ashore with the Bishop to help get ship's stores for the voyage. The feeling of subdued excitement before a ship leaves port seized me.

Our departure was somewhat delayed, as the Bishop and the Archdeacon had to spend most of the day with Government representatives, reporting on the needs of the areas stricken by hurricane, which they have just been visiting. Before we left, the Red Cross had delivered to the ship a very useful consignment of axes, hammers, nails etc., for the relief of those in need. In the Banks and Torres Islands there are about 10,000 people homeless. Thirty or so of the churches in the Diocese have been destroyed, seven schools and five dispensaries. With the destruction of trees, the peoples' livelihood - copra - has gone for several years, and the leaves which they use for roofing have all gone. John Bani, the parish priest, came on board to say farewell just before we left. He is an impressive fellow - not at all the pietist. He is trying to build a hostel for young men who come to work in Vila from other parts of the islands, for whom there is is no low-cost housing at the moment. His congregation will do the actual building themselves.

We were on our way by 4.00 pm, our course, due north. The sea was calm until dinner time. We all gathered round the altar at 5.30 pm for evening prayers (with that marvellous prayer for those at sea, "be pleased to receive into your protection the ship in which we sail", and all roaring out together "All Hail the Power of Jesu's Name"). Once beyond the shore of Efate, the sea was much rougher, the decks awash, and there was nothing for it but to lie on one's bunk. By midnight the sea had calmed a little, and I could open the cabin door without the wind and the water creating havoc. I lay on my bunk and watched the moonlight on the clouds and the water - like nothing else in this world: everything with a dim silvery coating.

February 22nd 1972
Dawn was as beautiful as night. In the small hours we had passed the island of Epi, and, as the sun rose, and as we gathered for Holy Communion, we were passing Ambryn, making our way through the channel between Ambryn on the East and Malekula on the West. The sky was vermilion and gold

over Ambryn, which is crowned by a magnificent volcano, 4,350 feet high, swathed in cloud. Then came Pentecost (known also as Raga), and Maevo, two narrow mountainous islands which we hugged, to save us from the full blast of Pacific rain and wind. Between Ambryn and Pentecost is, significantly, Selwyn Passage, and, between Pentecost and Maevo, Patteson Passage. Finally Omba, in the channel between Marvo and Espritu Santo, hove in sight. Small flying fish, darting like swallows over the surface of the water, kept us company. (We have not seen a bird since we left Vila.)

We dropped anchor in what looked like a beautiful little cove in Omba, Lolowai - actually the crater of a sunken volcano. On the landing stage, waving, was Mavis Salt, who I had worked with for two years at St Stephen's, Rochester Row, twenty years ago. She is now Diocesan Secretary for Education in the New Hebrides. I lunched with her, in her house overlooking the bay, continually interrupted by Melanesian school-teachers coming for help. After lunch, the Archdeacon drove us to the nearby school - he himself lives in the area - gravely damaged by the hurricane. But, dismayed as I was by the damage, on the fringe of the real areas of damage, I was even more appalled by the conditions under which this junior secondary boarding school of one hundred pupils permanently operates. The headmaster, one diocesan teacher, the rest, volunteer teachers from overseas. The equipment was derisory. But in this neglected Condominium, our Education Officer was first appointed only fourteen years ago.

John Chisholm and I had a happy dinner with Mavis in the evening.

February 23rd 1972
At 6.00 am, in torrential rain (protected by my Marks and Spencer collapsible umbrella!) I left the ship and climbed the

bull-dozed track from the landing stage to the little church overlooking the next volcanic cove. Chickens fled from my path! Half way along the path was the twenty foot root of an uprooted tree. By the church is the solitary white grave, surmounted by a cross, of Charles Godden, killed here in 1906. (It was here in 1864 that Bishop Patteson, seated on the beach, was confronted by a man bent on killing him, to avenge a murder committed by a British trader.) I celebrated Holy Communion within sight and sound of the sea. There were thirteen present, most of them apprentice carpenters from a nearby hostel.

Later in the morning, with the sun now blazing, the Archdeacon drove us along a treacherous track, strewn with palm branches and coconuts, to Navoda, where tomorrow three deacons will be ordained and I shall preach. The Bishop gave his ordination charge on 'The Good Shepherd', seated on a rough wooden stool, in a white alb, with his shepherd's crook in his left hand. His simple yet sincere and profound words were full of authority in the humble village church. The Archdeacon stood by him, in shorts and a shirt and bare feet. It was as dignified as any service I have ever known, and spoke eloquently of the authority of Christ.

Afterwards, we went round two more village schools, by which time I was melting in the heat. I came back to write my sermon, and stayed on board until John and I went to the Archdeacon's for supper. What a man! A leper, with one leg, and no sensitivity left in his hands, prepared the meal and waited on us. The house was crowded with books - poetry, biography, novels, theology - and a piano. On the cement floor there were only a few mats. His bed was in the dining room. He has served the Diocese - and the whole area - for twenty four years. He is on the Advisory Council for the New Hebrides.

The Archdeacon's house overlooks the cove where *Southern Cross* is moored. We walked along the shore of the cove in brilliant moonlight. If moonlight at sea is like nothing else in the world, what can one say of moonlight on such a shore? Tall palms stretching out to the moonlit sky, and the black feathery silhouetted leaves touched at their edges with silver.

My tapes of *Cosi fan tutte* and *The Marriage of Figaro* - and Patrick Miller singing Russian folk songs to his guitar - have now given huge pleasure in darkest Africa and the moonlit South Pacific.

February 24th 1972

By 6.00 am we had packed into the land-rover and were on the way to Navoda for the ordination. It is the roughest track I have ever traversed in a land-rover - or anything! Blue-green wood pigeons flew across our path. The little church was full for the ordination. The villagers from the three villages from which the village deacons had come, and to which they are being ordained, had turned out in strength. Some of them had started walking the previous day.

I had decided to preach on *St Stephen - the first deacon* - not least because of St Stephen's, Rochester Row, to which John, Mavis Salt, David Salt and I have had strong attachment - but also because I have learnt out here a great deal about Stephen Taroaniara, who was martyred with Patteson, the first Bishop of Melanesia, a century ago, and while the Patteson Centenary Year had been well kept last year, I doubt whether Stephen has had all that of a centenary. Eton, Oxford and the episcopate - rather than the indigenous layman - will have triumphed again! His death was very much in line with St Stephen. While he was dying of tetanus from the arrows shot at him, he pleaded that there should be no revenge on the islanders of Nukapu. There was!

After the extremely moving service, there was a feast for us all - pork and kumera laid out on long rows of banana leaves in the sun. I got to know two of the village priests, Walter and Francis, who are extremely promising - organising the 'National Party', an independent New Hebrides movement!

We did not escape from the gathering until 11.00 am. Five hours sweating is quite exhausting! I had a last lunch with Mavis.

Bishop Leonard Alufurai has now joined me in my cabin in place of the Archdeacon.

After lunch I was taken round the hospital and the leprosarium. Lolowai is really a mission station, surrounding a cove, which has become a centre to the surrounding villages. The hospital on one side of the cove is the heart of the mission station. It has a doctor and three nursing sisters who have trained many Melanesian nurses. It has about a hundred patients: thirty of them lepers of all ages. At the heart of the hospital is the chapel. The hospital serves a wide area. It is a work of which the Church can be proud. Yet visiting a leper hospital one is conscious at one and the same time of the outrage of leprosy, which drives one towards atheism, and of the work of mercy and redemption through the love of doctors and nurses. And from where does *that* spring? We had supper with the doctor and his wife.

Because Lolowai is quite a small place, it is possible even in a very few days to feel part of it when one has travelled around it, waving to people and smiling at them, and preaching at such an occasion as the ordination. So, as we prepared to leave at 11.00 pm, and our closest friends there came on board, and others crowded the landing stage, there was a sense of the parting of friends. And, as the boat slowly made its way through the dangerous waters of the reef, the bright lights of many torches waving to us from the shore, and echoing cries of farewell, sent us on our way.

February 25th 1972

During the eight hours of night, we had crossed the passage between Omba and Espritu Santo, the largest of the New Hebridean islands. When I awoke at seven, we were just about to dock at the little port of Santo: the second largest port of the New Hebrides. Even at half past eight the unsheltered road from the wharf into the town was burning hot. The town is an undistinguished continuation of that road - a few Chinese shops and a branch of the ubiquitous Burns, Philp & Co., a petrol station and a night club. We were at Santo to clear our papers before leaving the New Hebrides and entering the Solomon Islands, but there is a mission station at Santo, and I was expecting the clearing of the papers to mean a courtesy visit to the mission station. I had not expected the marvellous lunch which Harry Dabi, the Melanesian priest, and his wife, Clara, had prepared for us, nor had I expected Harry to be the superb priest that he is. The quality of his library revealed much of the man he was; but a week ago I would not have expected this conversation with a Melanesian priest:

"What is your favourite aspect of theology?"
"The Old Testament."
"Why?"
"Because our society is most like the society described in the Old Testament; but you can see how the New Testament would affect it."
"Who helps you most to understand the Old Testament?"
"Von Rad."
"Who is the character you like most in the Old Testament?"

"Isaiah. He makes me feel there is something I can say to the people here, and also that I'm not worthy to say it. He makes me think of 'Holy, Holy, Holy' and of doing something about this world around me."

He took me round his school. "That classroom we put up last Saturday. The other had blown down in the hurricane."

We came upon the young French Roman Catholic priest in the town, who immediately asked what was needed in the stricken areas - all of which are Anglican - and offered to be part of the joint aid committee in Santo.

In the evening, at Harry's octagonal church, there was a great Eucharist. The church was crowded, men, women and children, but again, more men than women, tall intelligent-looking men, with hair like lawyers' wigs of black. They stood like the great Melanesian carvings. John preached at the Eucharist. He was strong and simple with the right amount of drama for what was an 'occasion' in people's lives here. The sincerity showed through the drama, and the gentleness through the strength. John is loved by all the people. You couldn't ask for a better bishop.

The archdeacon translates expertly into pidgin - the last time I shall hear him. He returns to Lolowai tonight. (It takes quite a time for an Englishman to accept 'pidgin' as a real alternative language in its own right. I now have, as a gift from Mavis, the New Testament translated into pidgin. The word 'pidgin' is the eighteenth century Cantonese pronunciation of the word 'business'. It was born in the days of the East India Company. It provides now a common language for the many and diverse tribes of Melanesia and the Solomons.)

After the Eucharist, in the cool night air, about a dozen of us were again treated to a generous meal in the garden of the vicarage, the tables lit by the lights from the house. We were taken back to the ship at nine, and soon weighed anchor.

February 26th 1972

At dawn the sea was utterly calm, only the flying fish disturbing the surface, leaving a fretted 'landing strip' behind them. The sun shone in barely clouded skies. On the skyline were the grey volcanic outlines of the Banks Islands, the area of greatest devastation in the hurricane. But where then there was a 150 mph gale and vast waves, all was at peace. The calmness continued all day as we travelled northwards, past the Torres Islands. The sea was so still that at times the royal blue surface mirrored the large white cumulus clouds with an uncanny precision.

It was marvellous simply to read and sleep on deck most of the day. I suddenly realised how little 'free' time there has been in these last weeks. My reading has been 'compulsory' reading to put me in touch with the situation I happened to be in at the moment. (An outstanding book of 'homework' on this particular area, which has been a pleasure to read, has been Austin Coates *Western Pacific Islands*.) Today I have been able to take up Bertrand Russell's *Autobiography* again, for the first time since I entered Australia nearly a month ago. It really is a most moving - and surprising - book. Who would have expected to find him writing:

> "Ever since my marriage, my emotional life had been calm and superficial. I had forgotten all the deeper issues, and had been content with flippant cleverness. Suddenly the ground seemed to give way beneath me, and I found myself in quite another region. Within five minutes I went through some such reflections as the following: the loneliness of the human soul is unendurable; nothing can

penetrate it except the highest intensity of the sort of love that religious leaders have preached; whatever does not spring from this motive is harmful or at best useless; it follows that war is wrong, that a public school education is abominable, that the use of force is to be deprecated, and that in human relations one should penetrate to the core of loneliness in each person and speak to that...."

"Real life means - life in some kind of intimate relation to other human beings....the experience in one's own person of the emotions which make the material of religion and poetry....."

"Everyone who realizes at all what human life is must feel at some time the strange loneliness of every separate soul; loneliness makes a new strange tie and a growth of pity so warm as to be almost a compensation for what is lost.....the facing of the world alone, without one's familiar refuge, is the beginning of wisdom and courage."

"Life is a burden if those one loves best have others who come first, if there is no corner in the world where one's loneliness is at an end. I hardly know how it can be otherwise. Your problem is to face this with courage, and yet retain as much as possible of what is important to you....."

Perhaps these passages need to be read where today I have read them, on the wide sea, 'no stir in the air, no stir in the ocean', one tiny island vanishing below the horizon the only land in sight.

The sun was setting gloriously as we went into the saloon for dinner - a real feast of fish has been caught from the boat by the crew during the day - King fish - served with limes I had brought with me from Lolowai. We are a happy party at meals in the saloon - the two bishops, the sister, Philip Halliday, the Diocesan Engineer, who has just joined us, and Donald, the Bishop's young Melanesian secretary, who is a marvellous fellow - like James Baldwin to look at, a great actor - with a touch of Caliban about him, mischievous, mocking, loving, laughing, with a touch of sadness too. It is good that John has someone like him close to him. Travelling continuously from island to island without companionship would be too much to bear.

February 27th 1972

By the morning, we were ten degrees south of the equator and the Santa Cruz Islands were in sight.

I sat on deck reading, with much sympathy, the Second Volume of Bertrand Russell, until the contrast between the world in which he was writing and the world to which we were drawing closer every minute became unbearable. The world of Bertrand Russell - in the 1930's - was the depths of intellectual pessimism. He used such phrases as 'the mental night that has descended....', 'mood of melancholy', 'profoundly unhappy'..... Having all that civilisation could offer he could find little of purpose and delight, whilst, as we drew near the coast of Santa Cruz at Graciosa Bay, we were in pellucid waters, and villagers were to be seen waving from the shore, the thatched roofs of their simple houses clustered under the palms. It would have been romantic nonsense to suggest that these villages, having so little, possessed all things. A closer look at simplicity always reveals huge deprivations. But it was impossible, for the moment, not to be captivated by the surface beauty of the scene.

It was not long before we had anchored at Lueselaba, in

Bethlehem Bay, in the shadow of the mighty volcano, Tinakula, which rises stark out of the ocean. Tinakula erupted last year. To get ashore we got into the ship's launch, which took us near to the reef. Then it was a matter of jumping into the breakers, with water up to the knees, scrambling over the reef, and wading through the waters of the lagoon. Waiting on the shore to greet us were the Archdeacon of the Outer Eastern Islands, Dan Brock, and the nine priests of the archdeaconry. Dan is also headmaster of Bishop Patteson School, and the 340 boys of the school and the school staff were crowding the walk up from the beach to the school, also eagerly awaiting our arrival, with smiling faces, bare brown bodies, and loincloths - lavalava - of many colours - scarlet, orange, green, blue; some plain, some with floral designs. Many of the boys had - a surprising feature of these islands - blond or light brown hair on their heads, and soft golden hair on their black or dark brown arms and legs.

The school is a series of thatched huts as dormitories, classrooms and houses for the staff, overlooking the bay in an idyllic setting. A fine new open church has just been finished, and the main purpose of our visit was for the Bishop to ordain there two priests to serve in nearby islands. After I had lunched with the Archdeacon and talked to all the priests about their work on the islands it was time to rehearse the ordination, and for John to give his Charge to the two young deacons, now to be made priests, Levi and Robinson. For the Charge, all the priests came to the church. Their faces were a picture of concentration as John spoke to them. Then the church filled to overflowing with the school and with villagers, a congregation of 500 or so, and the ordination began. I preached again - from the appointed Gospel: 'The doors being shut, for fear, Jesus came and stood in the midst and said "Peace be unto you".' I spoke of the various fears that were likely to beset them in their village ministry - the fear that is shyness, fear of standing with the outcast, fear of standing alone, fear of *being* alone, and so on. (Their fellow priests will often be miles away and quite out of reach.) I spoke of Patteson's courage, without which we might not have been there in that church. Patteson, having waded ashore, as we had that morning and having been given a marvellous welcome, when he landed a third time and was departing, a crowd of four hundred men on the beach started firing arrows at him. Two young men with Patteson were killed, in that very bay, Edwin Nobbs and Fisher Young, both descendants of 'Bounty' mutineers. They continued rowing, though mortally wounded.

The boys sang with great vigour, and their attention during the service was rapt. It was an occasion they are never likely to forget. Neither am I. After the service, it was not long before dusk. It was almost full moon, and the palms, the thatched houses, and the bay in moonlight were unforgettable. We had supper with the Archdeacon and the staff of the School - about a dozen: the Deputy head had been at the Department of Education, King's College, Newcastle, last year. I went round all the dormitories to say goodnight to the boys. In some ways it was like a very primitive English public school, but if there is no *boarding* school for these boys from the small islands then there will be no upper junior school or senior school education for them at all. Each dormitory was lit by two hurricane lamps - at most. As yet there is no electricity for the School. That means nowhere to study after dark. The School is, of course, home to the boys for much of their childhood, for the islands are far apart, and there are not enough large ships - and fares would in any case be too great - to carry the boys home for vacations. Some of the boys are therefore at the School several years at a time. It says much for the 'extended family' that it can survive such withdrawal.

The situation is, of course, highly unsatisfactory. The British

Government should really be doing much more about education here. John has said to the Government that the Diocese is willing to hand over all schools, on certain conditions. But to do this at the moment would simply mean the closure of a number of schools the Church is financing - which it can ill afford to do. The trouble is there are no extra votes in England for increased grants for education in the Solomon Islands!

At nine, by moonlight, we made our way down to the edge of the lagoon and waded across it to the reef, waiting there for the launch from the *Southern Cross*. Again it was water up to our knees, and scrambling into the boat to make sure the breakers didn't carry it on to the reef. By ten, we were sailing away, and Tinakula was fading into the distance in the moonlight. Tired, but very thankful to have seen something of the Church at its best, in worship and action, I climbed into my bunk.

February 28th 1972
We have been sailing all day in broiling sun through what are usually extremely rough seas: the 200 miles between the Santa Cruz Islands and San Cristobel. There has been a swell on the ocean which has made standing on deck difficult and sleeping on deck only too easy! I have polished off Bertrand Russell and begun James Pope-Henessy's biography of Anthony Trollope.

These waters have a good deal of history about them from the sixteenth century, the Age of the Explorers, as the names of the islands have suggested. It was in fact a Victorian, Commodore James Graham Goodenough, a good friend of the Church in Melanesia, who persuaded a reluctant British Government to accept responsibility over much of Fiji, the New Hebrides and the Solomons. Like Patteson, he lost his life in carrying out his work: bone-tipped arrows killed him when he was on a goodwill visit to Santa Cruz on August 12 1875, and there his body now lies, five miles away from where we were yesterday, his grave marked with an iron cross, an identical cross to Patteson's.

But it is the immediate past which grips you more and more as you sail due west from Santa Cruz towards the Inner Islands. It was in the region of the Santa Cruz Islands that on October 26 1942, a large Japanese fleet, including four aircraft carriers, was engaged by a smaller Allied Fleet. Both sides suffered fairly heavily. On the same day the American liner *President Coolidge*, in use as a troop ship, and on the way to Guadalcanal, sank off Santo, having hit two American mines. On August 24 the Battle of the Eastern Solomons, between Japanese warships and American aircraft, had taken place off San Cristobel, which we shall reach early tomorrow.

February 29th 1972

We anchored in the middle of the night off Pamua, on the northern coast of San Cristobel. I got up at 5.45 am and got into the ship's launch at 6.15 am. Getting ashore here was even more difficult than at Lueselaba. There is no protecting reef to speak of, so you come in straight from the open seas. The launch brings you as near as it can, while the breakers every few seconds threaten to overturn the launch. So, at the word, you all stand up in the boat, and then make a jump for it over the sides, praying that all the breakers will be little ones! When I jumped, one got me amidships, so to speak, but Burton's Lightweight Suiting stands up to a good deal! I took my shoes off at the door of the Chapel of St Mary's School, and was kneeling down as though nothing had happened - but with a wet bottom - at 6.30 am, ready for Holy Communion to begin. The girls' school we were visiting is just on the verge of closing, amalgamating with boys' schools. All schools are being gradually 'comprehensivized' where possible.

After Communion, we breakfasted with the staff. The weather suddenly changed and there was half a gale and torrential rain. It had eased off by 9.30 am and the girls escorted us down to the beach. If the crew of the launch do not watch out and keep the launch at the right angle, the breakers come into it. The sooner, therefore, the collecting operation is completed, the better. So we - the two bishops, Donald, the Sister, the electrician and I - waded into the water to knee level, and jumped into the launch as quickly as possible. Five minutes in the launch and we were aboard the *Southern Cross* making for Alangaula and Pava, further east on the small island of Ugi, just off the San Cristobel coast.

At Alangaula the school is close to the beach, as it was at Pamua. We waded ashore there from the launch at 10.30 am. The Headmaster took me round the classes - the gardens are simply marvellous: looked after by the boys and girls - and then all the school filed into the chapel and sang lustily to us until John addressed them. By the time we left for the ship at midday the sun was again shining brilliantly on the palms that crossed the shore, and on the coral strand, and the sea.

In the afternoon, we visited All Hallows School, Pawa, occupying a most beautiful site overlooking the shore. It is the school with the best tradition in the Solomons - Bishop Leonard and Donald went there - but since Selwyn College was founded as a secondary school in 1970 it has become a mixed junior school. The school was well turned-out and the Headmaster, Jim Hunt, was obviously a specially gifted person. After John had talked to the school, and I had given a brief message, the boys and girls went off to do farming, cooking, gardening, building. We were taken round the school. I haven't seen a more lovely chapel since I left England, roofed in bamboo. There was a very good VSO, David MacIntosh, there from Wanganui Collegiate School, New Zealand.

We were on board by 4.30 pm and had prayers immediately. I have not yet explained that no one would dream of missing prayers - they are such fun! About twenty of us gather round the altar - Melanesian sailors with bare brown bodies and shorts, and passengers, most of us as scantily clad. We bellow a hymn into the wind and against the noise of the engines. John has usually chosen a hymn which, whatever else it is will be fun, eg 'O for a thousand tongues to sing', then John reads a short passage from the Gospels. He has the gift of reading very simply, naturally, and conversationally. Then he will gather up the hymn and the lesson and the events of the day in a short informal prayer. Then maybe another hymn - and, tonight, 'Good evening all and good fishing'. It's the only point at which all on board, except those on duty, meet together during the day, and with the language barrier (and the need for different foods for Melanesian and European) provides a meeting point we sorely need. It is a mixture of a riot of fun, and something that articulates many deeper aspirations. To be at sea in a small boat is always an 'elemental' experience.

When prayers ended, we were still more than a hundred miles from Honiara. A school of porpoises accompanied us part of the way, and then the Bishop's prayers were answered: we caught five large fish, each nearly three feet long!

March 1st 1972
The birth of Honiara was on this wise.

In March 1942 Tulagi, on Florida Island, opposite Guadalcanal, received her first raids, which were repeated until May 3 when Japanese forces landed. On May 7/8 occurred, immediately South of the Solomons, the first of the great naval battles of the Western Pacific, the Battle of the Coral Sea. American losses were worse than the Japanese, but the Japanese landing on

New Guinea was temporarily prevented. Shortly afterwards, Guadalcanal was occupied.

In June 1942, another vast Japanese fleet, with orders to seize Fiji, Port Moresby etc., and thence invade Australia, was intercepted and virtually obliterated, in the Battle of Midway, north west of Hawaii.

In July the Japanese started working on an airfield on Guadalcanal, the site of the present international airport, seven miles east of what is now Honiara.

Beginning on July 31, the US Army Air Force, from bases in the New Hebrides, began the bombing of Tulagi and Guadalcanal, and on August 6/7 made an amphibious landing in the region of the Honiara airfield. On the night of August 8/9 a Japanese fleet entered 'the Slot' and inflicted one of the worst defeats ever suffered by ships of the US Navy. The 'Slot' is the Sound around which are the islands of Guadalcanal, Savo, Florida, Santa Isobel and New Georgia. This worsened the supply points of the Marines ashore. They nevertheless reached the Japanese airfield and the Japanese dispersed to the hills. The Solomon Islanders gave huge support to the Americans. On August 21, the Japanese attempted to regain the airfield, but were repulsed. The American attempt to make the airfield operational went on for a month. Between August 29 and September 11 the Japanese landed another force. The Battle of the Bloody Ridge, September 12 - 14, followed. The Japanese were held, and retreated inland from the site of the present King George VI School, east of Honiara. In September and October the Japanese continued to lose ground. In October they launched their counter-offensive, with 20,000 fresh veterans. The Americans had 23,000 men there, exhausted, many suffering from malaria. On October 13/14 Japanese bombers eliminated the airfield and the Japanese Navy sailed into Sealark Channel, between Guadalcanal and Florida Island, covering the landings. (It is now called Iron Bottom Sound, because so much military material has been sunk there.) On October 23 the Japanese attacked what is now Honiara's Chinatown. The attack failed. The next day the Japanese infantry attacked. It lasted four days and four nights. It, too, failed. On November 11 the Naval Battle of Guadalcanal took place. Two vast opposing fleets became entangled - both fleets frequently hit their own ships. By November 15, after a series of engagements, the Japanese had lost two battleships, three destroyers and nine transports; the Americans, one battleship, two anti-aircraft cruisers and eight destroyers. The Japanese attempt at reinforcement had virtually failed.

During November, the American land advance continued. "If the earth beneath the shops and offices of Honiara, beneath the churches and government buildings could tell its own tale every inch of it would be a tale of death in war."

I recount this grim story because at dawn this morning we sailed up the incredibly beautiful waters of Iron Bottom Sound, with the coastal plain and hills of Guadalcanal on the port side of us. After Customs and Immigration, we drove from Point Cruz, the present port area, past the present police headquarters at Rove Creek - a distance of about a mile, which it took the Americans from November 4 1942 to January 1943 to advance - and along the road a half mile more to Bishop's House. And here I now sit. The Bishop's House and garden is not more than fifty yards from the water's edge - the garden ravaged by the hurricane last month. And half in the blue-green waters and half on the coral beach, in front of the Bishop's chapel, lies, vivid green, the rusted sea-weeded remains of an American transport. One cannot help thinking of all those - American and Japanese - who lost their lives amidst all this loveliness. But I recount this grim story also because, for good or ill, but for that wartime creation of an airfield there would be no Honiara today, and wherever else I might be, it would not be here.

Stage 9: Honiara - Kohimarama - Honiara

March 1st 1972

The capital of the Solomons, Honiara, is something over 11,000 people; that's all. It has a beautiful coastline that looks out on distant grey islands. It has its Chinatown; its housing estates; its 'residencies' - along the coastline; its sports ground; its cinema; its new Anglican Cathedral - a really fine open building, complete with Patteson relics - I shall be preaching there on Easter Sunday morning; its museum of Melanesian culture; its shopping parade; its Government House; and so on. It is the centre of urbanisation for the Solomons. More and more, the young in the villages of the islands are looking to it as 'New Jerusalem': where they will be able to buy their transistors and pop records. When you say to them: "Have you been to Honiara?" they reply "Not yet". But there's no doubt of their desire to get there.

I went into it two or three times today - to Immigration, for future visas - for postcards that were not 'too tourist to be true' - and found none; to the Post office and the Cathedral. But most of the day has been spent at Bishop's House, unpacking, and sorting things out, getting washing done, and repacking, and generally preparing for the next stage of the journey, which begins this evening, when I go to Bishop Patteson Theological Centre, Kohimarama, to give a week's lectures. If only the students knew how fearful of them this

'Canon James' is - 'who is a well-known writer and thinker in England'! (as the brochure says) - and, one might add, who knows next to nothing about their country! Part of me knows it will be different tomorrow, when I am with them, and have discovered that they smile, and are human, and are probably a little afraid of me. But today they are a very threatening group.

I have been sitting on the steps of the Bishop's House, looking out to sea for quite a while. Out here there is never the same set of colours. The light has curious effects. The clouds in the sky become isolated, white puffs against blue sky; then pink against blue; their shape standing out like 'cut-outs'. The sea, like a lake lapping the shore, will be quite still; and then one wave will appear from nowhere, a dark fold that grows larger till it becomes a wave; then that one wave gains a white crest, and the crested wave will go of its own accord to the beach, while all else remains calm and still.

March 2nd 1972
The Warden of Bishop Patteson, Eric Jones, (curate of St John's, East Dulwich in the 50's) came to fetch me in a truck, at Bishop's House, at 10.00 pm. We drove along the coast road - which had only just been re-opened after the hurricane - in full moon. We drove through miles of palm trees, close to the beach, and forded, ie drove through, several rivers. We reached Kohimarama by 11.00 pm. The College provides a three or four year course in theology, for laymen and those to be ordained. Some go on to a degree at the Pacific Theological College in Fiji. It is in the most lovely mountainous country, at the Western end of Guadalcanal.

We rose at dawn - 5.45 am - for Holy Communion and Meditation. My first day of lecturing - three lectures - has been very exciting. My subject is 'The Ministry and the Modern World'. Instead of lecturing to the College as a whole I am giving the lectures to the College in four separate groups. I think I shall get much closer to the students with four groups of twelve than with one group of fifty. When the students talk, I visibly make notes of what they say. I think this helps them to understand that I do very much want to learn what they have to say. And I do. Here are some of my notes today of what *they* said:

> "It is beginning that the educated do not usually come to church.... Old people are complaining that young people are introducing new life - dancing: not traditional dancing. Some of the young people no longer want to go to church. What they have learnt in school makes them not listen to old people. Our Catechists and readers are often old people. The young people want to go to cities. There is little to make them happy to enjoy life in the villages. They want to mix with other people. They are held by custom in the villages. In the cities they are free. You can wear what clothes you like. Nobody watches you."

After Evening Prayer, the Warden and his wife drove me out to a beach on the Western tip of the island, to a tourist hotel. There was no one on the beach but us. We sat drinking beer while we watched the sun go down into the sea. We came back to dinner, and I was in bed by 9.30 pm, exhausted by the heat, and the marvellous exchange with the students.

March 3rd 1972
The pattern today has been much the same as yesterday; Holy Communion at dawn, and four lectures. I wish I could convey the atmosphere of the little leaf-roofed open lecture rooms - I do not mean the temperature: that is always sweltering! I do not think I have ever lectured to a more responsive group, and I was warned to keep off the urban problem because they are villagers! What I say to them about the Church and

urbanisation clearly rings bells for them. I was worried that they would not talk and discuss. The difficulty now is to get through *my* material, because they want to say what the implications are for *them*. It sounds so condescending; but I never dreamt the students would be such good 'material'. It promises well for the Church of the future here. What is exciting (and having left school at fourteen I feel a fellow-feeling for them) is that half the students have never been to secondary school, and none of the rest have done more than three years, at the most, at secondary school - though all are capable of secondary school had it been available to them, and a good proportion will undoubtedly be capable of good university degrees - if the money can be found.

(I hope David Sheppard, working in South London on his book on the Church and Urbanisation, realises it will serve not only the Church in South London, or England, but the Church in places like this.)

At 7.00 pm this evening we had choir practice. The Melanesians sing naturally in parts. We sang mostly Welsh Methodist hymn tunes - they use Tonic Sol-fa! - but it was glorious *community* singing. We knew we had had an ecstatically happy time together through singing. It was odd to be so much part of this smiling, sweating, bare brown-bodied and trousered (shorts) company (who often unconsciously doodle with their bare toes with one hand while they're sitting and singing). I shall try and record some of their singing before I leave.

After choir practice, I had dinner with George Connor and his wife, (he is the New Zealander who teaches New Testament), Paul Moore, a Canadian, who also teaches here, and Dr James Berquist, now living in London, but a very American American, a director of the Theological Education Fund of the World Council of Churches, out here on a flying visit.

March 4th 1972
Saturday. I had a 'long lie' and only got up for Mattins at 7.30 am!

It's curious that one wouldn't dream of getting up at *7.00 am*
for *Mattins* in England - on a *Saturday*. But here I do not want
to be absent from the *community's gathering for worship*. I can't
quite make up my mind what this says about the community,
worship and me. The problem of worship is certainly greatly
diminished once there is a *community* - to whom one feels one
owes it to be present with them.

The Warden drove me into Honiara in the morning. I had been
driven to Kohimarama in darkness, so it was a drive, along the
coast road, worth doing. There are vast piles of rusting iron
work on the beaches - left over from the War - destroyers, etc.
- and half the body of a 'plane - a Liberator (Baltimore?) in a
field. I popped into the Bishop's House for a while. We picked
up a lad on the way who had sliced his hand with his bush knife
(everyone out here carries his own bush knife), blood dripping
on the car floor. In the afternoon, I finished off my sermon.

Paul Moore, the Canadian, gave a party for me in the evening.
The difficulty about an isolated place like this is that much the
same people must be invited, and much the same people will
come to any party. There are tensions between some of the
Staff - as there are bound to be in such an isolated community
- and the parties are therefore a little heavy going. You work
hard, knowing very well who is not really relating to whom.
Out of kindness I shall be invited out by different members of
the Staff each night I am here, who will probably invite some of
the other members of the Staff, who will probably all come out
of politeness, some not wanting to come at all. Fortunately the
'hard work' doesn't have to go on all the evening; 'melting' takes
place after a while. People are too exhausted by the heat to
keep up pretences and defences.

March 5th 1972

I preached at Holy Communion at 7.00 am. It meant much to me to be allowed to preach to the College, and they listened very well. I took the Gospel for the day, the Third Sunday in Lent; "Who do *you* say that I am?....The Son of Man must suffer and be rejected and killed....If a man will come after me he must take up his cross." I took the subject of 'Success and Failure', as a Christian must understand it, and related it, amongst other things, to the likely results of ministry to urban Honiara, compared with rural ministry.

At the breakfast that followed (bread and jam and tea), I decided to say that if anyone now wants to come and have a talk with me individually, he can. It was quite difficult to know how to handle this. In the time, I can't see *everyone* individually. I didn't want them to think I have my favourites (which I have!). The response in numbers has been just what I wanted, and those people with whom I felt I was establishing a particular rapport have said they want to talk. It will be good in the next days to have these individuals talks as well as lecturing.

It has rained heavily almost all day. It is remarkable how different the place is in sun and rain. In sun, the place is alive with light and life. In rain - Somerset Maugham sums it up just calling one of his novels, written in Samoa, *Rain*. Rain drips off everything - everything and every person. You keep under cover if you can. But the drenched hibiscus droop, washed out, and the palms just hang. There is not only dampness about, but darkness. Everything looks overgrown and rotting. It rains, but the rain does not refresh. Whereas, in the sun, life is positive, in the rain, it is negative. In rain, the dense forest looks abandoned, nature run riot, hopeless - in sun, it looks as though it is full of the power of growth and life. Only the frogs seem to thrive in the rain. In the sun, the lizards are darting everywhere. In the sun, the parched earth has a resilience: it sends up clouds of dust from the cars that pass by. The rain fills the grey-green places with empty silence. The rain is always a threat of further isolation. Indeed, the rivers that have to be forded between here and Honiara are now so swollen that we are cut off until they subside. Isolation here is, in part, psychological; but it feeds on reality! And isolation feeds depression. (Fortunately, life has been so full of good things for *me* recently that depression is another world.) Before Evensong, the Warden and I went for a drive along the coast road to the west end of the Island - a change from talking, while the rain goes on pouring down. We visited the Anglican junior secondary boarding school at Maravovo. A gentle and good headmaster. Two hundred and twenty brown-bodied young teenagers were all around the place. Some had been diving far out at sea to catch fish, and were triumphant over their catch. Some were messing about, and diving in the overflowing river, which we just managed to ford. I still can't get over the direct, open, smiling welcome which the children give one. Even the shy ones haven't yet learnt how to conceal the fact that they also want to see you.

On the way, and on the way back, we passed several villages, primitive and poor; all the housing thatched-leafed and on stilts. As I looked at the women, nearly naked, with pendulous breasts, and little naked children, I was overwhelmed with the feeling of being born *where* I was born, *when* I was born. These people still have to walk considerable distances for water (which is even then not what we regard as drinkable). The area is still malarial. Wages for simple labour in the surrounding plantations of coconuts are very low. I suppose the world *had* to happen this way: of slow painful growth towards civilisation - with each of us ultimately dependent on the generosity, and kindness, and sensitivity of our brethren - or the lack of it.

March 6th 1972

Besides lecturing, I have seen seven individuals today. I am immensely glad I decided to see them individually. It has not only been such a pleasure; I have learnt so much. I can't possibly put four hours of individual talks down on paper.

Clement Vaka has been able to go home to his island of Tikopia once in thirteen years since his education began! Willi Pwaisiho, from Malaita, has only been home three times in eight years. This is fairly typical for them. Ellison Suvi, from Malaita (who had been to school at Alanguala and Pava, which I visited last week - and would also have been away from his island home for a long time) said: "In England you have 'classes' to divide your peoples? Our peoples are divided into those who go to village schools only; those who have left their island to go to primary school, but did not get into secondary school. (When you go away you feel very sad, you feel you have failed if you have to come back to your village with no more schooling.) Then there are those who go on to secondary schools. And there are, nowadays, 'lieus' - young people who hang around and muck around in towns. They have no respect for our culture.... Many people talk about reviving our culture, but it is all talk, no action. I want to see loyalty to chiefs taught again.... This new bishop: he make change too sudden. He have plays in church."

Sam Misitana, from Malaita, asked me: "Young people do not now think of their bodies as holy. In the past, if a young man had sexual relations with a girl of the same village he would be sent away or murdered. Today the church has taught us not to kill, and not to send away, but the enmity is still there. What do you say is the way of love for us?"

Ellison Vari said: "There has been a bad gap between clergy and people, but now there is a new gap - between new clergy and old clergy."

What worries me most of all, after seeing these attractive students, is their unanimous interest in 'reviving custom'. They are all people who have had education which has taken them away from their villages, and I suspect they feel - unconsciously or consciously - guilty. I remember Professor Monica Wilson's lectures in which she argued that in Africa, over the past century, there has been an enlargement in the scale of people's contacts and consciousness. Where once African societies were small-scale, they now exist in what are new and altogether larger environments.

"Those who praise small-scale societies" she writes, "have rarely lived in them, in isolation, for long. We anthropologists have.... It is the business of the anthropologist to show the Peter Pans who refuse to grow up, who reject the responsibilities of largeness of scale, what tiny societies are like ....To seek to return to smallness of scale is no cure for our present disorders....In a large civilised society which is heir to countless civilisations in the past....there are greater heights and depths than in an isolated, pre-literate society."

I have tried to discuss this possible guilt with the students. They appreciated it. They don't *really* want to go back to many of their customs.

After Evensong we spent an hour making a tape of their favourite hymns for me to bring back with me. This was a very happy time. They really *love* singing, and they really enjoyed doing this. We had fun. They are not beautiful singers. Their voices are harsh and raucous, and they do not attend to light and shade. But their directness comes over in their singing -

almost all their favourites are Welsh Methodist tunes. With a Welsh grandfather, this suits me!

The Warden's wife has been increasingly ill since I arrived here. She had major surgery a few months ago. She was carried off to the hospital at Honiara this afternoon - in a truck, the only hope of getting across the swollen rivers. She came back, after forty five miles of pummelling in the truck. The surgeon has gone to Hawaii for a week. Come back next week! There is no 'phone here, so you have to go to the hospital to find out if the hospital is working! This is one of the meanings of 'isolation'. It's no good simply attacking urbanisation - if it means a surgeon on the spot.

At 9.00 pm I popped into the library. It was full, with about thirty students, all silently working at their essays. (They will be up at 5.30 am.) It is marvellous to see this application.

March 7th 1972
Lectures and interviews - and rain - all day. The curious thing about rain in this area is that you can *hear* it raining - like an approaching train, getting louder - from five minutes before it arrives.

At 5.30 pm, I went to the headquarters of the Melanesian Brotherhood, a mile away, and after Evensong in their chapel, gave the twelve novices and four Brothers present a talk. The Brotherhood was founded in 1925 and there are nearly a hundred of them now. They have no pay, remain unmarried, go wherever they are sent, and commit themselves to the Brotherhood for periods of three years at a time - after their novitiate of two years. They have undoubtedly been responsible for a great deal of the best work of the Church in Melanesia. Indeed, the villages would probably not now be Christian but for them. They go now to New Guinea and Fiji as well as

Melanesia; organised in 'households' - not more than twelve to a household. They meet as a Brotherhood roughly once a year. Their dress is a black loin cloth and a white sash. Novices wear a crimson loin cloth. Urbanisation and education are bringing new problems to a Brotherhood which was rural and uneducated.

I went to dinner with a priest and his wife whom I had known when he was a student at Lincoln Theological College. He is unhappy here, and leaving. It is 'too old-fashioned and conservative' for him. My own feeling is that it is not good enough to come to a community with a certain tradition, without great academic resources, and say "This is what I believe, in consequence, this is what I will do - though it is not your practice." I am reminded of the words in St John's Gospel: "I have many things to say unto you, *but you cannot bear them now*." It is unloving, rather self-centred, and, maybe, cruel, to say "This is what I believe: take it or leave it." This chap hasn't been cruel. He would hate to be thought unloving. But I think he has been thoughtless and impatient. As it happens, I have not myself found it necessary to 'tone down' even my most radical views. They have wanted to hear them and discuss them. Indeed they have been more open to new ideas, without prejudging them, than most audiences of English priests and ordinands I have addressed. I think - by the evidence of their chuckles - they have rather enjoyed it all. I've no doubt it is a community eager and ready for change; but it is one which needs to be respected - neither 'engineered' nor flouted.

March 8th 1972
After lecturing all the morning, I left Kohimarama, having made many new friends. I so hope some of them can see England - as I have seen their country - at some stage of their ministry.

As I was getting into the truck to drive away, they all came out of their various lodgings to shake me by the hand. Again, I was struck by their very personal warmth.

The drive to Honiara meant fording the four rivers - eight, now, because of the rains. Two of them were very dangerous. The rule is that someone walks into the river; and if the water is above his knees, the truck should not attempt it. The person who walked into the river was a very tall Melanesian! The water was just above his knees. We risked it, and survived, though coming out of the water at the last bank we got stuck in the mud! However, we backed into the river, and found another way up the bank.

After dinner, the Bishop, Donald and I went shopping - at 8.00 pm - in Chinatown. I bought some shorts - to be prepared for more jumps into the water from the ship's launch next week! I retired to bed early, to read. Whilst I was at Kohimarama I had spent what time I could with the students in the library. It seemed one way of bridging this inevitable gulf between staff and students. In the library I had begun an exciting book which I obviously ought to have read years ago; *The Death of Christ* by the American Professor John Knox. (It is now a Fontana paperback.) It seems just the right preparatory reading for my lectures in Holy Week at Selwyn College. It is a book which is at once radical and devout, courageous and humble.

March 9th 1972
This is one of the rare 'days off' that have emerged from this sabbatical so far. There will be another tomorrow.

John Chisholm has been able to spend a good deal of time trying to re-make a garden out of the wilderness caused by the hurricane. It is coming along marvellously. It has been really refreshing to sit in a chair, in the shade of a tree, reading and thinking, and writing. It must be almost the loveliest spot in the world for a garden - no sound but the waves gently breaking on the shore, a few yards away; the ocean empty but for the distant islands, and a few fishermen, not far out to sea, motionless in their canoes. The sun has been blazing from cloudless skies most of the day.

I have finished *The Death of Christ.* I'm glad John Knox faces the question which has often bothered me: How could Jesus be *conscious* of being what the Gospels claim for him, and keep his sanity - and his goodness and his humanity? But I am particularly glad to have read at this time an undoubtedly great book - which in tackling the question of the vocation of Jesus helps me to rethink the general question of vocation. Is it *just* the relation of one's gifts to the needs of a particular bit of the world? Or is there a transcendent purpose for us all - for Jesus, for my friends, for me, for the ordinands of Kohimarama *and* for the primitive villages nearby? What do we mean by the 'Chosen' people? This is a crucial area for faith/agnosticism. What exactly was Jesus' 'vocation'? What might have killed it - or never brought it alive?

In working over the Early Church's conclusions concerning the significance of Jesus' death: that Jesus won some kind of *cosmic* victory, and that Jesus offered some kind of 'sacrifice' for cosmic sin - both of which conclusions I was relieved to find Knox finds unconvincing - and in trying with Knox to find more convincing conclusions, I've had a chance to do what I have needed - and wanted - to do for many months: to reflect quietly and dispassionately upon Christ and the Mystery of Good and Evil. I have come away from England for many reasons, some positive, some more negative, but not least because the failure of the Church of England to accept what I judge (for what it's worth) to be *essential* reforms (and the absence of any prospect of their being accepted in *my lifetime*), coupled with a particular experience of 'spiritual wickedness in high places' in the Church, has made me need and want to think out again fundamentally - that is, over against the large questions of vocation, Good and Evil; my own future. Here in Honiara - seventy two days away from England, and 14,000 miles away from Southwark - I have felt able to reflect *dispassionately*. I do not find my lack of passion makes the situation of the Church of England any brighter, or the 'spiritual wickedness' less heinous. But perspective is all: the perspective of the total mystery of Good and Evil.

While I was thinking and writing, three Melanesian women swam into view - twenty yards from the shore, fishing for octopus! That is *their* world of vocation!

In the evening, I went to the cinema with Donald, who, as I've said, is the Bishop's Melanesian secretary. The cinema is an adapted US corrugated semi-circular hangar-type construction, surviving from the War. The film was *The Longest Day* - all about D-Day. We seemed to be bombed and machine-gunned from 7.30 pm till 11.00 pm! The Melanesians in the packed cinema took sides enthusiastically. They clearly knew all the US film stars. John Wayne received ecstatic cat-calls whenever he appeared, and Robert Mitchum. When a German pill-box on Cap-Something-or-Other was being overcome, cliffs scaled, and lots of Germans were being killed, there was wild cheering. Fortunately, no one seemed to be reflecting that people actually were killed on June 6 1944, and that people were bereaved - wives, children, mothers, fathers. It was a sort of 'Western' - a good dramatic story - like, come to think of it, the crucifixion often is.

When Donald and I got back, John was in trouble which might have been very serious, having set light to petrol on his hand from a hurricane lamp.

March 10th 1972

I celebrated the Holy Communion in the Bishop's Chapel at 6.30 am, not least to give John's hand a chance to fully recover.

After a couple of hours reading and thinking - I've started John Macquarrie's *Principles of Christian Theology*, which I ought also to have read years ago - I then went to visit the Melanesian Museum in Honiara and on to the Library. It has an airmail copy of *The Times*, and I spotted all sorts of odd pieces of information (the first English newspaper since I left England). Out here the radio news is quite difficult to get. Lord Salisbury is dead, and the Bishop of Newcastle has resigned. But I couldn't wade through over two months of *Times*, and quickly got on with what I had gone to the Library to do: read the War Histories on the Guadalcanal battles, over the territory which is now mostly familiar to me. The photographs and detailed maps make it all a fantastic story. Guadalcanal must have been the Thermopylae of the Pacific War.

In the evening, the Bishop's cook's night off, we went to one of the local hotels for a meal. The food was good, but it was very much a tourist place. I am beginning to hate more and more the tourist! He doesn't want to see the *real* Guadalcanal. He will pay anything for the bogus - so long as he can be photographed in a group of villagers in 'typical' native costume. He will pay them to do anything - carve, undress, dance, smile, take him to bed, wait on him in pseudo-native garb. I hated finding young lads, whose schools I had visited, as waiters in this hotel. Of course, it *could* be a good job. But - 'beggars can't be choosers'. The tourist will do anything but treat the people as real people. Tourism is the great escape: the great prostitution - in every respect.

Stage 10: Honiara - Santa Isobel - Gela - Savo - Honiara

March 11th 1972

We should have set sail on the *Southern Cross* today, but the journey is postponed because of engine trouble, and we shall have to wait, no one knows how long, until it is repaired. This is a good example of how constantly subject to frustration John's plans are out here. An equally good example is this evening's announcement on the Solomon Islands Broadcasting Service, giving, first the cancellation of the visit of the *Southern Cross* to several islands, immediately followed by the programme of the visit as if it had never been cancelled! In fact, the cancellation of the sailing - for a day - suits me very well; for I, too, have had 'engine trouble': the diarrhoea which has - I won't say 'dogged my footsteps' - from time to time since Nigeria (in spite of Entero-Vioform!), and which is very exhausting when it comes, has decided to attack today. I have done very little but lie flat, sleep, and read a hundred pages of John Macquarrie. The trouble is, one lies flat amidst an onslaught of moths, grasshoppers, the occasional cockroach, and, my particular horror, the 'rhinoceros beetle' - a flying beetle an inch wide and two inches long. I could well do without the insect side of God's creation! And, seriously, what I have learnt out here about the complexity of the life-cycle of the parasitic organisms that cause malaria, makes me wonder how anyone can fit it into God's plan and purpose.

March 12th 1972

The Bishop celebrated Holy Communion in his chapel at 7.00 am, and I preached. The chapel only seats forty, but there were well over one hundred present, most of them standing outside. Nothing demonstrates the love that people have for him more than this fact that when he is around there will be a company of people, high and low, rich and poor, Melanesian and European, who will want to worship with him. It is as things were in Westminster twenty years ago. His simplicity, fun, saintliness - of a very down-to-earth kind - and love, draw people. It is not particularly remarkable that people should gather here on a Sunday. But weekday mornings and evenings there is also always a company of worshippers. The people *enjoy* worshipping with him. Hardly a service goes by without some piece of almost schoolboy wickedness; but they also catch from him the meaning of worship. Not many people are convinced of the existence of God these days by logic alone, but few people could remain entirely unmoved by the worship that goes on in John's chapel.

I am very glad John has this 'company', because, the more I see of his job, the more it is clear that it is one of the hardest episcopal jobs there could be. First, there is the sheer physical demand - the voyaging and the heat. Secondly, there is the weight of responsibility for such a manifold organisation - staff, schools, theological college, ships, cathedral, hospitals, finance, etc. I know how much John longs to delegate, and tries to, but at the moment it can't be done a tenth as much as he would want to. He compares the situation here very unfavourably with New Guinea, where he was assistant bishop, and blames the British Government, which has for years failed to provide anything like appropriate money for education and medicine for the so-called 'Protectorate'. Thirdly; there is the problem of 'going Melanesian'. John can't win: if he doesn't go Melanesian, the Melanesians will criticise; but the backwardness of the

Melanesians, with obvious capacities left unfulfilled, is tragic. For instance, some of the students I was with last week could not really *count*. John is himself longing to go Melanesian, and all his plans are to this end: but there are mammoth problems. A fourth problem is the size of the diocese. Many places cannot be visited more than once a year. No matter how approachable John is when he arrives, matters requiring his judgment have often gone too far by that time. Few people ever love their judge! Of course, there are many reasons, dating from the past, ecclesiastical and secular, which account for such a situation, and little of the fault lies with the Melanesians.

The Franciscans and a Community of Sisters are in Honiara. Brother Daniel was here for lunch - a very good person indeed, but what I've seen of these religious communities so far makes me wonder whether people have not put too much faith in them as the 'answer' to the problems of urban Honiara. They are, of course, untrained for the urban world, and unskilled at discerning what is required; and not all that available to meet changing needs. Their *poverty* is not particularly conspicuous in a world in which many people live in greater poverty than themselves; the chastity of monks and nuns living in parallel communities is undoubted, but does not specially speak to this urban community; and their *obedience* is not 'notable', for though they are very good people, they tend to seem over-concerned with keeping *their* way of life; and the urban world - and the urban church - can easily go by them.

Tonight we drove through the 'labour lines' - the accommodation for unmarried men and for families of workers coming, in the main, from other islands. Such places need the hard slog of day-to-day pastoral and social work. Honiara needs people who will 'get amongst it all' - Melanesians.

If the *Southern Cross* is delayed for long, John wants me to turn my attention to Honiara itself. I have seen something of the islands, and have had a chance to question a good many people, and while I am out here, I might as well 'do my thing' and try and help the Church here to come to grips with 'urbanisation'.

March 13th 1972
We spent an appalling morning.

The Malaria Eradication programme is in full swing in Guadalcanal, which means that, at six month intervals, the interior surfaces of every room are sprayed with DDT insecticide. Imagine, in stifling heat, having to put the furniture of every room into the centre of the room, taking down curtains, pictures, etc., and then, after spraying, putting them all back again. Of course, it is an opportunity for a rapid spring-clean; and the only way you survive is to treat the whole thing as a joke. The real sufferer is the cat, who has to be put in a box out of the way for three days, otherwise there are disastrous results. The spraying over a period of years gradually eradicates malaria, which is really all that matters. This year's Annual Report of the Solomon Islands is not very comforting for people who live where the Bishop lives. 'In the sprayed areas, *apart from the low-lying north coast area of Guadalcanal*, vector densities were, in general, very low......The north coast of Guadalcanal presents a problem with high vector densities coupled with predominantly early-evening biting-habits providing favourable conditions for malarial transmission.'! Moral: Keep away from mosquitoes during High Tea!

I spent quite a while driving round Honiara with Donald in preparation for making some kind of comment for John on what should be the shape of Urban Ministry here. Donald has a detailed and intimate knowledge of the place, and has an answer for all my questions as he waves to this friend and that as he drives around.

I wanted to identify the areas that require specialist ministry and the various residential areas. The residential areas, apart from those that are ribbon development along the coast road (usually upper crust, like Government House and Bishop's House!), are in between the many ridges that run at right angles to the coast. These ridges are close to one another, and may be several hundred feet high, and wooded, (hence the heavy fighting during the War that captured and surrounded and re-captured them one by one: the Battle of Bloody Ridge, etc.) The housing estates each therefore have a real sense of locality, divided off from one another. The houses are prefabricated: two or three bedrooms and a verandah.

The more you look closely at a place like this, the more fascinating it becomes. For instance, the Chinese problem. There are only 428 Chinese in all, and half of those are under twenty. But all the shops but about two or three are run by Chinese, and their money goes out of the country. (They often educate their children in Australia.) Here is the beginning of a racial problem.

Another population fact, with social repercussion: there are twice as many men as women in Honiara. Over half the population is under twenty.

I greatly enjoyed watching lads playing football (soccer) on the sports field by the Cathedral. They play with bare feet, but I've never seen such dexterity with the ball. One of the good things about this place is the fine physique of most people, in view of considerable poverty. The lads are also natural actors. Football for them is very much display to one another, almost like dancing: "Look at me!"

March 14th 1972
There is still no news of the *Southern Cross*. It will come any day.

We shall be away for ten days, which means that if I'm to do an 'urban report' I must do it now. The Annual Reports of the Solomons and the reports of the South Pacific Commission, eg on the Development of a Social Welfare Service, give one a good deal of material to work on; but statistical data and social research are always limited, and mostly non-existent.

Various things come to light as one goes on talking to people; eg that some of the clashes between groups in Honiara are still tribal. Although Pidgin is the *lingua franca*, people tend to 'settle' as squatters in Honiara in their language/tribal groupings. These are the slums before housing has been provided. The Church has an important role here.

I have done a draft report which, after analysing the situation, and comparing and contrasting the village and urban worlds, identifies areas of residential ministry, and also suggests the development of ministries to every educational establishment, to the hospital, to the prison, to industries, to Government, to Radio in Honiara, but above all concentrating on 'training the trainers' who will be able to train lay people for ministry. The new Cathedral gets a regular congregation of 800, but they are mainly 'passive' at the moment. The real need is for training for youth and community work of a very demanding kind. The town is still small enough to be one Team Ministry. A good many of the residential areas would not warrant a full-time priest; They need a 'local somebody'. Every ministry which can be secularly financed should be. But the lack of Government money is crucial. I have said already that the Government does not want the Churches to relinquish education. There is not the Government money to pay for it. Government's direct par-ticipation in Education at the moment is mainly in secondary and technical education, in teacher training and further education. The money allocated for Social Welfare for all the Protectorate this year is three tenths of one per cent of the total budget expenditure, ie £11,500 out of £3,500,000. The Government Report says, 'The main burden of social welfare continues to rest with the Churches' - a nice way of saying that there is no one else who will shoulder it. A place like New Guinea/Papua, which has had colonial status, has received so much more financial aid than this 'Protectorate', which term the Government has interpreted as limiting its obligations - with tragic results for the people of the islands.

In the evening I managed to persuade John to come with Donald to see a Laurel and Hardy film - the first time John has been to the cinema since he came here as bishop. It was excruciatingly funny - mostly custard pies.

March 15th 1972

This place is lovely at all times, but at some hours, some days, it is enchanting. The house is perfectly oriented for dawn, which every day it is worth rising early to see. But some days you can sit on the verandah at six, overwhelmed with what takes place before your eyes. There is a rain tree between the house and the sea. It is perfectly formed, a central stem and a mushroom of branches. It is silhouetted almost every morning against a pale blue sky that gradually becomes filled with flame and gold. The dappled surface of the sea reflects the sky and catches all the colours. Usually, over the distant islands, there are great chariots and mountains of cloud. They, too, are flame and gold. Then comes the time of the sun's rising over the horizon. You cannot look on it. All the scarlet fire is gone. It is just radiant, molten gold.

At various times there are curious illusions. On the horizon there appear sometimes to be dozens of islands, but most of them are in fact one. The curve of the earth's surface - presumably - allows you only to see the higher ground, hence the illusion of several islands. But why this illusion should appear only on certain days I do not know.

I have sat on the verandah most of the day putting the final touches to my report, and preparing a Lent address for the Cathedral. John has now sent the report to all sorts of people, from the High Commissioner to the students at Kohimarama.

The service at the Cathedral was quite a surprise. I had presumed that there would be only a handful of the faithful in a side chapel. When I entered the Cathedral, and saw the large crowd watching a football match in the adjacent sports ground, I longed to be watching the football! But, at half past six, the football match stopped, and the Cathedral filled with men and women who came straight from the football match!

After the service, Canon Norman Palmer, a gifted Melanesian priest, who will head up the Honiara team ministry, came to dinner with his beautiful wife. It was a joyful occasion - the last night ashore for ten days; for we had heard the *Southern Cross* would be with us in the morning from the repair base, the sheltered harbour in the Florida Islands, Taroaniara.

March 16th 1972

A quiet day, reading and thinking for the most part: more John Macquarrie, and preparations for Holy Week lectures at Selwyn College. After I'd given a Lenten address at the new little church of All Saints in the centre of Honiara, which the Franciscans and the Sisters run, we went on board the *Southern Cross*.

March 17th 1972

At dawn we were close to the coast of Santa Isobel, and by 7.30 am we were anchored a mile from the shore, at Kolotubi. There was no one in sight to greet us, so it began to look as though we were not expected. A radio message had been broadcast yesterday of our revised programme (much out here still depends on radio messages), but here few would have radios. There was no certainty that we were not expected, because the village is a few miles up the river from the coast. We could only tell when the ship's launch had taken us to the river's mouth, had found its way through the sand bar that runs almost across the mouth, and had taken us up the river, and we had walked a mile or so from the river to the village.

The ship's boat was launched. I must confess I was a little uneasy when I realised the sailors did not know where precisely to enter the river: all they could do was to look over the side of the boat for sandbanks and take swift avoiding action, whilst the breakers were sweeping up from behind, threatening to overturn the boat if it turned at the wrong angle. However, we gradually found our way into the river: a gloriously wide, thick, green river, heavily wooded on either side. There was no one to greet us at the river bank, where the path to the village began; but as soon as we were spotted, the drums began to beat, and the bells to ring, and the villagers came out to greet us. The houses of the villages were quite the loveliest I have yet seen on my travels. They were built on stilts, but what gave them their beauty was the pitch of the thatched roofs of sago leaves, which gradually widened out from an acute angle at the top, so that the roofs were almost horizontal as they overhung the walls. We shook hands with all the villagers, who looked more under-nourished and primitive than most others I have seen in the Solomons. There seemed also to be more evidence of disease. Yet in the new Church, built recently by the people, with beautiful carving, when John addressed the villagers, the children were responsive and the singing was like nothing on earth! The women's was more screeching than singing - English tunes like 'The Head that once was crowned with thorns', but at a much higher pitch than we would dream of singing them.

It is always fascinating to see over the altars here, for 'Holy, Holy, Holy' TABU, TABU, TABU, pronounced *Tambu, Tambu, Tambu* - the word, of course, which owing to amateur orthography, has come through to the West as 'taboo' - and is now also the common phrase (like 'Verboten', or 'Trespassers will be prosecuted', or 'No Entry') for forbidding access to certain places, or the pursuit of certain activities.

We did not know what was ahead of us when we left the village. We walked to the river, and the first incident was almost pure Laurel and Hardy slapstick. I slipped down the very steep and slippery river bank into the river, covering the backside of my new grey shorts with thick brown mud. It is incredible the joy such an incident can give *other* people - of all races!

The ship's launch had brought us near to the river's mouth, when suddenly the engine gave out, and all attempts to restart it failed. We were fast drifting on to the sandbank, the bar at the river's mouth, a good deal of it quicksands. The sailors had forgotten to bring the oars with them (Never again!) and there was no other launch on the *Southern Cross* - a mile away out at sea. How could we get through the bar, across the breakers, and out to the ship?

Mercifully, on the sands of the bar there was enough driftwood to provide us all with a makeshift oar. Donald, carefully treading on the sands, retrieved the wood. Then, after some very anxious moments as the breakers pitched against the boat, we all managed to form ourselves into a tolerably disciplined rowing crew. John became John Snagge for a while, crying "In - Out"; and I managed to think of some appropriate sea shanties, 'Blow the man down!' etc., and in a while, we were safely at the ship's side. Of course, the sun all this time - from the ship to the village and from the village to the ship - had been blazing down upon us. If we had been exposed much longer we would have been severely burnt, quite apart from any other dangers.

An hour's steaming brought us to our next port of call on Isobel, Susubona. Here part of the landing stage had been washed away after the hurricane, but it was not long before the crew had rigged up a temporary ladder. At 5.00 pm we had Holy Communion for the village close to the sea, followed by a 'Parish Meeting'.

Again, the villagers - many babies slung across backs or fronts, and crawling on the floor - looked undernourished. Few could use hymn books or prayer books in their own language. As I shook hands with people and looked at them at close quarters, the unmistakable marks of dire poverty were upon many of them.

'Out here' - rural Nigeria, Uganda, in the Solomons or in urban slums, wherever you may be - you either choose to live the life of a Government Officer, who rarely learns the local language (very few in the Solomons have ever done so) and never really get *deeply* involved with the people (at Honiara the whites tend to live a 'Club' life together) or you know that for life you can never again escape the sight in the mind's eye and the feeling of responsibility in the heart for these people. Either you are 'members one of another' with them or you are not. Of course, there is a real dilemma. I remember the relief with which I came across the Abbé de Tourville's saying: "You cannot play Providence to the universe." True, but surely you cannot escape some responsibility for it either.

In the service this evening, I think I enjoyed most of all what went on in the aisle. Several infants just beginning to walk had been rigged out in rudimentary 'Sunday Best' for the occasion, unfamiliar knickers and top. Pride in these garments and displaying them to each other, quickly dissolved into boredom, followed equally quickly by acute irritation. Knickers and top were gradually removed and became useful instruments of battle. Even 'Clobber my neighbour' became boring after a time; and one young lady flung her knickers from the aisle to mother, deep in prayer, sitting in the middle of the pew, who caught them on the side of her face. Later, the same young lady burrowed through kneeling bodies to retrieve her knickers, and was most aggravated that, try as she would, she could not successfully fit them over her head. Mother remained deep in prayer!

March 18th 1972
We sailed, at dawn, further westward from Susubona; and, after four hours, were landing, (that is to say, we were stepping knee deep into the water) at Samasodu, another coastal village. After shaking hands with all the villagers, John gave a talk to them gathered in their village church, and so did I, and so did Kathleen Holgate, the very good Diocesan Adviser on Education, who is travelling with us. At 1.30 pm we left there, and after an hour's steaming along the lovely coastline, dense with palms and with tree-covered highlands beyond, we were at the next village of Dedeu. The senior men of the village helped us out of the water, and led us past a boathouse of hollowed-out canoes, along a beautiful grassed and tree-lined avenue, to the village. One of the senior men, who showed me the canoe he is in the middle of making, is also in charge of the decoration of the reredos for the side chapel of the Cathedral at Honiara. It was lying where he works on it, in the open, waiting for more shells. When the pattern has been chiselled in the wood it is filled with mother-of-pearl from the inside of certain shells. After another village meeting in the Church (and more 'screeching'!), we were escorted down the mile-long avenue back to the shore and got into the launch. It was about half-past three when we climbed aboard the *Southern Cross*.

Another hour westward along the coast (Santa Isobel is the largest island in the Solomons: it is 120 miles long, but narrow) and we were at Litogahira, where there is a Senior Primary School of 115 boys. The Headmaster led us from the launch up through woods to where all the school was waiting in the sun outside the school chapel. After an address of welcome to the Bishop and me, I was astonished to be presented with a most magnificent conch shell, at least a foot long and six inches wide. I was, of course, delighted.

After shaking hands with all the boys, we then went to the school hall, where the boys vigorously sang us some of their favourite songs. A football match followed, with about twenty-two a side, and with many of the *Southern Cross* crew joining in. I was painfully sunburnt with all the walking I had done to and from the villages and to the school chapel, so I was quite glad to get back to the ship for the night, after a memorably happy day.

March 19th 1972
At 6.30 am, we left the *Southern Cross* and went ashore to the school, for Holy Communion. I preached to the boys, and after breakfast they sang us some more songs in the school hall, before they all came down to the beach, at nine, to see us off. I was very impressed with the school. Yet, perhaps some estimate of the situation of education here is gained from the simple fact that only two boys went on from this school last year to Secondary education, two to the Honiara Technical Institute, and four to some other kind of further education. Over ninety per cent went no further than Standard Seven, at which there is a Protectorate-wide examination - by aptitude tests - into Secondary School, at, roughly, fifteen years of age. 1,800 children in the Protectorate took the examination last year.

But the simple fact is that less than fifty per cent of children in the Protectorate go to school *at all*. Of those, less than fifty per cent go on from Standard Four to Senior Primary School at twelve years of age (they start school at seven). They must pass an examination which is rather a farce. The majority of teachers in Standard One to Four are untrained. The exam is really a test of the *teachers*. The low standard of written English makes it quite clear that English in many classes has not been spoken sufficiently, so the ability of a class to communicate in English may be small. Thus of any one hundred children - less than fifty go to school at all, only twenty go to Senior Primary School, only five go to Secondary School.

Here is a wastage of human ability comparable to the wastage by apartheid in South Africa, but this is largely due to Britain's neglect of its educational responsibility to its Protectorates - largely, for there is also an apathy towards education on the part of some parents, especially towards the education of girls.

Our next port of call was Kia, six hours journey to the west, a small town of a thousand people in an inlet at the extreme western end of the island. All the houses of the town are built on stilts in the water on a winding coastline. As the houses are these characteristically beautiful Santa Isobel houses, it is difficult to imagine any town in the world more lovely. The Church, too, is a fine building at the water's edge, and has the best Melanesian decorated reredos to be found anywhere in the Islands. We had Evensong there at five - John preached, and there was a church meeting afterwards.

As the sunset happened to be the most glorious I have seen since I left Britain - the sun sets the far side of the inlet, silhouetting the canoes in the sea and the distant trees on the other side of the water - it was all unforgettable. After taking some photographs - but knowing that no camera could ever capture this - I sat in the stern of the *Southern Cross* just watching the sun go down.

March 20th 1972
At first light we left Kia. Dawn over Kia was almost as beautiful as dusk. We had ship's prayers as soon as we sailed, but the open sea was rough, and we said them sitting down. While we were saying the Lord's Prayer, my roving eye caught sight of a solitary Melanesian, fishing from his canoe in calmer waters just by the reef. That lone Melanesian was my prayer for the morning: his significance and insignificance - and mine

A frigate bird flew round us for part of the morning. You miss out here the gulls of England following the ship near the coast; instead, there is this isolated, large, lonely creature - its bat-like wing span can be as much as seven feet across - coming close to make a continuous investigation and haunting the ship till it finds something better to do.

Lunch today was delicious - fish, speared late last night from the ship, tied up at the landing stage in Kia; a slice of fresh lime from a lime tree in Kia, followed by two slices of fresh pineapple, also from Kia.

John and I spent quite a while discussing 'paternalism' this morning. Before I came out here I had often heard it said that the Church here is 'paternalistic'. I have seen few signs of it. I have seen many evidences of its being *paternal* - in response to the need of a father. 'Paternalism', as I understand it, means 'treating someone like a child when they ought to be treated like a grown-up'. When you see how primitive people often are here you see how cruel it would be to treat them as though they were more educated and sophisticated, and were used to isolated responsibility. John in his talking to the people, for instance, at Church meetings, often talks as a father: "What I want to see here at Kia.....", but what he is wanting to see, and is trying to establish, is a pattern of training, consultation and government which will increasingly give people more experience of responsibility. Of course, the temptation to be paternalistic is huge - especially when 'my people love to have it so'; when they have been used to chiefs and tribes, and when many still want a bishop to be an old-style chief.

At each church meeting John asks "Now have you any questions you would like to ask me?" In no village have I heard anyone respond with a question - except a senior priest. No one would dream of asking a question of a chief. No woman would think of speaking in public. This is not *John's* desire! And, wherever there is education, the questioning is coming. It would be possible to refuse to be treated like a father - to refuse, for instance, to have the kind of greeting which the people love to provide at each village - the lining up to shake hands; the hymn singing; the address of welcome, as though this were almost a 'royal' visit. But surely this would be ungracious and uncharitable, and would probably so offend as to remove the kind of mutual confidence that is absolutely necessary if there is to be advancement into less paternal patterns of authority.

We sailed eastwards along the coast for nearly ten hours, all the while past land now virtually uninhabited, which a century ago had been densely populated. The cause of the depopulation is complex: the introduction of European diseases; the loss of the will to live when 'alien civilisation' has arrived; emigration to Australia as forced labour through 'blackbirding', and head-hunting. Not far short of a million men and women disappeared from the face of the New Hebrides and Solomons early in the last century. There is much in the story which Europeans can only read with shame. Perhaps this accounts for part of one's anxiety that the West should now do its duty towards these lands, and one's joy that the Church is at least trying to be a father to the thousands who might otherwise be forgotten people.

We arrived at Buala at about 4.00 pm. Here we could pick up fresh water and also visit two more schools, Tasia Senior Primary Girls' School and Jejevo Senior Primary Boys' School. I preached at the Girls' School Holy Communion. Afterwards we went round the School, and had supper with the Headmistress.

We had been joined at the School by Bishop Dudley Tuti, the second assistant bishop. He is a most saintly and remarkable man. He had walked over to meet us at Kolotubi - a two-day walk over the mountains from the other side of the island - and after waiting in rain for us to arrive, owing to the engine's failure, had walked back again.

After supper, Bishop Dudley suggested he should take me back to the *Southern Cross* in his canoe. On the principle of 'try anything once', I agreed. The *Southern Cross* was moored at a jetty on the mainland. The Girls' School was on an island that was half and hour's journey by canoe - with outboard motor attached - from the shore. To me it seemed the most precariously balanced craft I had ever travelled in. (But one cannot really compare a punt on the Cam with a canoe in the South Pacific!) The moon was a thin crescent, otherwise all was darkness. I think I might have been more composed had not the kind Bishop Dudley uttered words intended to console me just before we departed: "The canoe is the most reliable of all vessels" he said confidenty; "If it happens to capsize, you have a good chance of righting it, and you lose *nothing but the load!*"

The canoe, which the Bishop, of course, manages with consummate ease, is his main means of transport. The point is worth underlining, for although air transport has improved immeasurably in the last decade - there is an airstrip even here at Buala - and although boats like the *Southern Cross* call from time to time at places large and small around the Islands, this vast area is bereft of regular, reliable, cheap transport for the mass of people. For better or worse, schools, villages, towns are isolated. There is no newspaper. The outboard motor and the transistor radio have caused a small revolution. But this Island Diocese will always inevitably contain some of the most isolated communities in the whole world; with the unavoidably huge cost of ministry by Church or State.

March 21st 1972

I preached again at 7.00 am at Holy Communion at Jejevo School. It was good to meet Alex Palmer from King's College, London, doing a year of voluntary service there. At 9.30 am we were taken back to the *Southern Cross* and for four more hours we sailed eastwards till we reached Kamaosi. The *Southern Cross* dropped anchor, and Bishop Dudley, who knew well the place we were visiting, suggested his canoe - which had been tied to the *Southern Cross* - would be better than the launch-approach where we were due to land. The two bishops, Miss Holgate, Donald, two Sisters and I therefore got into the one canoe, and away we went for half an hour or so till we reached the landing stage of the Kamaosi Rural Training Centre and Primary School. From the landing-stage there was half an hour's walk, single file, along a track through towering forest and over log and bamboo bridges. I heard the sound of a conch shell being blown in the distance, followed by wild shouts and screams. Suddenly there burst upon us twenty black 'dervishes', sparsely clad, with foliage on their heads, with ear and nose decorations, brandishing spear-like poles and clubs. They surrounded us, shrieking and gesticulating. It was the students' surprise welcome, brilliantly done: a wonderful ironic laugh at the whole image of the way Melanesians might not so long ago have received a bishop. They kept up this skilful war dance round us - coming to within an inch of our faces and bodies again and again, yet never once touching us - for ten minutes of our walking, till, beyond a triumphal arch of palm and flowers, some of the Primary School were lined up, who then marched ahead of us to where the rest of the School was on parade, singing a most lovely Melanesian melody and clapping rhythmically with their hands.

We took an hour to go carefully round the Centre, which could be one of the most important places in the development of the Islands. It is really an agricultural and engineering college in the making - teaching carpentry, canoe building, outboard motor repairs, land and cattle cultivation, etc., whilst, at the same time, the students are taught English, mathematics, science and other basic subjects. A chapel is at the heart of the Centre; but this is a project not of the Church but of the Island of Santa Isobel's local Council. It is, of course, run on a derisory budget, and the buildings are mostly sago palm and bamboo. We went round the junior primary school as well. John talked very powerfully to the students and schoolchildren, in the Chapel on the significance of the place; and, after tea in the Headmaster's house, we walked back along the forest trail to the canoe - followed by the senior students bearing a dozen and more large pineapples and quantities of sweet potato. All this had to be got into the canoe as well as ourselves. Donald, as adept with the canoe as Bishop Dudley, realised what a deep sense of insecurity I felt in it and was merciless! Sitting behind me, he was able to rock the boat at will. The end seemed near again and again! We were all convulsed with laughter most of the way back to the ship.

It was only two hours along the coast to Suva (Santa Isobel, not Fiji). It was twilight as we got into the launch. John said quietly to me "It'll be a miracle if we survive this: we've got to get through the reef." It was soon dark, and for a quarter of an hour, the launch made its way through the seas outside the reef, looking for lights from the shore to show us the way in. The lights soon flashed on the beach, but not precisely enough to keep us off the rocks at first attempt - but no damage was done. Then, with the eyes of some on the breakers and with others using the oars - and the Bishop using his staff - to feel a way through the rocks, we gradually found an entrance. As we stepped over the side of the launch into the water, the choir of villagers, gathered round hurricane lamps, began to sing a hymn. We kneeled down on the shore, and the bishop gave the blessing. We were then led up to the village church, but only by a few hurricane lamps. It was a simple gathering, and I found myself making the simple reflection there that if Christ had not lived and died, and if the Church did not believe in His living presence, the villagers would not be gathered there that night in their little church, and I would not have crossed the seas to be with them.

After the meeting in Church, the villagers had provided a meal for us in 'the rest house' - a simple but lovely house for any visitor to use, especially their visiting priest. As we sat at table round the hurricane lamp, the light throwing shadows on the faces of those around me, I was reminded of Van Gogh's *The Potato Eaters*. It was a bowl of sweet potatoes that was before us.

We returned to the *Southern Cross* another way, walking along the coast for half an hour until we were at the point nearest to the ship. The launch found it no easy task to pick us up, and it was with a very wet seat that I shook hands as I stood in the sea and said farewell to Bishop Dudley, and to Fr. James of Kolotubi, who had been with us ever since we left his village four days before; and so took leave of Santa Isobel.

March 22nd 1972

In October 1880, the commanding officer and four sailors from *HMS Sandfly* were murdered by headhunters in the Florida group of islands - between Santa Isobel and Guadalcanal. A few weeks later, another vessel of the Royal Navy indiscriminately shelled villages in the area by way of reprisal. In May 1881, *HMS Cormorant* was sent to the area to bring the real culprits to justice. It carried as passenger John Richard Selwyn (son of Bishop George Augustine Selwyn), second Bishop of Melanesia. With great courage, the Bishop went ashore alone, and persuaded the local chief to talk to him and surrender the murderers - including the chief's own son. The ringleader was hanged from the tree from which he had shot the commanding officer of *HMS Sandfly*.

Extraordinary as it may seem, this action was the beginning of the end of headhunting in the area, and of the pagan religion that held sway there. All the chiefs of the area became Christians within months.

It was to this area - still known as the *Sandfly* area - that we came overnight. At daybreak, we waded ashore from the launch to Nagotano on Sandfly Island. The Bishop confirmed two young girls and a young man - the young man had been deaf from birth. The Confirmation was followed by Holy Communion. I thought the community was as primitive as almost any I had seen, and there seemed to be some fairly primitive verbal aggression going on, shortly after the service, between one group and another as we returned to the ship.

After about an hour, we reached Olevuga, on the island of Gela - another beach landing. Again, a fairly primitive community. But - for the record! - a young man asked a question when the Bishop provided the opportunity.

We sailed on for two hours more to another school, Hagela Junior Primary School - a small school of about sixty boys and girls. They were lined up on the grass above the beach. We went to the chapel, and I preached to them on my impressions of Melanesia.

Then another two hours and we were at Siota, on 'Small Gela'. The boys of St Peter's School welcomed us with a dance. Again we went to the Chapel and I preached once more. Two strange villages and two strange schools - requiring four landings from the launch, wading ashore, about 800 hands shaken, two sermons preached and small talk to strangers, many of whom only understand a little of what one is saying - is probably enough for one day. Certainly, though there is a distant storm, I am ready for bed.

March 23rd 1972

During the night, there was a tempestuous wind with thunder and torrential rain, and lightning every few seconds. When I got up at 2.00 am to fasten things, I saw several canoes broken from their moorings, being driven past the ship. In the morning, the wind had abated, but it was grey, sultry and drizzling and the seas were still angry.

We could not land at the village we were due to visit, Belaga, even by launch, but had to be taken ashore at Siota again and walk for an hour or so. The track was sometimes through forest, sometimes along the rocks overlooking the shore. Sometimes it became indistinguishable from a stream. After a while we came to a river over which three tall palm trees had been placed as a bridge - over sixty feet long. Sometimes the trees were together, sometimes less close. Over the middle of the river they bounced up and down as you walked on them. As I gingerly made my way across, a step at a time - with my Mark's and Spencer's umbrella up - I felt I was in training for Billy Smart's Circus. But not much further along the track was a bridge of only one tree. When I had crossed *that* I felt I had nearly passed out - in more ways than one!

As soon as the service began in the village church on the shore, filled with 150 villagers, the torrential rains returned. The building was more permanent than most, ie it had a corrugated iron roof. The rain was almost deafening, and made it impossible for John to speak for any length of time. With characteristic kindness, there was a 'light breakfast' ready for us - rich soup, chicken and sweet potato, and 'custom' pudding, a purple substance made of yams and nuts. The coffee was made with coconut milk.

John particularly wanted to visit the village, for its priest, a man just over fifty, had had three heart attacks in the last year.

The torrential rain showed no signs of ever stopping, and there was no way of escaping an hour's drenching walk back. All the way, the path was now a stream. John, dressed in black oilskin, cap and coat, and carrying his crook, looked anything but a bishop of the Anglican Church; but whereas this was 'holiday' for me, and 'once for all', for him it was the normal round of duty.

We went to Vurenimala, just after midday. It was a very poverty-stricken village: mothers with terribly misshapen breasts, nursing babies, and with protruding stomachs, probably the result of constant attacks of malaria. Yet many of the men were in their best white shirts, and the women had done what they could to be at their best. A very good, articulate, young man, in question time, spoke for the people and asked that a priest who was not exercising his ministry - at their previous request - should be re-instated.

Our last 'port of call' (ie jump into the water) on Small Gela was Siarana. The villagers had made a triumphal arch on he beach, of bamboo, palm and frangipani. During Communion I sat at the back, watching the people (and letting my eyes wander out of the window to the cockatoos, red and green and white, in the coconut palms) reflecting on why we were there.

The 'triumphal arch' and the people's obvious joy made me want to ask "What *is* this all about?"

I think for anyone to talk clearly and authoritatively about the Life of Jesus to any community, (especially one that may be eaten up with village quarrelling) is a job worth doing. To talk to this kind of community about the necessity of education, and of sending their children to school, is also very worthwhile. To speak on 'leading by serving', and to call for people to lead in various ways - priesthood, teaching, etc., - could hardly be more valuable. To try and raise up a democratic church here - with church and community synonymous - is to try and develop a democratic community. To speak of the needs of others, of what is happening in the world at large, and to represent the wider family of man (John had spoken of the needs of those stricken by the cyclone) is, I am sure, an important piece of work.

To be a shepherd to leaders - priests and teachers - already here, is also a good work. Just to serve people by providing an unforgettable occasion for them once in a while, is also something one has no need to be ashamed of. A headmaster yesterday said he was "thrilled the Bishop had gone to the trouble of visiting them". To visit is to recognise and value. When we left tonight, we were loaded with pineapples. We had done so little to give people such joy as seemed to be theirs at our visit, but I was in little doubt that it was good for us to have been there.

March 24th 1972
We had decided last night to anchor in calmer waters outside Siarana, and to sail early this morning for Savo, the volcanic island nearest to Guadalcanal, known there as 'Queen Victoria Lying in State'. It is a remarkable likeness!

We sailed at three, and by six were close to Monago. We went ashore for Holy Communion. The first woman we shook hands with, one of the choir on the beach, was terribly disfigured with a goitre.

Instead of going continually 'to and fro' from the *Southern Cross*, John thought we should walk by way of the coast track to visit the next villages. (The day was as beautiful as yesterday had been impossible.) We therefore walked on a few miles to Bonala. On the way, the marvellous butterflies of the Solomons, in size and colour, (it must be one of the best parts of the world for them) hovered about us, flitting in and out of the trees and flowering shrubs that lined the way. We were a happy party, joined by more and more people on the way. Melanesians have the lovely habit of holding each others fingers as they walk. Where the language - and some kind of social distance - may create barriers, I have found this simple act breaks all such barriers down. If only the English could recover the sense of touch!

Bonala was another primitive community - like the islanders of the West coast of France. Their fishing lines were suspended from bamboo contraptions in the sea in front of their homes. In church, I was struck, as I have often been, by the beauty of the faces of the young, but how, by forty, all trace of that beauty has gone. It was a Church full of 'locals'. And all the way through the New Hebrides and the Solomons it has been the same. This is a church of the people.

On the altar, in most of the churches, are metal shell cases for the flowers: the fruits of war!

We walked through the village of Pikoli - to which we would be returning - and on to Panueli, where there was a meeting, in the Council House by the sea, of the Island's Council. A decision needed to be taken concerning a school that had to be moved.

Eric James

The President of the Council chaired it, and John spoke. Half a mile along the coast were the vast nests of a bird unique to the Solomons, the megapode, which buries its eggs in the sand, and runs off and leaves them - as it had this morning.

We returned to Pikoli at midday, when the church was now packed for the Confirmation of thirty-two boys and girls. The singing of our Victorian melodies was as vociferous as I have heard anywhere on the islands, and during the Communion an aggressive choirmaster urged the choir to redouble their efforts by shouting at them, like a farmer shouting at an obstinate mule. "Blessed is He that cometh.....Hosanna in the Highest" must have beaten the record set up the first Palm Sunday. But it was the voice of the people, not of ecclesiastics. A crowd of villagers from all the villages we had visited that morning, and the President of the Council, saw us off from the beach. I was quite sad to be putting my feet into the sea from the *Southern Cross* launch for the last time. We set a straight course for Honiara, and by 5.30 pm we were home - and dry.

Stage 11: Honiara - Selwyn College - Honiara - New Guinea

March 25th 1972
The return to Honiara was like returning from another world - which, indeed, it was.

There were letters again from England.

It was a stormy night, and the sound of driving rain on the roof of the house, and of the waves pounding the shore, kept me awake. I found myself in 'the slow watches of the night', which 'no less to God belong' again trying to comprehend the 'mystery of iniquity' - an appropriate theme at the beginning of Holy Week.

With the lectures to Selwyn College next week my mind also hovered around the extreme difficulty of having a faith that is both intellectually presentable, eg to Selwyn College, and presentable to the primitive islanders where we have been these last ten days. Today, for instance, is the Feast of the Annunciation of the Blessed Virgin Mary. John Macquarrie, a more conservative scholar than many, says of the stories of Christ's nativity: "There can be little doubt that the stories that have come down to us are legendary rather than historical." Few of our best biblical scholars would now disagree with him. But I am surprised that having said that, he goes on to use Luke 1. 38, as an example of the 'free response' of the Blessed Virgin

Mary, and, indeed, uses it twice: "Mary's words 'Let it be to me according to your word' are a great confession of dependence and obedience, freely accepted". It is this kind of double talk which simply will not do - especially from a theologian. There is bound to be a certain amount of double talk in different situations, eg the pastoral and the academic situation, but there is no excuse for it in 'Principles of Christian Theology'.

My anxiety is that the boys and girls at Selwyn College, part of the five per cent of whatever intellectual aristocracy there is in the Islands, the professional class of the future, will find out at Selwyn that religion is part of the village 'custom' which you can only continue to subscribe to by betraying your intellect. In founding Selwyn College, two years ago, John did a brave - and necessary - thing. He wrote on the wall the end of a simply primitive and authoritarian religion out here.

I spent most of the day preparing lectures, but in the afternoon I went to see a rugby match between Selwyn College and King George VI Secondary School - a Government school: Selwyn's rivals. I thought it would be good to set eyes on some of the boys and girls to whom I shall be lecturing in the next days.

March 26th 1972
I helped at the Cathedral. It was Palm Sunday. There were about a thousand people there; a cross-section, from the High Commissioner and his ADC to people of extreme simplicity.

I then sat in on a meeting of the Melanesian Commission of the Diocese at the Bishop's House from 11.00 am until 3.00 pm - thirty high-powered Melanesians discussing, very ably, just how they get the Government to do what it ought to be doing about Education. Six of those present were elected politicians. It is the extraordinary contrast between primitive village peasants and these people I have been with today which is continually surprising. And these people have come from the very villages I have been visiting in the last ten days.

Discussion was often heated, and those involved uttered truths from experience in the midst of their excitement: "People do not believe in Government: they see the officers of the Government once in a blue moon. They believe in the Church - because their catechist and their priest are with them day by day." Yet there was also evidence of changing patterns of authority. "We want our priests to tell us what to do; then we shall try to do it" said one person. Others said that now it is wrong to expect the directives to come from the bishop and the priests.

At 3.00 pm, Howard Brock, the Bursar, came with his wife to drive me out to Selwyn College - seventeen miles south-east of Honiara. I shall be staying with Howard and Eunice for the week. They are fairly newly arrived from Adelaide.

The Acting Headmaster, a thirty-three year-old New Zealander, Richard Roberts (they are waiting for the appointment of a new headmaster) had gathered most of the staff to meet me over tea. I was especially glad to see John Pinder, recently married, whose parents live five minutes' from St Stephen's Lodge, SE1. He has been giving good service to Melanesia for nearly five years. There are fourteen others on the staff, but only three of them are Melanesians. Almost all the staff are astonishingly young, most of them necessarily somewhat inexperienced. I gather from them that experience of teaching - and of the Church! - is coming quickly, and, often, painfully.

After tea, I went straight to Chapel, and gave my first address to the 80 girls and 160 boys. I thought I would try to get to know them as casually as possible, so I went then to the kitchen (they do their own cooking at weekends) and, after supper with Richard Roberts and his wife, two people with whom I felt an immediate sympathy, I went round some of the dormitories; serried ranks of double bunks. In one dormitory there was an inspection for lice in the hair! The students come from all parts of the Solomons. It was very nice to be able to say to them: "Kia? You come from Kia? I've just visited Kia - a marvellous place." And so on. I'm so glad I'm *ending* my time in the Solomons *here*.

March 27th 1972

Teaching in classes - sixteen periods in four days - preparing lectures that are given in Chapel once a day, at 5.30 pm and seeing individuals, staff and students, is taking all my time.

The day begins with the beating of the drum at 6.00 am. I have a cold shower and make my way in the dark across the campus to the Chapel, to celebrate Holy Communion at 6.20 am. Usually about a third of the school is there. Classes begin at 7.30 am. I do most of my preparatory work in their new library, avidly used by the students, although at the moment it is hardly more than paperbacks and newspapers.

I lunch and dine, one by one, with each member of staff. It is clear that in this isolated situation they greatly appreciate having someone from outside to talk to.

The generator is turned off at 10.00 pm. and the lights suddenly go off. You need to be in your bedroom by then - with everything prepared for the early morning. There is no light in the morning until daybreak.

The light goes out in five minutes' time! Tonight I shall not be sorry.

March 28th 1972
The reactions in class to my lecture last night had been very interesting. Many of them take some convincing that 'urbanisation' has come to the Solomons. I ask them "Which of you want to stay in Honiara?" "Which of you want to go back to the village?" Most of them want to stay in Honiara, and even those who say they want to go back to the village wouldn't want to go back if it hadn't the benefits of urbanisation - tractors, drugs, transistors, outboard motors, etc.

It takes quite a lot of courage for many of the boys and girls to ask me questions, for English is not their mother tongue, although it is the only language allowed in school. I knew that one boy wasn't speaking in class because he wasn't sure he could manage the English well enough. Without my asking, he produced this in writing:-

"Why do you want to stay in a village?"

Looking at it from a Christian point of view:-

1   I believe that the knowledge I gain at school is a gift from God. Therefore the people who really need this gift of mine would be the isolated and less fortunate ones living in the villages, for they do not have the same chance as I do. I think these people need careful attention, too. 'True happiness comes by giving'.

2   Also, I think someone who knows something of this changing world should stay with the rural dwellers in order to communicate to them what is happening in this country and to help to solve such problems as cultural interaction. I think it is important to create some kind of link between the urban dwellers and the rural dwellers.

3 I want to live in the village in order to encourage our people to maintain our culture. To my mind we don't want to be too British or American, for what is good for them is not appropriate for the Solomons.

Economically

The riches of this country depend on agriculture. Therefore we should go home and help people or teach people how to farm the land and grow better crops. If some incentive is formed in the villages, I think there will be less flowing of young people to urban areas.

Political Views

Our local Council members had very little education, therefore they need someone educated enough to replace them. They have done their part, and it is our time now, for we know something more of this changing world, both of internal and external affairs.

If we go home we shall be able to plan better developments which will suit our future conditions.

Finally, I would like to say: "The implements of yesterday are no longer of use today". Similarly, "the students of today should be the leaders of tomorrow."

These are rather 'boy scout' opinions here, and the writer is nineteen years old; but if a school can get students to think like this, it can be thankful. The students are very pleased when they shine. One boy came to see me to talk over a problem. As he left, I rather absentmindedly used the South African greeting "Go well". He replied: "Stay well, umfundis." - letting me know he, too, had read Alan Paton's *Cry the Beloved Country*. He was delighted with himself!

I lectured this evening on 'Changing Patterns of *Authority* in a Changing World'.

March 29th 1972

It has rained almost continually since I arrived - not just rain, but rain so heavy it is often deafening, like coals being poured from somewhere. Last night there were over four inches of rain, and when I first went out across the swamped campus there were hundreds of toads jumping and shouting for joy, their sound like an engine being started. It was a nice day for toads! We are not far from the path of yet another cyclone. My thoughts are often with the Bishop, who has gone to visit more of the stricken areas, in the *Southern Cross*. The people of the Diocese could not take another cyclone this year - nor could John. And the *Southern Cross* is not the boat to be on in a cyclone.

They seemed to have understood what I was saying last night about 'Authority' but it puzzles them: they have been brought up in societies with such fixed structures. And their Junior Schools have also often been fairly rigid. "Would you tell us again how we can *earn* authority?" said one questioner. It seemed a new idea to him. I had given them various examples of people in authority - Chief, High Commissioner, Archbishop, Queen, Pop Singer, etc. This provoked the embarrassing question "How is the Archbishop of Canterbury appointed?" I unfolded the gory details, wishing that any other question had been asked. When I had finished, the questioner said innocently: "Please, sir, *why* is it done that way?" Why indeed!!

The girls are very slow to ask questions. In fact, not one has asked a question yet - a reflection of their position in their society, I think; for they are often more intelligent than the boys. It will take quite a time for the experiment in *co-education* really to succeed. During the first part of the afternoon the students are engaged in market gardening and other outside work, which teaches them to grow new crops and use new methods of husbandry. The school is self-sufficient, to a limited degree. I enjoyed visiting the piggery this afternoon. The students - girls and boys - were obviously proud of what they were doing.

It was a good introduction to my lecture on 'Worldly Holiness'!

March 30th 1972

The older students have clearly got the point of my statement that I would 'judge the success of Selwyn College by how much more freedom it gave them, and how much it helped them to cope with that freedom responsibly.' They have quoted it approvingly in the first paragraph of their student magazine, duplicated and distributed today. The older students are thirsty for freedom and are given a lot of it here. Several have raised the question of compulsory school chapel. Personally, I do not see how you can both encourage people to think freely and with integrity and say, virtually, that no matter what the result is of their thinking, they must come to school chapel at all the specified times. Most of the staff want attendance at chapel to be voluntary, but some of those in Authority in the Diocese tend to say "the Melanesians do things as a group: it would disturb this 'group' feeling to make chapel-going voluntary." There is truth in the statement that Melanesians do things in groups, but it is so easily prostituted simply to support the views of those who want to go on seeing a chapel full of students! Melanesian students probably are used to acting as a group more than Europeans. Melanesians are also more and more concerned with individual integrity - and the responsible use of freedom. They are aware that there are defects as well as virtues in the 'group' approach - the escape from individual decision and responsibility. I wonder what attitude would be taken if the Melanesians decided as a group *not* to come to chapel!

On the surface this seems such an ecclesiastical subject. But I think the students are right to see the integrity of the Church and their own integrity are involved.

It has been a good subject to talk out in the classrooms on Maundy Thursday.

I have found it very useful in my lectures to have the script of the play from which the film *This Man* was made (the film I saw in Perth, Australia). It is by Francis Bogotu, a Melanesian, now at Lancaster University. The play is about the clash of Melanesian and Western culture.

> "I am looking for myself;
> I am looking for a man who will answer to my name.
>
> "Sometimes I want to love - ah, love!
>
> And sometimes I think I float above the town,
> To watch myself hang around,
> Stay here, drink there, work today, sleep tonight.
> So I think - who is that stonehead in the long pants?
>
> Is it me?
>
> And I'm not the only one -
> Plenty of us, walking, laughing,
> Putting on the style.
> But in the quiet hours of the morning,

When we wake before the dawn,
Thinking - who are we?

We are the ones who do not know:
But we need to find out soon,
For tomorrow we ourselves have sons to teach.

I have opened up my mind
Like a giant rubbish-can
And have welcomed into it
Everything the European throws away.

In there among the rubbish
Are the good and useful things,
But how to recognise them from the trash?

So - who are we?
We are the modern people.
We are the new time men......"

The whole script I find as moving as when I heard it in the film. Here, because it is peculiarly theirs, the Melanesians own product, it is listened to with rapt attention.

March 31st 1972 – Good Friday
I realised when I began to prepare what I had to say to the School this morning that I had never spoken to a school before on Good Friday - they are usually on holiday. Certainly I've never spoken to a school on Good Friday whose mother tongue is not English. I felt it was a day to try to say what is at the heart of the Cross very simply. I didn't think there was much chance of succeeding, but I had more success than I expected.

At 9.00 am, I said:

"I am looking for myself...I am looking for that man who is me." How does the death of Christ 2,000 years ago help me?

When I look at the death of Jesus on the Cross I see one unmistakable, unavoidable fact; that evil is a very real thing in this world.....

But it doesn't just happen in Jesus' death and nowhere else. I have to take it seriously in my life.

Don't ask me to tell you how evil got there. I don't know. Don't ask me to tell you *all* about evil. I don't know *all* about it. But if you are looking for yourself, do not pretend there is no such thing as evil. And do not pretend it is not something very mysterious. The mystery of evil is something deeper than any of us will ever be able to understand in this life. We can understand some things about evil, but not all.....

But if you are looking for yourself you will see - if you look at the death of Jesus on the Cross - another unavoidable, unmistakable fact: that *good* is a very real thing in this world. And the longer you look at Jesus, the more you will see clearly the nature of Good. But good doesn't just happen in Jesus' death and nowhere else.....

If you are looking for yourself, do not pretend there is no such thing as good; and do not pretend it is not something mysterious - something higher, wider, deeper than we shall ever understand in this life.

But when you look at the death of Jesus you see that there is something going on between good and evil, which to describe we have to use words like 'battle', 'fight', 'war'. It's not like the Battle of Savo here, with ships and guns. But watch Jesus in Gethsemane and you see a spiritual battle. Watch him all the way through his Trial and Sufferings. Some mysterious kind of battle is happening.

It's as though Jesus said: Evil is real. It looks like the last word on things. But I, Jesus, believe that Good is real, and that good is the last word.

> Nothing is going to kill the Good in Me.
> Nothing is going to stop me loving.
> I shall suffer all that evil can do.
> Nothing will - in my life - give evil the last word.

Jesus tells us that there is a *battle* between good and evil. But the battle doesn't happen in Jesus' death and nowhere else. Jesus tells us how to battle against evil: never to stop believing in the power of loving; which we can co-operate with - and share......

If I am looking for myself I shall find something of myself if I see the mysterious power of Good and Love as the lost important things in life: that they can win the battle against evil.....

> The Death of Jesus shows us the centre of life.
> The Death of Jesus shows me the centre of myself."

Of course, that's not all I said. And all I said doesn't say *all*. But 'enough is enough'.

At 12.00 pm we had an unforgettable happening, anunrehearsed Passion drama. Ken Watkinson, an Englishman on the staff, a gifted producer, had just marked out various sites, and told various people what he wanted them to do. We all 'assembled' - just as a crowd - in the centre of the campus. Ken started reading sentences from the Story of the Passion. Students, as the disciples of Jesus, came into our midst. 'Jesus' went over 'the brook of Kedron' (after the rains - a dyke running with water) to what is in fact a flower garden. A Land-rover full of 'soldiers' - and 'Judas' - suddenly came careering across the campus. Then followed the Betrayal. The Arrest was too realistic to be anything but blood-curdling. It might well have happened in a number of the countries I have been through. The 'soldiers' so obviously enjoyed manhandling 'Jesus'. The Trials - the Chief Priest had a mitre on; Pilate was High Commissioner - took place in three areas of the dining room. The crowd of us - students, staff, villagers - crushed in. It was all curiously real. Some climbed trees to see in through the windows. By the time 'Jesus' was led out, the 'soldiers' were really enjoying themselves at 'Jesus'' expense; so was the crowd. It was too real. Howard Brock (the College Bursar with whom I'm, staying) got pulled out of the crowd to carry 'Jesus'' Cross when He couldn't make it any further. The boy who was Jesus - unrehearsed - did incredibly well. That's to say, I had difficulty in keeping my tears back, and didn't really succeed. He looked as though he was going through it, and, I think, was. The Cross was two bamboo poles. They - and 'Jesus' - were tied to a tree. After 'Jesus' died, we were drawn away from the site to where music was suddenly blaring forth, interrupted by a recorded Solomon Islands news Bulletin. The death of Jesus, arrested last night in Honiara, was one item amongst many - the fall in the price of copra; the position of a cyclone; the news that a sudden storm had damaged the chancel of Honiara Cathedral etc.

Howard Brock and his wife - they have been very kind to me - drove me back to Honiara in the afternoon. It has been a memorable Holy Week, not only for nine inches of rain in five days (there were fifty-three inches here during the week of the cyclone). When I got back, John had returned from the hurricane areas. On one island, two houses out of a hundred had been rebuilt - the materials for rebuilding have been destroyed. In another, there had as yet been no rebuilding. A plague of caterpillars has followed the hurricane. All means of livelihood have been destroyed. But the villagers, with blind faith, had always done what they could to restore the altar of the Church. They themselves are living in four foot temporary hovels.

April 1st 1972
A day of recovery, and more preparation. I spent a lot of time on the sermon for the Cathedral tomorrow, Easter Day.

April 2nd 1972
"As it began to dawn....." there was an almost cloudless sky, and a marvellous sunrise. It has been a perfect day of brilliant sunshine.

The Cathedral service was one I shall not easily forget. It was packed to the doors, and beyond and around. I am rarely satisfied with a sermon, but I am grateful this year for this opportunity to re-think what I believe, particularly with the help of John Knox's *Death of Christ*, and with the pressure to express it clearly in a strange environment. In many ways my Easter Sermon was my Good Friday sermon, but that is largely what I believe: that Easter Day makes explicit what is implicit in Good Friday: the victory of love. For me, the Empty Tomb can add little to the Good Friday victory, indeed it can detract from it - people can put their faith in a magical removal of a body from a tomb instead of in the Easter Gospel, which is the Victory of the Love of God in Jesus: the victory of Good over Evil: unquenchable, undying Love.

During the service, mynahs, with yellow beaks and brown and white feathers, fly constantly in and out of the Cathedral. My religious self said "The sparrow hath found her an house.....even thy altars". But my unregenerate self longed to say - especially when they interrupted the sermon: "For God's sake, someone, interfere with those mynahs!"

For breakfast we went back to Bishop's House, where the congregation of his chapel were having breakfast on the lawn - more kumera, etc! The very English Director of Education was there (who told me that Cambridge had won the Boat Race: he had stayed up for it). It was an opportunity to say in as gentlemanly a fashion as I could manage how disgusting I thought Britian's contribution is to education in the Solomons. He smiled charmingly and said (a) that "it is four times what it was" (so is 2/- four times sixpence), (b) that "we mustn't give people here a set-up which they cannot afford to maintain after Independence." This seems to me to be Parkinson's Second Law of Parsimony. (The First, which I had used against me several times in England by Bureaucrats is "We have tremendous sympathy with you, but if we helped *you* we would have to help everybody."!)

We went off to Selwyn College at midday for their Easter Feast. Three hundred sat down on the grass to eat off banana leaves, pork, kumera, and cassava pudding, which had been cooking in special ovens made in the ground since the previous day. I managed to nibble a respectable amount and consumed the contents of a coconut. After the Feast, there were games, including a very good football match between the school and the town. After Evensong, the Bishop dedicated the new Library of the College. Then there was a 'Hula'. In England it would be called a 'Hop'. And no one would be able to tell the difference by the boys' or girls' dresses or by the music - electric guitars, drums, and a singer who managed to look 'sent' most of the time. The main difference is that boys and girls sit separately, and when a boy wishes to dance with a girl he comes to her and makes what they call in ecclesiastical circles 'a profound bow'.

April 3rd 1972

Easter Monday is a holiday in the Solomons as well as in England. It was another lovely day, and John thought this would be a good day for repairing what he euphemistically calls 'the swimming pool' - part of the coral rock formation in front of the house which the tide fills and empties. The hurricane had ravaged it. John had invited three young masters from Selwyn College to lunch - John Rolfe, from England, and two Australians, David Wippell and Terry Ward. They were 'voluntary' labour to remove the boulders now blocking the middle of the pool and form them into a dam at one end. (As John said, characteristically, "What better day to roll away stones?") It was in fact a magnificent day for sun; jumping in and out of the water; having a light lunch out of doors; doing a piece of work that needed doing - with beer and music; and talking about education, when we needed to sit down.

In the evening there was a farewell party for the Bishop. (He is going to Britain via Australia and New Zealand. We leave by the same 'plane on Thursday.) Most of the guests were Melanesians. I spent a lot of time talking to Baddeley DeVesi, now in the Secretariat here. After Junior School, the Diocese sent him to senior school and teacher training college in New Zealand. Then, after a spell as a teacher and as a headmaster, he went into politics. But he became cynical about politics here and entered the Inspectorate of Education. From there he was seconded to the Secretariat. All this - and he is only twenty-eight. Clearly he has a considerable part to play in the future of these Islands. But without the Church he would be one of the uneducated masses. That is the simple truth.

April 4th 1972
Bevin Meredith, one of the assistant bishops in New Guinea, who is going to have a look at the Church in some of the villages on the Island of Malaita, came to dinner. He had come straight from Bouganville, and was able to bring us up to date on how the copper mine is influencing life there. The good news is that the mining company is employing islanders who have trained for all the truck work, and have sent back to their countries of origin most of the people originally drafted into Bouganville. Alan House, the Director of Education, whom I had met on Sunday, also came to dinner. I found him an attractive and intelligent character. But it was clear to me how frustrating it must be to be a civil servant here. When you have a heart and mind, and see what could be done, how galling it must be to be denied the money to do it, and to be met in the ignorance of the issues by the Foreign Office in London. You are almost bound to serve up stock face-saving answers. One of the Under Secretaries, visiting here recently, stunned everyone by asking "What *is* copra?" It only happens to be the chief source of the livelihood of the Islands! It must also be dismaying to know that this place has been for years 'the end of the line'. Always there have been places like India and Kenya far ahead in their demands upon the British, and their 'leverage' to achieve their demands has always been greater. Of course, when I said I was coming here, most people in England said, "The Solomon Islands? Where are they?"

April 8th 1972
My last day in the Solomons today. It has coincided with something odd that happens here. The wind has changed direction, and the sea currents, and, with the change, the colour of the sea has entirely changed, because the calcareous substance that is secreted by marine organisms to form coral has been swept down to this part of the coast, where it remains for eight months of the year, covering, for instance, the

rusting remains of the US transport at the water's edge. Today, a vast expanse of the sea near the coast is an opaque sky-blue, contrasting with the royal blue further out.

It has, in fact, been very much the 'last day'. I have been gathering my things together in a leisurely fashion. But for an hour after lunch I went down to the water and bathed in the 'pool'. I doubt whether I shall bathe here again, and in this kind of water, for many years; pure, translucent warm water. I sat for some time on the rocks against which the waves break in glorious spray.

I recalled one of my first strong memories: when I was a child, and we were finishing a family holiday - I suppose I was five or six. For the first time in my life the mystery of time overwhelmed me. I had seen a wave in the sea, and suddenly I realised I would never see *that* wave again. All I could do then was to cry. My mother trying, at the time, to get four reluctant children to the railway station, could do no more than chastise me. Today I remembered again my inconsolable grief - though today I could smile at it too. I shall not see Guadalcanal again for many years - if ever. Today I smile (an ironic smile, it is true) and say "That's life!" But I confess that the mystery of knowing things or possessing them for hardly more than a moment is perpetually for me one of the greatest and most painful mysteries of life - "sunt lacrimae rerum" - "Tears at the heart of things". And the tears are not easily turned to joy.

Brother Daniel of the Franciscans came to dinner, after a final Communion in the Bishop's Chapel. It was a quiet last evening here, and a happy one.

April 6th 1972
John got up to make a cup of tea at 4.15 am and there was no more sleep! At 6.30 am the tourist vessel *Arcadia*, painted

white, anchored off Honiara; a glorious sight in the sun. At 7.00 am we left for Henderson Field, the airfield which was the cause of all the fighting on Guadalcanal. A happy company of people had come to see us off - schoolgirls, Sisters, Franciscans, schoolmasters from Selwyn, some of the Honiara priests, and Donald. It was fascinating to see from the air the green island of Guadalcanal, and then to begin the 870 mile flight to New Guinea, over many coral islands, archipelagos, and atolls, Savo - the Russell Islands, the New Georgia Group, including the tiny island now called Kennedy Island, to which John F Kennedy swam when his ship was sunk during the War. They were like an exquisite necklace of jewels, dark green the centre and bright turquoise the surround, set in a fabric of blue. We crossed the Solomon Sea, and there again were such islands, lovely beyond words, first the Kiriwina Islands, then the Dentrecasteaux Islands, then New Guinea itself. We crossed the north coast near Popondetta, where I shall be next week. Then we flew over the densely wooded Owen Stanley Ranges, passing Mount Lamington, which exploded laterally in 1951, killing 4,000 people, and Kokoda. John's brother was killed near Kokoda during the War - his body was found eighteen years later. It was his brother's death that in part led John to come and serve in New Guinea - before serving in the Solomons.

As we dropped down on Port Moresby we passed over the new university. It was clear that the Solomons - and New Guinea - though all 'South Pacific' - belong to two different worlds.

Stage 12: New Guinea: Port Moresby and Popondetta

April 7th 1972

Theodore Woods was waiting to welcome me at the airport at Port Moresby. I had not seen him for ten years. At Trinity College, Cambridge, he was a medical student, having resisted the pressures of family tradition to get ordained - his father is Archbishop of Melbourne; his uncle, Bishop of Worcester; there are bishops in his bloodstream! Eventually it all caught up with him, and I last saw him when he was a curate in Leicester.

But the Woods tradition has taken a fascinating turn in Theodore. In 1967, he came out with Jean, his wife, and his children, to work in New Guinea - Philip is now seven; Jo, five; and there are identical twins, Alison and Rachel, two and a half. He had done ten months voluntary service as a teacher in New Guinea in 1959. He came out this time - never having taught except as a volunteer - as Principal of St Aidan's Teacher Training College. Now, at thirty four, he has a very interesting and important job. He is Principal of the In-Service College of Training for Teachers, which is responsible for the further education of all teachers in New Guinea. There is no actual 'college'. He has to deal with the provision of courses of further training and with the principles of selection for them. This involves working with local district people, with church authorities, and with national educational authorities. There are 7,000 teachers in new Guinea, fifty per cent of whom have had no education after primary school. hence the importance of the work.

Of course, you cannot be involved in a job like Theodore's without being concerned with every aspect of education in New Guinea. Of a total population of two and a half million people, only 235,000 are in schools to start with, and in the Southern Highlands only twenty five per cent of school-age children are in school. Of those at school, fifty two per cent 'drop out' at Standard Six or before - not only voluntarily, but because of the shortage of high schools - only forty per cent of those who completed the primary final examination in 1970 could be given a place.

Since 1970, all education has been unified, with a national education system, two thirds of education agencies are 'church' (mostly the lower levels of education). Theodore is therefore very concerned with the *aims* of church school and state school education. With an actual decline of children entering high school (from sixty seven per cent in 1965 to forty per cent in 1967), he is concerned with what happens to the 'failures' - which also relates to the aims of schools. Is the aim to get pupils to pass Standard Six? - so as to get money? - and stay in town? Is it to prepare them for life in the village? The self-respect of the 'failure' is as important a subject in New Guinea as in England. But whereas in England it is the failure of the Secondary Modern child who didn't get into the Grammar School, here it is the failure to get into the Secondary School at all. Education for *all*, a 'Comprehensive' Education system, would need resources which are simply not available at the moment.

Theodore has been quite marvellously diligent in arranging for me to 'see' Port Moresby, and to get some kind of insight into the problems of Papua New Guinea, in only four days. This morning, Jean and I went to the market at Koki, always a fascinating way of seeing a slice of life. We were there an hour, and then I went to the Franciscans' Church and Primary School nearby. Some real community work is obviously going on there. Theodore then collected me to go to the 'Outrigger' Motel, where he had arranged a lunch for me with four very interesting people: an Australian, Dr Jim Farrell, who has been in Papua New Guinea for ten years, and has an American Doctorate in Education. He is virtually Theodore's 'boss'. He was Principal of Port Moresby Teacher Training College, but is now Superintendent of Curriculum and In-Service Training for the Department of Education. He had also invited a most lively person, Vincent Eri, from a village near Port Moresby, who was for many years a primary teacher. After teaching, he went to University, and was the first person in the Education Department to get a degree. He has recently written a magnificent novel, *The Crocodile*, which I read in Honiara. He is now First Assistant Director of Planning in the Department of Education. The third member of our party was Miss Pamela Quartermaine, Deputy Principal and Dean of Women at Port Moresby Teacher Training College. She has written a good many of the text books in use. The fourth guest was McKenzie Daugi, from Gona, for many years a primary school teacher in Anglican Bush schools here. He is a man with an intense interest in the community. He was trained as a teacher at St Aidan's College. In recent years he had been the District Education Secretary. He has just completed a very tiring election campaign in the Northern District, and has won a seat. So he is one of New Guinea's one hundred MPs - 'MHAs' (Member of the House of Assembly). This is the last government before Independence, which is due to come in about 1976. It was one of the most fascinating lunches I have ever attended - politics, religion, education, community, literature: conversation never slackened.

I went round the Teacher Training College with Pamela Quartermaine after lunch; at 3.00 pm Canon Ian Stuart, who has been Rector of Port Moresby for ten years, came to drive me around it. He has just had published a large illustrated guide book to Port Moresby. He is a young bachelor, and was a missionary in the bush for a number of years, in the northern coastal area, before he took on this place.

In the last census, in 1966, Port Moresby was 42,000 people. In the intervening years it has probably put on another 30,000. It is just a century since Captain Moresby discovered it. Now it is the Administrative Centre of Papua New Guinea, It is a city of no great beauty, but it is spread out around a harbour of very considerable natural beauty.

Ian Stuart gave me a lightning tour of the place: everything from the upper crust housing to the squatters in houses-on-stilts in the sea; from the first wooden church, built by the London Missionary Society, to his own new church, dedicated in 1968 - where I shall be preaching on Sunday evening. (The first Anglican priest came to Port Moresby in 1890, but there was no Anglican church until 1914, when St John's, the predecessor of Ian Stuart's new church, was built. It was badly damaged and looted during the Second World War, when the town was heavily bombed by the Japanese, and when everyone was expecting it to be captured by the enemy, which it never was.

It was an exhausting day, and it was a delight to spend the evening relaxing with Theodore and Jean. Theodore is such a gifted person - with his hands, at making things - he has made his own clavichord; with music - he is a very good organist; at administration and ideas. He is a born leader, and is often bursting with enthusiasm. But people don't find it easy to keep up with him; so, in a way, he's a 'cat who walks by himself'. That has its pain.

April 8th 1972

It was a harassing morning. Dr Penelope Key - whose brother, John, I have known since he was an undergraduate at Pembroke College, Cambridge, and whose father I have known as Bishop of Truro - took me round the Port Moresby General Hospital, where she is Acting Consultant in Obstetrics.

There were several shocks to the system. There was the company of mourners, weeping, at the door of the mortuary, unwilling to leave until the burial of their near relative had taken place. There was the milling crowd of out-patients, stretching down a corridor. I would have lost all hope. There were the wards in which it was not easy to tell who were the patients, for all ages and sexes could often be found in one ward, in and out of bed; the mothers who would not leave their children. so slept with them in bed; the husbands who would not leave their wives, so slept on the floor under their beds. There was the literally faceless young man, whose face had been held in the fire in an attempted murder. He was blind, but, with what served as a face, laughing.

Penny herself taught me a great deal in her comments as we walked round. She said that trained men in New Guinea often resent the authority of a woman, and ordinary men often resent treatment by a woman. She explained that villagers would not come to hospital at all unless relatives could come too, and talked of the tremendous difficulties the language barrier sometimes presents. How do you begin to deal with psychiatric disturbance if you cannot speak in the language of the patient? She talked of the problem of where you should spend the limited available money. Although there is 'status' in a new large hospital, it is clear that a great deal of hospital treatment can be prevented if money is spent on District Health Services. Penny has spent a number of years working in the rural areas, walking over the mountains as a matter of course; so she knows what she is talking about. Nearly ninety-five per cent of the population of New Guinea still live in rural areas; and, in some of them, between ten and twenty per cent die before they reach the age of five. The malnutrition in early years exposes the child to fatal infections and also affects intelligence.

A rapid mortality decline has been achieved in recent years in many areas, through, for instance, control of malaria, or through new roads making skilled midwifery more available. I was not surprised that between fifteen and twenty per cent of all hospital admissions are for respiratory diseases - in Lae thirty seven per cent of the hospital admissions are due to pneumonia.

I was fascinated by the title of an article that I spotted in a copy of the Papua and New Guinea Medical Journal - 'Poisoning with Angels Trumpets', - but disappointed to find that it referred simply to poisoning through eating the flowers, leaves or fruit of a flowering tree - which I first saw in Nkambo Mugerwa's garden in Kampala - with hanging white or scarlet trumpets, which children love to 'blow', - with unexpected results.

Penny gave me a copy of a very interesting inaugural lecture by the Foundation Professor of Clinical Science, Dr I Maddox, of the University of Papua and New Guinea. It, too, had an intriguing title: UDUMU A-HAGAIA: which, being interpreted, is: "Open Your Mouth'! Dr Maddox has been living in one of the worst areas of housing in Port Moresby, by the sea, to see for himself what its implications are for medicine. In New Guinea today there is one 'medical officer' for every 20,000 people. Compare the UK: one to every 1,855. Nevertheless I was heartened to see 'gangs' of medical students going round the hospital, as in Britain. These were, of course, young black New

Guineans, and I was introduced to some fine New Guinea doctors already at work in the hospital.

Theodore picked me up from the hospital and transported me to the marvellous new University, leaving me in the hands of three students. We went to the refectory for lunch - mutton chops - and, again, it was encouraging and exciting to sit in a dining hall crammed with New Guineans. It lacked nothing of the boisterousness of any, in term, English university refectory. Here is a great deal of the South West Pacific's future. After lunch, I went round all the new buildings, some still being completed: splendid dramatic concrete architecture, well landscaped, with a main entrance and forum of many stairs on which the students clearly love to sit. A lecture room of orange chairs thrilled me, and I spent an hour or more, finally, in the air-conditioned library. My student hosts could not have been more courteous or informative - one reading anthropology; one, economics; and the other, politics. They were a wonderful sample of *new* New Guinea. The new Vice-Chancellor is Professor K Inglis, the Australian who wrote the excellent book *The Church and the Working Classes in England*. He will have quite a task in the University. There has been sexual chaos in it. In a recent survey, only sixty per cent of the students said they saw any point in premarital chastity, and less than a third, even if they saw the point, indicated personal acceptance of such a standard. What the survey revealed in print has been confirmed in the experience of those pastorally responsible at the University - it is, of course, not only 'sexual chaos' but culture chaos.

In the evening, we went to three one-act plays in the university open-air theatre, until it was rained off; and so were we.

April 9th 1972
I went to Church, Low Sunday, in Hohola, a suburb of Port

Moresby. It was an almost entirely New Guinea congregation, very much like Melanesia; indeed, several of the congregation were Melanesians, at college or university here. One was the brother of the captain of the *Southern Cross*. It was a happy congregation of a hundred; but I cannot believe it will hold people from the villages, now in the town, for long. It wasn't yet geared to the world of Port Moresby. It was much more a club for those who hadn't found themselves in this world (which is one important role for a church, but only one). A New Guinea priest celebrated the Holy Communion and preached. Theodore spoke afterwards. He is excellent in all that he says and does. It is such a shock for me to have known an attractive but immature under-graduate, and to come here - asking only for friendship! - to meet a young man with very great and developed capacities. He would make an excellent Bishop of New Guinea or Melanesia tomorrow! But I suspect the days of Bishop Woods have passed, and only the secular world will now be able to find room for his gifts of episcope.

Again, he and Jean had laid on a splendid lunch party, a barbecue in the garden. Professor Antony Clunies-Ross, Professor of Economics at the University, and his wife and children, came. His wife is a professional 'medic'. The Assistant Director of Agriculture and Fisheries, John Natera, and his wife, Eileen, also came. He is a New Guinean; she, Australian - a much experienced Community Development Worker in Port Moresby. Another New Guinean, whose surname I never discovered, Geoffrey, also came: the Assistant Director of the National Tourist Board. We thrashed out social and economic problems of town and country, and, of course, 'tourism'; and the question of what of past culture should be encouraged. Do you want a merely backward-looking music, for instance? How do you encourage a contemporary New Guinea 'style' in music, art, and literature?

After lunch, we meant to drive out to the mountains, but it rained heavily, so we only got as far as Bomana, seven miles out, to the vast War Cemetery for Commonwealth people killed in the South West Pacific area. I found it very movingly beautiful. John Chisholm's brother was in the Book of Remembrance.

In the evening, I preached at Ian Stuart's church in town: a small, almost entirely white congregation; a kind of Anglican chaplaincy to Australians abroad. However, this kind of person needs to be ministered to, and Ian clearly had a special ministry. Theodore played the organ. That was a delight.

April 10th 1972
Eileen Natera, with her Community Development experience, had asked whether she could drive Theodore and me around Port Moresby. We went to all the various settlements which have sprung up around the town, mostly of different tribal groupings. My Western sensibilities were often shocked: four taps to two thousand people in one settlement; housing barely more than covering; sanitation, the beach. But most of the people could afford more, and it would probably be provided if they wanted it. I gathered, from Mrs Clunies-Ross, the doctor, who was also with us, that there was no conclusive evidence that such - what I regard as - low standards had had any adverse effect on health. Should 'higher' standards be imposed on people? Should they be encouraged, educated, engineered to want them?

As we went past the House of Assembly it was all being painted up for the new Assembly. This is another situation, inevitable out here, where the question of what is the will of the people is difficult to discover and implement. The Australian Government made up its mind that the Territory should be given independence before it was screamed for. The great bulk of the people still scarcely comprehend what it implies. The framework of government to be provided is almost entirely foreign, mostly Australian. The proceedings of the present House baffle many of the present indigenous members. Most of them see them as primarily a forum in which to ventilate demands for local developments - roads, bridges, etc. The great majority of villagers (ninety-five per cent of the country) are isolated from meaningful contact with the distant House of Assembly. The rugged topography, dense vegetation and impassable swamps, which cover most of the country - and ocean waters - assure this. Most of the people know no language but their local vernaculars. At the 1966 Census thirty-six per cent of the population over ten years of age said they spoke Pidgin; thirteen per cent said they spoke English; seven per cent said they spoke English and Pidgin. There are hardly any newspapers. Radio receivers in the villages are still rare. Territory-wide travel must be almost entirely by air, which means it is accessible only to a very few. All this tends to make the villagers averse to anything that might disturb the present relationship to their 'sugar-daddy' Australia. Bishop George Ambo, for instance, one of the Anglican Assistant Bishops, is very much against independence yet.

Unlike most countries I have visited, Papua New Guinea lacks national unity and a real nationalist movement. It has not had to wage an anti-colonial struggle. It has only a small indigenous elite, as yet. Its political parties are weak. It has not yet found any outstanding national leader. But Australia has decided (like a local government laying on water or electricity) that Papua New Guinea should have independence.

Just after midday, I flew back over the Owen Stanley Range, in a little fifteen-seater Otter aircraft, to Popondetta. It's normal flying altitude is about 10,000 feet, which means that you get a magnificent close-up of the mountains. You say to yourself "This really *is* New Guinea": the densest vegetation imaginable. There are no roads across the mountains, but the famous Kokoda Trail begins not far from Popondetta. It was by this Trail that the Japanese, having landed troops at Gona, a few miles from Popondetta, in July 1942, made their overland advance on Port Moresby, reaching, after bitter jungle fighting, a ridge only thirty-two miles from the town, where they were halted.

Brother Brian of the Franciscans, (who was a very good friend of mine, Brian Harley, when I was a student at King's College, London) was waiting for me at the airfield with Paulus Moi, a Papuan, at whose Profession as a Franciscan I am to preach on Sunday. They transported me in a Daihatsu truck to the Friary, four miles away at Jegarata. When we arrived, it was nearly dusk, and the daily ration of torrential rain was beginning. My little guest room - in spite of the warmth of the Brothers' welcome - seemed forbiddingly barren; an electric light, a hurricane lamp, a thin shelf, a small table, a bed, a blanket, a towel and a mosquito net were all its contents. Nothing at all to hold clothes. But, Evening Prayer in the Friars' octagonal chapel was very happy. There were about a dozen young Friars, mostly from New Guinea and Melanesia, and Reg Box, Brother Reginald, Provincial of the Pacific Province, whom I have known for twenty years, and Peter Hand, now Brother Simon Peter, whom I first met as a boy of fifteen in Southwark Cathedral in 1940, when he was a Priest-Vicar there. Supper was fish and vegetables. I retired soon to my room, only to find it now full of moths, mosquitoes, ants, winged and other insects, flies of all sorts and kinds, a three-inch grasshopper, and, my pet aversion again, the flying rhinoceros beetle. (One of these horrible miniature monsters lay dead on the floor as malevolent in death and immobility as the other did in life, careering around the lamp and the room.) There was only one thing for it: take refuge under the mosquito net. Outside it, all the evening, the lamp attracted even more winged things. (I'm afraid I shall never be Franscican enough to say "Brother Rhinoceros

Beetle" or even "Brother Moth"; though out here, only this afternoon, I saw the most lovely butterfly I have ever seen, with glorious blue sheen on its frail wings. I would willingly have called it *Sister* Butterfly - but sex gets difficult here: *Sister* Red Admiral, or *Brother?*) I became oblivious to it all for I had begun to read Joseph Conrad's *Lord Jim*.

Before the lights went out I had read: "No one ever understands quite his own artful dodges to escape the grim shadow of self-knowledge," and a dozen similar nagging sentences. There is a mystic quality about the book from the moment you are told Lord Jim is a parson's son, and from the time his boat takes a thousand pilgrims on board....."As if the obscure truth involved were momentous enough to affect mankind's conception of itself." But the oft repeated phrase "He was one of us" helps to establish the book as not only about a man, but about Man. It's a book about the going away that can either be escape or pilgrimage, search, and exploration. The dust cover of the Penguin is a Brangwyn.

This place is like a very happy prison camp! It is like what I have always imagined Changi to have been in the War. The Friary consists of several two-storey buildings, each hardly more than open frames, with partitioning walls, with a verandah or balcony to each floor, and an overhanging corrugated iron roof. There are guest rooms, brothers' rooms, bathrooms, library, offices and dining room. In the middle is the open octagonal chapel with a central altar. The buildings are surrounded by trees, palms, teak, cassia, etc., and flowering shrubs, great and small. The elephant grass between the trees and shrubs is like a swamp at the moment. I wear sandals but no socks, as the water, almost wherever you tread, comes over your toes. When the sun shines, the large butterflies of every colour flit from bloom to bloom on the flowering shrubs. It is difficult to see the birds, but they keep up a constant noise - not so much a song, rather a series of notes, four or five very recognisable, slow, deliberate notes, as though they were starting off a choir - which never comes in.

Not far beyond here, partly within sight, is the chapel and buildings of the Evangelists' College, which the Friars run, and the chapel and buildings of the Sisters of the Holy Name.

If you were to ask what is the main point of this place I think the Brothers would say, first of all, to live as a Brotherhood. Even in a few hours the quality of the life together has 'hit' me, and made the frustrations of the place comparatively insignificant. They are a very relaxed community. In Chapel, one of the brothers from Tonga often plays his guitar. You cannot imagine a happier group of different races and tribes together, and in this part of the world it is quite important to show that this is possible.

April 12th 1972

This morning I have at last got the 'bucket shower' to work - which is pretty essential in this climate. A 'bucket shower' (in case you don't know, either) is a bucket with a perforated disc as part of its bottom. The perforated disc is movable. You move it so that the perforations don't show, when you want the water to stop. First, therefore, you fill the bucket, push the perforated disc to 'open', and pull it up on a pulley. It is frustrating - I mustn't say more here - if the perforated disc won't budge, ie no water. But to pull the bucket, full up with water, with one hand, and to soap and wash what St Paul calls your 'less honourable parts' with the other is an acrobatic feat of some distinction.

I have three lectures to give on Saturday and a sermon on Sunday. I have spent most of the day preparing them. The Gospel on Sunday is 'The Good Shepherd', but there are no sheep or shepherds in New Guinea. (In the Solomons there was no wine, and bread was an unaccustomed luxury.)

The only book I have brought with me of what is called, or what might be regarded as 'of a devotional nature' - the kind of book which can profitably be used in the Community's meditation time - is Dag Hammarskjøld's *Markings*. I have slowly worked through *Markings* a dozen or more times since I first came upon it in 1965. But again, as I begin to read it, each page seems to have something more to say.

Today I was astonished to find Hammarskjøld refers directly both to my TS Eliot quotation "Old Men Ought to be Explorers" and to *Lord Jim*.

He writes: "Old men ought to be explorers! Some have to be - because the frontiers of the familiar are closed to them. But few succeed in opening up new lands."

And again:- "'At the frontier of the unheard of -' The unheard of - perhaps this simply refers to Lord Jim's last meeting with Doramin, when he has attained absolute courage and humility in an absolute loyalty to himself. Conscious of guilt, but at the same time conscious of having atoned, so far as atonement is possible in this life - by what he has done for those who are now asking for his life. Untroubled and happy. Like someone wandering by himself along a lonely sea-shore."

The 'community' of people who are 'on to the same things' or who somehow manage to say what you have been struggling to say, is as important to one as one's friends, or as, for instance, the community I am actually living with at the moment. Hammarskjøld says "Friendship needs no words - it is solitude delivered from the anguish of loneliness." When you recognise in writings a kindred spirit, like Hammarskjøld, or Conrad, or

Eliot, you receive from them a kind of friendship which also delivers solitude from 'the anguish of loneliness'.

April 13th 1972

I have spent most of today in Popondetta itself, a growing town of 2,139 people in 1966. I went first to the Vocational Training Centre, which provides a practical training course for students who have completed primary school and who will not have the opportunity to go on to high school. It teaches the boys carpentry, brick making and laying, furniture making, motor maintenance, fishing, agriculture and trade store management. It also trains in 'simple business skills' that will help those who later became 'self-employed'. The girls' side of the Centre concentrates on instruction in house management, baby care, community studies, craft work and gardening. It is a twelve month course, but some stay for two years.

I specially wanted to see the 'Tapa Cloth' made here, for which the Centre has quite a reputation. I have now seen examples of this work in Fiji and the Solomons. John Chisholm has a cope and mitre made of it. It is made from the bark of a tree, and simple designs are painted on it with dyes from berries. I managed to buy a few rectangular pieces. The girls of the Centre are now making the cloth into handbags and lamp shades, but each rectangular length of cloth is made separately, and is, to me, something to be displayed for itself.

I went on to the High School and spoke to two forms - my first chance to speak to New Guinea school children. About half of them, boys and girls, came from within three miles of the school, but some were boarders. The questions were very intelligent. "How many churches are there for the people of London? Have there ever been enough for everyone to be a churchgoer?" "Are there more Christians in the villages of England than in the towns, as there are here?" "If only a small percentage of those baptised in England go to church, what does the Church do when those who are baptised but do not go to church bring their children to be baptised?"

I was very impressed with the self-government of the school. When my session was finished, they were just off to brief their elected class representatives who were going to the Student Council, which was then meeting the Headmaster. How much better this than prefects appointed by the Headmaster!

I then went along to the office of the Inspector of Education. A Papuan Inspector very clearly and courteously explained his job to me in that area, its problems and opportunities. He was a Lutheran who had obviously been taught by an Australian!

The two Brothers who came into Popondetta with us, Comins and Augustine, were both from the New Hebrides. One of them speaks English very beautifully indeed. It is a delight to hear him read in Chapel. Part of the happiness of the 'outing' was to talk with these two. There is no doubt the Franciscans are now 'indigenous' here, and it is marvellous to see.

April 14th 1972
It was odd to receive Holy Communion this morning, my birthday, from Peter Hand SSF - whose fine aquiline features I can still so well remember when I first set eyes on him over thirty years ago, standing under an arch in Southwark Cathedral, when he was a young priest and I was a lad of fifteen out at work on the South Bank - and from Brian Harley, whom I have known as a friend for well over twenty years, since my days at College. It was odd to be so far from London - 12,500 miles - and yet to be so much at home in the community. When I set out on this journey, I was for a time acutely aware of not belonging, of being ripped away from a particular place and particular people. And meeting again so many people I have

known in the past could have meant one was tossed from this person to the next, from pillar to post. But I seem to have been given again, for I have had it before - an awareness of a communion beyond the individual. I hardly dare put it into words, they are so vulnerable and fragile, so easily knocked over and trampled on. Someone would only have to say "*Beyond the individual?*" in a sceptical tone of voice to make me hesitate! But I regain my courage if I think of that individual who is me. Then I am sure that only a fool thinks *any* individual - not least himself - can be 'explained', described, accounted for, with *no* Beyond. This doesn't make room for 'any old Beyond'; but it makes my faith - I think that's the right word - in a 'communion beyond the individual' less open to ridicule.

My forty-seventh birthday has provoked other reflections in me. In these last eighteen years which may remain to me before so-called 'retirement', I want to live a clear life, clear with meaning, and to get on with it as un-selfconsciously as I can. I have seen enough in the last months that clearly needs to be done to fill a *million* lives.

The problem is how to avoid the ecclesiastical, yet not jettison those good things for which the Church of England as an institution stands, and which it undoubtedly still provides in many places - and which many look to it to provide; how to avoid the ecclesiastical without forsaking one's brethren, who, with the highest motives, remain in the ecclesiastical machine; without adopting a 'holier than thou' attitude, or that naive idealism which does not reckon with the inevitability of sin within the church. You cannot live, for instance, in this Community of Franscican Brothers, born of the Church of England, and take an entirely condemnatory attitude to the Church of England. I owe it too much to do that.

At 11.00 am this morning, in Popondetta, I dropped in on a

meeting of about twenty clergy from this area, all Papuans. It was good to have a brief chat with each one about their work. There is a tremendous difference between the old and the young priests. Most of the old priests had hardly any education at all.

The Archdeacon, a young Australian, Martin Chittleborough, then drove me out to his home at Agenahambo, about twenty miles in the direction of Kokoda, not far from Mount Lamington, in the heart of the country. Within his parish is what has been thought of as the top Secondary School of Papua New Guinea, Martyrs Memorial School. It was at this school that Prince Charles stayed a night in a 'bush' house when he was at Geelong Grammar School. I was taken round the School by the prefects: the gardens, dormitories, and classrooms. I gave the assembled school a quarter of an hour's talk. There were several teachers from England. It clearly is still doing a superb educational job in the Territory. I had a long talk with the Australian Headmaster, Ron Morris, who had done a year in England, at St John's, East Dulwich, in the 50's.

The Archdeacon's wife, Ann, has her birthday on April 15th, so does the Rector of Popondetta's wife, Valerie Thulborn. Hearing that it was my birthday today, they decided to throw a party for us all, and to invite Brian to bring out a truck-load of Brothers. We had a superb time. There was a marvellous barbecued meal - the fire and the cooking looked after by the Papuan Brothers. The evening ended with dancing - there were nurses and teachers there too; and while people were recovering, there was chance to tell a shaggy dog story or two.

The drive back to Popondetta, over the rough road, sitting on a form in the back of the open truck, was memorable. There was a beautiful night sky and a great number of fire-flies. The cool night air was gloriously refreshing. It was near midnight when we arrived back at Jegarata. I immediately scrambled under the mosquito net in the darkness, knowing that the rising bell would call as usual at 5.30 am.

April 15th 1972

I have given three lectures to people who have come in from around, as they do for this day every year. They were a very receptive audience - Brothers, Sisters, teachers, priests and lay people from neighbouring areas, and a retired Bishop of Quebec, Bishop Russell Brown, who teaches at Martyrs' School. It is not often they get a 'speaker from outside' and I had no doubt it was a worthwhile day.

I had a shower, and then, through the kindness of Martin Chittleborough and Neville Thulborn, I joined them in continuation of the celebration of their wives' birthdays. We went to dinner at the local hotel and on to the film of *Far from the Madding Crowd*. I had not been able to see it in England. I was glad to see such fine acting and superb photography of Wiltshire and Dorset. How Hardy was fascinated by the dark side of life!

April 16th 1972

I preached this morning at the Profession of Brother Paulus Moi, who has served his three year novitiate. I felt very privileged to preach on such an occasion. Paulus is a specially good Papuan young man. (His brother was the first qualified Papuan doctor in the Territory.) The church was crowded. I do not think one can ever fail to be moved when one is present at simple and sincere self-offering - at a marriage, for instance. Paulus is the second Professed Papuan in the Franciscans (others from the New Hebrides and the Solomon Islands have already been professed!). It is so good that the Anglican Franciscans around the world now have over a hundred Brothers and just under fifty novices. There can be little doubt that their way of life is one that is near to the heart of the Gospel. That is not to say one has no questions about 'monks in New Guinea'. I personally wonder whether a young Papuan should be asked to make *life* vows of celibacy. You learn so much about yourself at every stage of life. Few people, if any, are in a fit state to promise their life away before the age of thirty. The Franciscans might answer "What then about promising life-long fidelity in marriage?" To which I would answer: "Good question!" 'Poverty' *here* - as in Honiara - is in many respects above the living standards of most Papuans. (The food, by the way, has got better every day I have been here!) 'Obedience' is now interpreted much more liberally as 'respect for one another'. As I've said, it is the example of Brotherhood, God-centred Brotherhood, that makes this place notable.

There was an atmosphere of joy about the place all day, so that Evensong nearly came to a halt through laughter. It was the Old Testament lesson that literally started the rot. It was the passage in Jeremiah which tells of his escaping from the well by 'old cast clouts and rotten rags'. The new translation we were using referred to 'Jeremiah in the mire', which, not only to Papuan ears, sounded curious! but the 'cast clouts' phrase, in modern English, sounded like a church jumble sale.

Translation into English here has its surprises. I looked up in Pidgin the Gospel on which I was preaching this morning. ('The Good Shepherd': John 10.) What could be more clear than 'I kam bilong stil' ('E came to steal'), 'na bilong kilim' ('and to kill'), 'dai na bagarapim tasol' (literally 'and to bugger-up him', ie to destroy)? It is, of course, in the main, the unrefined English of the nineteenth century traders, transliterated words with Melanesian grammar. I find it's quite difficult to get used to the idea that the centurion at the Cross ('Kepten bilong 100 soldia') said: "Tru tumas, dispela man i pikinini bilong God."! - ("Truly this was the son of God")! It makes you wonder how modern theologians would get on out here. One of the Fransican Brothers suggested to me that since in Pidgin 'foundation' and 'bottom' are both 'as' (arse) 'The Ground of our Being' should be translated 'As bilong yu mi'!

The day ended with me receiving a resounding defeat at table tennis from a Tongan Brother. I fear that, with my Colonialist unconscious, I assumed I would thrash him. The same Brother, Afu, in the music-making that was part of the Community Recreation, performed brilliantly on a double-bass he had constructed out of a tea chest, a piece of cord, and a plank. The cord, which could only be plucked, was fixed at its bottom end to the tea chest. The other instrument of the trio, besides a guitar, was a rake, to which had been loosely attached a score of metal beer bottle tops - a remarkably effective cymbal and castanet. St Francis, I think, may have turned in his grave - this way and that - to the rhythm of the music.

April 17th 1972

I celebrated the Holy Communion in the Brothers' Chapel this morning. It was a privilege. Then, after breakfast, I was driven over to Gona, on the coast, fifteen miles north of Popondetta. I wanted very much to see Francis Cumberledge, who had come out here in November from Portsmouth Diocese, where he had been curate to Bill Todd, with whom I was a curate in Westminster. Francis had been a VSO at Martyrs Memorial School, succeeding Theodore Woods there, and had then gone to King's College, London, to train for the priesthood. Already at Gona he is much loved. I was glad to see the church and the school at Gona - Headmaster and VSO from England - and the hospital. After seeing the latter, I was specially glad that it is being replaced by a permanent building! The villagers from each surrounding village had agreed to spend a day helping with the building work. Men, women and teenage boys and girls were all pushing wheelbarrows, mixing cement, etc. The Sister-in-charge of the hospital, Nancy Vesperman, was laid up with a poisoned foot, but it was good to talk with her about the place. She has been out here for ten years. (Any small cut or bite here has a good chance or turning septic. Almost everyone goes round wearing at least one elastoplast strip; but this continuous danger of poisoning is, of course, serious. I am a two-strip man myself at the moment: a bite on the foot and the knee-cap, both septic.)

I was glad to find Nancy Vesperman reading *Medical Care in Developing Countries* by Maurice King, the Professor of Social Medicine in Zambia with whom I dined in January. He calls the book 'A Primer on the Medicine of Poverty'. Wherever I have travelled in 'developing countries', people have talked of the value of the book, and one could see that with one's own eyes at Gona. Maurice King believes patients should be treated as near to their homes as possible, with the smallest, cheapest, most humbly staffed and most simply equipped unit that is capable of looking after them adequately. He is a great believer in a health service 'from the bottom up, not the top down'. The book - which I have now dipped into in various places around the world - explains in language which is clear even to me, how a doctor in places like this should spend his time; how a hospital here should be built; what drugs should be stocked; what should be the scope of the hospital. But the hospital is discussed in the context of providing a total health service. The preface deals in a very down-to-earth way with how and why a doctor in an affluent country should serve in a developing country for two to five years between the age of twenty-five and thirty-five. I have found it compelling reading. It is never merely hortatory.

When I got back, one of the Brothers brought me the stones which one of the students, training to be an Evangelist, had just given him. He said a sorcerer had said he had removed them from his stomach. The student had been ill, and, because he was getting no better, had resorted, in his anxiety, to the sorcerer. The stones were undoubtedly ordinary gravel. The sorcerer had apparently put his mouth up and down the man's stomach, and then produced them to the student from his mouth. The student, who felt no better, felt guilty he had gone to the sorcerer, and had lost faith in him, and realised the stones were probably concealed in the sorcerer's mouth all the time. The incident revealed what is proved time and time again out here: that 'primitive religion' is not buried very far below the surface of people's lives. But, of course, superstition in England might reveal much the same thing.

The incident also revealed the need of priests and teachers out here to have a true theology. I was a little worried at the way, for instance, an outbreak of 'Cargo Cult' - the specious promise of material benefits, if only you follow what a particular religious man tells you to do, resulting in the last months in the swindling of thousands of people - is 'answered' by a 'model sermon' not by a true theology but by threats. ("If you go over to 'Cargo' all those things that the Book of Revelations speaks of will happen to you.")

The fact that the Anglican Church thereby succeeds in persuading people away from 'Cargo' may then be taken as evidence that its theology is right. But to me it is more like a naked power struggle. The Anglican Church is undoubtedly powerful in Northern Papua. Its influence with the people is probably greater in some things than the Administration. Similarly, it is tempting to answer sorcery with a theology of evil which simply will not stand up to modern theological scrutiny. I had hoped to see more evidence that the men in training around the Friary were being given a more adequate theological training for the 'survival' New Guinea world and for the last decades of the twentieth century.

April 18th 1972

This morning I got up again in the dark. It is an odd way of going about things! The rising bell goes at 5.30 am. You get out of bed, out of the mosquito net; feel for your soap, towel, toothbrush, toothpaste, razor, shaving cream and hairbrush; make your way along the open balcony in the darkness, down the outside stairs, to the wash basins, where, in the darkness and silence, other people will be shaving too. By the time you are showered, shaved, dressed, and have walked to the chapel across the gardens, dawn will have come, and it will be light enough to read a book.

I, personally, think it would be more sensible for us all to get up half an hour later; so that we can *see* what we are *shaving*! But this morning this odd way of going on became a kind of lived out parable. I had been thinking of something Dag Hammarskjøld had written, about faith and finding one's way again - that it was 'like playing Blind Man's Buff', deprived of sight, you grope your way around, and pass your fingers over the faces of your friends, and recognise them; you discover what has been there all the time. This morning, the groping around in darkness was real enough - and as Hammarskjøld says, deprived of sight, you have in compensation to sharpen all your *other* senses. But 'as it began to dawn' - and it was a particularly marvellous sunrise - and as I saw who people were, and the palm trees and shrubs and buildings - that, too, was vividly real - as though I was being allowed to see things, being *given* things, for the first time, or being given them back again. I found myself thankful for the 'groping in the dark' (which there has been for quite a time now) which *is* a way of discovery - (and there always will be 'our side of discovery', through touch, and sight, and intellect, groping for the truth). But I was thankful too for the sense of dawning Light (for instance, an awareness again of 'communion beyond the individual'). I wouldn't want the 'groping in the dark' way of discovering the truth ever taken away from my humanity, painful as that groping is, but you do not simply *discover* the *dawn*. It is *given* - like existence, and breath, and much of the world as it is. I had the overwhelming feeling this morning that the Day Light was 'given', and that I must simply see myself and other people in or through the 'Light', and put my blindfold away. At Mattins, appropriately, the set Psalm was twenty seven: "The Lord is my Light and my Salvation."

I very much wanted to see some more of Theodore and Jean Woods before I left New Guinea, so at 8.45 am, I said a fond farewell to the Friars. Brian drove me to the airfield, and a DC3 was soon conveying me back to Port Moresby. It was a perfect flight, with only three passengers on board, and marvellous views of Mount Lamington. The day was mostly another 'catching up' day: essential, every so often, when you're living out of a suitcase for several months - washing clothes, etc. But, in the course of it, I discovered the locks on my attaché case, and the main hinges of my suitcase, have rusted here and broken. Cases get a hammering at airports, and loading and unloading will already have meant handling my cases over fifty times on this journey. With all this, and with the extremes of climate - at Popondetta there are over one hundred inches of rainfall a year - I suppose I must not complain at the unexpected expense.

In the early evening we drove out to Burns' Peak, with a marvellous view over the whole of Port Moresby. Then Theodore and Jean and I drove fifteen miles into the country for dinner, at the nearest equivalent to a 'pub' one can expect New Guinea to offer.

April 19th 1972
I have spent rather an episcopal last day in New Guinea. David Hand, the Anglican Bishop of New Guinea, had invited me to

lunch with him. Bishop George Ambo, a Papuan, one of the Assistant Bishops, was there too. Bishop David has a house with a glorious view high up over the harbour of Port Moresby. He has been out here over half his life, and is in his fifties. There is no doubt he has been a great Bishop of New Guinea. He has been a man of vision, always developing the work, and pressing further into the Highlands. He has also done a great deal to see the work in the fast-growing towns developed - Lae, Madang, etc. He is an indefatigable pastor to the individual. He has taken indigenisation very seriously. He is a man of considerable influence with the Administration. He is *a man*! Typically, he has decided to do a fund-raising walk over the Kokoda Trail in a month's time - with the Archbishop of Sydney and Bishop George Ambo. It is 170 miles long, and it will take a fortnight. He hopes, by this 'sponsored walk', to raise money to end the Church's dependence on overseas giving. It is, as a walk, from Gona to Moresby, over the Owen Stanley mountains, no mean task. He is getting in training for it, running round (and up and down) Port Moresby, in the small hours. At lunch, with Bishop George as well, we had a fascinating discussion on evil. Bishop George is also a person of great authority, with Papuan and European alike. We were talking about witchcraft and sorcery. Whereas Bishop David has said "I have been in places where you can literally *feel* the evil around you", Bishop George surprisingly took a more detached attitude. "I have no doubt of the power of the sorcerer over people. When people are gifted people, and they give themselves to do evil things, they can be very powerful; and their power over people can be very great. But I do not believe in the sorcerer's claims, and I believe his power is mostly psychological." I was surprised to hear Bishop George take this attitude, because, politically, for instance, he is conservative. I think it is rather good that publicly Bishop David speaks out for Independence now, Bishop George, particularly aware of the Papuan villagers, publicly speaks against it. One sometimes hears it said that bishops in a diocese need to speak with one voice. Here there is a marvellous personal unity with creative disagreement in opinions.

In the evening, I met the Bishops again at a party which was meant to welcome Bishop John Howe, the Anglican Executive Officer. Unfortunately, yet another cyclone had grounded his 'plane in the extreme east of New Guinea. However, it was a good opportunity to meet Members of the House of Assembly, and leaders of other Christian bodies out here.

The New Guinea ABC Broadcasting Corporation had 'phoned asking me if I would make a comment on my visit for their news bulletin. A rather nice Papuan girl interviewed me. I realised she was having difficulty in taking down what I was saying - she wanted me to say something that would relate to the House of Assembly being opened by the Governor General next day. I therefore asked (hoping to avoid mistakes) whether I might write down my comment for her. She readily agreed. I wrote briefly that I had been travelling through many countries in Africa which had received their independence. Before Independence they had - rightly or wrongly - been able to blame the Colonial power over them. After Independence they had to confront their own problems - Health, Education, etc. I said I had been particularly glad to visit New Guinea on the verge of Independence. Now it would have to choose how it spends what money it has - on a University? On training the 7,000 teachers, half of whom have no education after primary school? On Hospitals? It would have to decide on priorities. I said that countries newly independent celebrate their past a good deal - music, art, and so on. I was more interested in the future. I had been glad to see Vincent Eri's new novel *The Crocodile*. What I would love to see is a 'New Guinea style' in literature, art and music.

The young lady was delighted, and said it was just what she wanted.

The news at night said: "An Anglican clergyman, Canon Eric James, visiting New Guinea, has said it is time for New Guinea to face her own problems. She cannot have 7,000 teachers educated and have more university graduates." Total misrepresentation! I ought to have learnt by now, I suppose. I was frustrated, annoyed, and dismayed; but decided it was useless to try to do anything.

April 20th 1972

The gifted Theodore has bought three new brass hinges for my suitcase, removed the offending rusty steel hinges, and fixed brass ones. The case now looks good for another three months. He has saved me eighteen dollars - eight pounds, ten shillings.

At 11.30 am I kissed Jean and the twins goodbye (the other children had said goodbye to 'Uncle James' before going to school), and Theodore drove me to the airport to catch the 12.35 pm to Townsville, Queensland, Australia. Seeing Theodore again, and meeting his wife and children, has been one of the very great delights of these months.

At the airport, Theodore bought me the Port Moresby Newspaper, the 'Papua New Guinea Post Courier'. It had banner headlines - two historic words for this land of promise: "FIRST GOVT!" A national coalition government had been formed of all parties except the United Party, in time for the opening of the House of Assembly this morning.

Stage 13: Australia: Townsville and Sydney

April 21st 1972

The 700 mile flight to Townsville in a Fokker Friendship was at times disturbingly bumpy. We flew fairly near the path of Hurricane 'Faith', which was stationary, blowing itself out 130 miles south of Port Moresby.

We crossed the Great Barrier Reef, and landed first at Cairns, 200 miles north of Townsville, to clear Customs and Immigration on entering Australia. The green sugar cane fields, tidy rectangles in the coastal plain between the hills and the sea, looked more pastoral and domestic than anything I had seen for a couple of months.

We flew along the Great Barrier Reef to Townsville, where John Clarkson and his wife Lorraine and their two small boys were waiting for me. John is a close friend of mine from my King's College, London, days, though I have not seen him for eight years and had never met his wife. As a Lancing College boy he had involved himself a good deal in the work of the College Mission in Southwark, St. Michael's Camberwell. He is now Rector of Mundingburra, a suburb of Townsville. He drove me straight to his home. The trees in the garden of the Rectory were greatly damaged in the cyclone that had hit Townsville earlier this year. The spire of his church, St Matthew's, had been entirely destroyed.

It was just gone five when we reached the Rectory. At six, John took me to the local Rotarians meeting, where, besides meeting a good many very typical Queenslanders, I heard an interesting talk on how the railways of the State operate today. I went back to the Rectory with John to 'baby-sit' while his wife went out to a church. At midnight, John drove me to the 'colonial' type Victorian residence of the new Bishop of North Queensland, John Lewis, who had invited me to stay with him for the weekend. Most of the roof of his house was temporary, for much of it had been ripped off in the cyclone.

I spent this morning with John Clarkson seeing Townsville. It's odd to think it is as near the Equator as Fiji - on the same parallel. You can think of Townsville as a large dry tropical city, 1,000 miles north of Brisbane (the capital of Queensland). It is situated on the shores of Cleveland Bay, at the mouth of the Ross River. It has a population of 71,000, rapidly expanding. It is the major transport and communications centre for the vast North Queensland area (one and a half times the size of France). It is linked with the complex of 'beef roads' now being built to pastoral and mining lands in northern and western areas. The port serves an area stretching beyond Mount Isa, 1,000 miles to the west, where there is a vast copper mine. Sugar is the main commodity it exports, but minerals and meat come next, and around the docks there are huge meat works, a copper refinery to process ore from Mount Isa, a nickel smelting plant, and so on.

The city is also the gateway to Magnetic Island, only five miles across Cleveland Bay from the city centre. It is one of the main centres for cruises to the Great Barrier Reef, forty miles away.

John and I drove along the sea front, still much damaged, then up Castle Hill, a vast granite promontory which overhangs the town, dividing the port from the hinterland, and one side of the town from the other. We looked at the new university, opened in 1969 (with a most beautifully designed Library), and rather modern barracks for 5,000 troops. (It is to some extent a garrison town: a useful fact at the time of the cyclone.)

In the afternoon, the Bishop interviewed me on the local radio. I rather enjoyed this. The Bishop is just younger than I, and was only made bishop last year. He has spent most of his life in Adelaide, serving in the Society of the Sacred Mission, (he was their Provincial in Australia), and had recently set up their house in Japan. I liked his humour and general approach to things. He was in the Australian navy during the war.

In the evening, he threw a party for those of his clergy and their wives who could conveniently get into Townsville. (There are about fifty clergy in the Diocese: but only about a dozen are based around Townsville). As we had both enjoyed doing the radio interview in the afternoon, to start a general discussion, after beer and savouries, we adopted the same method again. It was a happy and relaxed evening.

April 22nd 1972

I browsed through some of the Bishop's books this morning and came across a book of Dick Sheppard's I had never seen before, an anthology, published in 1928 called *Fiery Grains*. His preface almost exactly echoed what I feel about "institutional religion" at the moment. But what I most enjoyed discovering in it was a verse of John Masefield that has meant a lot to me ever since a Trinity Hall friend of mine, John Kitching, first drew my attention to it:-

> Man with his burning soul
> Has but an hour of breath
> To build a ship of truth
> In which his soul may sail -

Sail on the sea of death,
For death takes toll
Of beauty, courage, youth
Of all but truth.

After lunch, the Bishop drove me out eighty miles to the west, to Charters Towers, a country town which was a gold mining centre a century ago. It had a 'wild west' atmosphere about it, with mostly Victorian shop fronts and 'colonial' houses. The 'pub' doors were bat-wing, the type you expect a holstered cowboy to burst through any minute.

Almost all the way, the country was the same, with an unpretentious loveliness about it. "This is our country" said the Bishop. "Gums and grass - give or take the grass". In a way, it was ridiculous to drive two hours there and two hours back just for a Church Fete, which the Bishop was to open - had we arrived on time; but we burst a tyre *en route*. But I was delighted simply to mingle with ordinary Australians, young and old. It was like any English Church Fete - the useless embroidered coat hangers; pots of tomato chutney; the junk stall (with an attractive Victorian 'slipper' bedpan). The old ladies spent most of their time having tea inside, out of the sun, enjoying a good gossip. The youngsters gathered round a group with electric guitars and a loudspeaker that deafened all. I heard more harmless platitudes in an afternoon than I have heard since I was last in a similar gathering of English middle-class people. "What I always say is: it never hurts anyone to do a good turn" etc. etc. There was a nice old Bishop from Madagascar there, Bishop Miles.

It was good to talk for four hours with the Bishop in the car. I like this combination of a really human being and a monk. He can't help telling stories and telling them well. "I was once on leave here from the Navy. A day in Charters Towers and all our sweat sores from the tropics healed up. When we came here, half of the lads went riding and the other half went boozing. In the evening, one half couldn't sit down and the other half couldn't stand up."

As we were about to return to Townsville, I realised I had some kind of fever on me: dizziness, aches in every joint, alternately hot and cold, sore throat.

I went to bed as soon as supper was over, at half past seven, and sweated the night through.

April 23rd 1972

I got up at 5.30 am to get a sermon ready, and preached for John Clarkson at St Matthew's at 7.00 am and at the Cathedral at 9.00 am. The fever was still with me and I didn't feel like 'church'. But had I felt more like it I doubt whether my judgement would have been any different. The services were of a type that would appeal to a small ecclesiastical - Anglo-Catholic - 'club'. My sympathies were with the Australians who were not in church: there were very few who were. (Of the 6,000 Anglicans in John Clarkson's parish, not more than 250 were in all the churches in his parish.)

I stayed to lunch with John and his wife and family. (He is one of the most loving and gentle people I know.) I slept for an hour, and then went to visit the local girls' school, to see the daughter of one of the Australian priests I had met in New Guinea, and then called it a day. I thought I would read something familiar which would also prepare me for some of the journey ahead. I took to bed with me E M Forster's A Passage to India. It gripped me for the next hours, and, by the time I had finished it, the fever had left me (not so the mosquitoes!).

April 24th 1972

The Bishop's housekeeper got me up at 5.30 am and gave me a good breakfast to set me on the way to Sydney. She has been a 'ministering angel' - you have need of and appreciate such people on your travels, especially when you are 'below par'. The Bishop took me to the airport for the 7.55 am 'plane. John Clarkson and his family were there too. We flew via Brisbane, the Great Dividing Range, which at one time was the barrier to the opening up of Australia's interior, but is now the major source of her timber, water and power - over a thousand miles of rougher country than the English usually credit to Australia. And then - Botany Bay, and Sydney Harbour: a most glorious sight from the air.

Frank Cuttriss, whom I had never met, was at the airport. Bishop Donald Shearman (now Chairman of the Australian Board of Missions) whom I had got to know at the Lambeth Conference and had met again in Perth, and who now lives in a suburb of Sydney, had thought it would be good for me to stay with the Cuttriss' in the centre of the city. (The Archbishop of Melbourne had also told me to write to them.) With great generosity they had written to me in Honiara a warm letter of welcome. Frank's church (where I shall be preaching on Sunday) is right in the centre. His Rectory is only two miles away, in Double Bay, the Chelsea of Sydney. Sydney is a Diocese in the control of extreme Evangelical churchmen with a negative theology of the world - no drinking, no dancing. Frank is one of the handful of clergy who people like me regard as oases in this desert. He comes from Melbourne, and, ten years ago, was in charge of the task force of clergy dealing with the new areas of expanding Melbourne. In his early fifties, he and his wife, Elaine, who has a tremendous interest in art and politics, are obviously key people in any creative dialogue in Sydney between the Church and the world. Frank has been doing this rather special beleaguered job for nearly ten years.

It was immediately clear to me that, though I should see little of the inner-city work of the Church in Sydney, Frank and Elaine would introduce me to as fascinating a collection of people, and give me as good a spy-hole on this great city, as anyone could provide. Not much time would in fact be available - I am here only until Sunday afternoon - with most of Monday now gone, and tomorrow, ANZAC day, Australia's public holiday, centred round the memory of two World Wars.

As soon as I had unpacked, Frank and his wife took me off to lunch at a most marvellous Chelsea-type restaurant. (His wife had also recently returned from three weeks in New Guinea and was ready for a 'treat'). We then drove around the Harbour to see the new Opera House, to be opened next year. The Opera House, by the Sydney Harbour Bridge, is as thrilling a sight as I expected it to be. But Sydney Harbour is much more vast than ever I imagined, and around it a very varied city has grown up - a city that has already captured me in a way that Melbourne failed to do. It is a lively modern city; but it has escaped rectangular modernity. Its new office blocks are never far away from parks - and the Harbour. There are imaginative new creations - fountains for instance - at unexpected points. In the sun, this afternoon, I found myself thinking that if you celebrated this city in music, at least one movement would have to be full of *joie de vivre*.

April 25th 1972

As it was St Mark's Day, I celebrated the Holy Communion at St James' at 8.00 am - very much like St George's Camberwell: much the same date, the early 1820's. (In the vestry was a picture of David Sheppard in 1956 signing autographs for Islington choirboys after leading England to victory!) Already the city was alive with be-medalled ex-servicemen getting ready for the ANZAC parade. At 10.00 am I went into the city again to see something of the parade, in which 20,000 soldiers and ex-servicemen were involved. It is incredible how all this has survived in Australia, whereas it is now nearly dead in England. I suppose we have other occasions and other ways of celebrating our national identity. As I looked at people in the park, the crowds and the ex-servicemen, I was surprised to find how much I enjoyed it all. It was a celebration, an occasion for pageantry (in the Diocese of Sydney, so opposed to ritual!). The parks were packed with groups of people chatting together in the sun, enjoying old times: there were bowler-hatted ex-officers, little ordinary men and big ordinary men. There were bands and pith helmets, scarlet uniforms, bagpipes and kilts, but above all there was the feeling of solidarity born of a great and mutual experience. I don't think that feeling should be under-rated or despised.

Just before lunch, Frank and Elaine and I set out on a marvellous drive along the miles of coastline surrounding the city. You soon forget you are near a city. It is like Bournemouth, then like Devon, Cornwall and the Lake District. The Harbour itself is so large that few city churches are far from some view of it. There are dozens of bays and coves and river estuaries full of yachts and power boats, and beaches crowded with young surf riders, whilst, on the landward side, there are glorious forests of firs and gums. We were never further than twenty miles from Sydney, yet we had been for half a dozen hours in an environment which must excel that of almost any other great city in the world.

We were back at the Rectory by 5.30 pm. Frank and Elaine had invited thirty guests to come to the Rectory at eight so that I could meet them. They were a fascinating group: some long-haired young people, and professors and lecturers from the University and their wives; the new head of the YWCA out here, Ann Bailey (who had worked with Janet Lacey at Dagenham, where I was born), and so on.

I talked for half an hour or so. One couldn't have asked for a more creative evening's discussion.

April 26th 1972

I had to spend the best part of the morning at the offices of the Union Steam Ship Co. of New Zealand, going into the details of the last part of my travels. My visa to China has not come, but the limitations of my cash mean that I have had to give up the idea of going to Nepal. Risking insolvency when I get home, I have now planned some time in Singapore, Hong Kong, Calcutta, Delhi, Bangalore and Ceylon.

Opposite the travel agent was a forty-seven storey tower, opened in 1968 by the Duke of Edinburgh, with a viewing gallery at the top, 1,000 feet up. It provides great dramatic views of the Harbour. Two large white liners were close by the Opera House, one tied up at the dock near the Bridge, the other gradually approaching the Bridge, tugs keeping it in mid stream. It was a fine sight in the sun.

I wrote letters in Hyde Park for one hour, then Elaine took me to see several art galleries. The Hans Heysen paintings of gums are my particular delight. Sydney is alive with creativeness. How sad that so many of the Christians here should pass by it all on the other side. In the evening, Frank and I went to *Godspell*. I had already seen it in London, at the Round House, and had been thrilled by it. The Sydney production was just as excellent.

April 27th 1972

I had asked Frank and Elaine to suggest some reading that would put me in touch with what they regarded as 'Australia'. My bedroom floor soon became a pile of books covered with Malcolm Lowry's novels and Patrick White's. But the novel that I decided upon was George Johnston's *My Brother Jack*, clearly largely autobiographical: the Melbourne childhood and growing up between the Wars of two very different brothers. It is as original and poignant a story as I have read in years, painfully observant and evocative.

Elaine wanted me to read a biography of John Gorton by Alan Trengross. In England, we know very little about Gorton except that he was Prime Minister for only a very few years, after Harold Holt's death by drowning, and that he was ejected from office after public criticisms of his private behaviour - in a night club, and with the daughter of a Senator at the American Embassy.

I am very glad to have read this biography. At seven, Gorton's mother died, and he was then brought up by his father's wife - not the same person. He was sent to Geelong Grammar School (where Prince Charles was sent for a year), and to Brasenose College, Oxford. His friend was John Buchan's son (now Lord Tweedsmuir). John Buchan had said to his son "I like your silent Australian". Then there were hard-going years, trying to make his father's orchards pay. He had married the sister of an American undergraduate. There were more terrible ordeals in the Second World War. He was shot up and considerably disfigured. It was a record of very great bravery. Then there was the gradual political climb - and fall. However good or bad Gorton was as Prime Minister, there is reason to think the 'scandal' was in part the creation of political opponents. Whatever the truth of it, I was glad to have met a human being through the biography whose life has - as well as its blotches - a glory to it the politicians in England - and the mass media - have prevented us from seeing.

Thursday in Sydney was a full day for me. I spent an hour or so with Ann Bailey at the YWCA. After a lifetime in Social Service in England, Nigeria etc., I knew her observations of the Sydney scene would be invaluable. (She and Gwen Rymer had worked closely together in England on experimental youth and community projects.) After I had talked to Ann, I was clear about the kind of questions I wanted to ask at the headquarters of the Council of Social Service for New South Wales, where I was meeting the 'opposite numbers' to those I see often in London on the London Council of Social Service. They could not have been more helpful. I came away armed with accurate information on many of Sydney's social problems, which, in a sunny city like Sydney it is easy to pretend do not exist. Homelessness; 'Youth in Community' (there are two million people under twenty-five in New South Wales); Alcoholism - a huge problem, with 56,000 arrests for drunkenness in New South Wales, in 1966; the Aboriginal Problem - between 10,000 and 20,000 live in the Sydney Metropolitan area.

The Archbishop of Sydney, Marcus Loane, who does not cultivate publicity and is not known for speeches on social matters, yesterday hit the headlines by "calling on the Federal Government to relieve poverty" - the result of unemployment and spiralling prices. Today the Government has replied with furious denials and telling him virtually to mind his own business. It is undeniable that Australia is a very affluent nation. Its income per head is surpassed only by the United States and Canada, and most Australians take home weekly earnings that are within several pounds of the national average. But several groups have been squeezed outside the protective circle - certain pensioners, families with low incomes and high rents, and certain immigrants and aborigines etc. The Archbishop is a meticulous person. His speech has been all the more powerful because his evidence is from the undeniable experiences of the Churches involvement in social work and because he is not 'over-exposed to the media', as they say.

In the afternoon I nodded into the Cathedral - and out again.

It is more like a mortuary than any Cathedral I have ever seen. When I called next door at the Diocesan Office, I bumped into the Archbishop. Outside the office was a jumble of Press and TV cameras and vans. He had clearly 'touched a nerve'.

My purpose in calling at the Diocesan Office was to discover what action had been taken on the Report of the Diocese of Sydney's Inner-City Commission of Inquiry, published in 1969, and to hear of the social work of the Church of England in Sydney. The latter is very considerable. But I was not surprised to find the Church in the Inner-City in Sydney as 'up-against it' as in other great cities. The Director of Inner City Work, Paul Barnett, had been burgled twelve times in four years. He said there was a good team of workers in the inner-city ministry, but the suburban parishes had a very limited understanding of the problems of the inner-city Church. I particularly wanted to gather this information as the Australian Broadcasting Commission had recently shown on nation-wide television a film of the Church of England which, when it had been shown in England last year had caused much controversy. In Australia, the Church Information and Public Relations Office has also rushed in to attack the film. The ABC, hearing that I had appeared in the film and had something to do with its planning behind the scenes, came to interview me at 3.00 pm.

I was able to say that, when the programme was planned, I had said to the producers "You probably can't win with this film. Most of the clergy of the Church of England are in the country but most of the *people* are in the towns. Your film to be accurate about England must be mostly about the towns and the clergy in the *country* will rise up in wrath because it has so little about them in it. Secondly, what the Bishop of London said in 1895 is still true today. "It is not that the Church has lost the cities, it has never had them" and if you are to be accurate, your film must therefore mainly be a story of that situation - and the bishops and the suburban clergy will rise up in wrath. I suggested to the producer that they include film of the Church experimenting in 'failure' areas and in new towns - which they did. I said in my broadcast that there were justifiable criticisms of the film, but that the reactions to it had fulfilled my gloomiest forebodings. A number of the country clergy, the suburban clergy and the bishops, even of the urban dioceses, had behaved like scalded cats. They had not even been willing to be as honest as the Bishop of London in 1895. I added that nothing I had seen in Melbourne or Sydney had made me feel that the Church in the Inner-City was any more 'successful' there than in England. I paid tribute to those who continue to minister in the inner-city.

At 5.00 pm I went to a gathering of the clergy of the eastern suburbs of Sydney at which a film was to be shown and the Archbishop was to speak about his Kokoda Trail walk. It was an excellent film, including many of the people in New Guinea I now know, and many familiar scenes. The speech by the Archbishop was also fascinating. He spoke at length without notes. He speaks with a deadpan voice. He is very much the scholar. He hasn't an ounce of music in him and has little interest in the theatre. He is a teetotaller. He is a pronounced Evangelical very concerned about Sin - with a Capital S! He is a 'conservative' in relation to the Bible. The stories I have heard of how he deals with the clergy who do not share his views have horrified me. But at this meeting and when I talked with him, I found myself quietly admiring his bravery and his integrity (evidenced in his speech on Unemployment and Poverty). It is interesting that the Kokoda Trail walk has so captured his imagination. He walked a good deal of it in the War, thirty years ago. He reminds me in some ways of my erstwhile Dean at Cambridge, Professor John Burnaby, who, as shy as Marcus Loane, once told me his happiest evenings were his annual reunion dinners with the soldiers with whom he had served in the Great War. I find myself wondering if Marcus Loane had had more experience like his wartime experience (he is a Public Schoolboy who has never had a parish) whether his attitude to human beings would be more expansive and broad. I'm told he is a good deal 'warmer' now to people who do not share his pronounced views than he was even a few years ago.

In the late evening, Frank and Elaine drove me round the Harbour to see the City at night - marvellous 'city lights' across the expanse of water. What a city it is!

April 28th 1972

I spent the day with Bishop Donald Shearman at his new home at Wahroonga in the suburbs north of Sydney. (Until last year he was Bishop of Rockhampton.) I had longed to meet his wife, Fay, and their six children, and they were a glorious family to be with. Now Donald has taken on the chairmanship of the Australian Board of Mission, with particular responsibilities towards New Guinea, the New Hebrides and the Solomon Islands, We had much to talk over after my travels.

We managed to fit in an excursion to the nearby National Park, not far from where Frank and Elaine had taken me on ANZAC day.

April 29th 1972

A barbecue lunch and a barbecue dinner today (and a sermon prepared for tomorrow). The lunch was with Dr Geoff Oddie and his wife. He lectures in Indian History at the University of New South Wales. It was a further chance to prepare for what lies ahead next month. Geoff had lived a while in Bangalore - and in London. He and his wife were two of the most delightful people I have met in Australia. Dinner was with Roger Scharr and his wife. He is curate of St James's and had invited several of the local clergy, those who did not belong to the 'Protestant Underworld' - which meant that none of them were *parish* priests: The Archbishop of Sydney would not have licensed these chaps to his *parishes*. What a 20th Century tyranny! The evening was very relaxed. I found it inconceivable that these good fellows and their wives were regarded as 'unsound'.

April 30th 1972

I packed my bags and preached at the 9.00 am and 11.00 am services at St James's. It was very much a 'gathered' congregation of intelligent people who have taken refuge from the extreme Puritanism of the Diocese. It was not 'High Church' - (except for Sydney!): but what would be regarded as very 'middle of the road' in England. The 9.00 am was a large Parish Communion with breakfast together afterwards. The 11.00 am was a beautifully sung service - Herbert Howells *Collegium Regale*. The organist and choirmaster, Walter Sutcliffe, had been trained under Harold Dexter at Southwark Cathedral. He is also the chief double bass in the Sydney Symphony Orchestra. It was a very moving service, and I could see why such a large number of people were willing to travel into the centre of the city on a Sunday. Frank Cuttriss has an astonishing memory for people. He stood at the door and seemed to know everyone by name - 400 or so people all told. I have never seen anyone exercise this gift with such a large congregation - that, too, is why people come to St James's. He is such an excellent pastor.

Frank drove me straight from the Church to the airport (I had said goodbye earlier to Elaine) and we had a farewell lunch together. I am deeply grateful for the gift of Frank and Elaine's friendship. They have been incredibly generous to someone they have never met before.

At 3.00 pm, the Boeing 707 Flight 727 took off in cloudless skies, north-west into the sun. It is just under 4,000 miles to Singapore, half of which are over Australia and most of those arid desert. For long, long stretches it is red, with great black scars and craters, like the surface of some planet in outer space. What hills there are, are black and barren. Sometimes a long straight road stretches from horizon to horizon, or a massive black fault appears, like the Great Wall of China, from the air. There is an occasional river and lake, but, oddest of all, huge areas of long parallel folds, parallel with mathematical precision. The Plougher has ploughed long furrows. From the air it is uncanny and unnerving, this uninhabitable four-fifths of Australia. It is like the Dark Night of the Soul, or like "the Beginning:.....the earth was without form and void....." Vaughan Williams' *Symphonia Antarctica* came into my mind. The frozen wastes of the South are so different from those burning torrid wastes, but from the air there is little sense of temperature, only waste and void. And in the middle of it all, utterly remote from anywhere, appears - and disappears - Alice Springs.

We crossed the Australian coast 400 miles south-west of Darwin, and flew on another 1,000 miles across the Indian Ocean, south of the Timor Sea, to Bali, in Indonesia, and then on another thousand miles across the Java Sea to Singapore.

The sun was setting blood-red over Bali as we began dinner - Salmon Alaska, Breast of Turkey Maitre d'Hotel, Dauphinoise Potatoes, Buttered Zucchinis, followed by Passion Fruit Pavlova, Cheese and Coffee. It was difficult to think of Sunday Morning in South London, until the Cockney, sitting next to me in the 'plane, going back to England for the first time since he emigrated eight years ago, (and who had slept soundly all the way across Australia), turned to his wife and said: "Lovely drop of turkey, gel".

Stage 14: Singapore

May 1st 1972

Singapore lies one degree north of the Equator - ninety miles. It is hot and wet through the whole year, with little variation of temperature - between seventy nine and eighty three degrees Fahrenheit.

When I got out of the Boeing 707 at 8.45 pm, the hot air hit me like something you could touch. I soon spotted Alastair and Mary Macdonald in the crowd, behind the Health and Immigration and Customs barrier. Alastair I had prepared for Confirmation in 1954, when I was a curate in Westminster. He had finished at Cambridge, and was beginning life as a Civil Engineer. Out here he is building a dam.

I have longed to visit Singapore for many years. In part, I imagine, it is the drama that surrounded it in the War: that terrible day in December 1941 when we learnt that the 'Prince of Wales' and the 'Repulse' had gone down off Singapore, with 840 officers and men; and the following fateful February, when the beleaguered City fell.

I came to know as a friend John Leonard Wilson, the then Bishop of Singapore (later Bishop of Birmingham), whose courage in captivity is a story that still sheds a radiance upon the dark pages of Singapore's wartime history. But my desire to see Singapore is, in part, something much older than the

Second World War. Singapore is inseparable in my mind from all the romance of the East - Raffles (who founded it in 1819); the East India Company; and, at the turn of the century, all that moved the pen of Conrad, and, later, of Somerset Maugham. It was the Raffles Hotel in Singapore, of which Maugham wrote that it stood 'for all the fables of the exotic East.' Last night I half expected to meet the captain of a schooner round every corner.

But Singapore has greatly changed. Even people who have been away for only five years say that. About the size of the Isle of Wight, twenty six miles across and fourteen from north to south, it now has a population of over two million.

Chinese	1,579,866	78%
Malaya	311,379	14%
Indians	145,169	7%
Others	38,093	0.5%

Its initial population, when Stamford Raffles first arrived, was one hundred and fifty people.

I had forgotten that May Day in such a Chinese dominated republic would be a public holiday, so there was nothing I could do today but see the sights. (Not that Chinese Communism has much power here. It had, until 1960, but the People's Action Party, a one-party Government, which claims to rule on a socialist-democratic basis, has developed the country so much, in terms of public housing, education, employment and social services, and has led the country into such prosperity - because of rapid industrialisation and a building boom; unemployment is at present at its lowest level - the Communists do not get much of a look in.)

Mary Macdonald and I went down early to the Harbour, and a

wizened Chinese took us out in his sampan, fitted with an outboard motor. I have never seen a harbour filled with so many ships. It was like sailing round a great armada, or a fleet drawn up for review, but a merchant fleet of ships, small and great. There, laid out before our eyes, was the truth of Singapore: that it is really a great warehouse. Entrepot trade, import and export, collection and distribution, accounts for most of its national income.

It was sweltering hot in the harbour, and 'velly smelly'! And so - to Raffles Hotel! To the Coffee Bar, not to the 'world renowned Elizabethan Grill'. (Sir Stamford, we gathered, would have turned in his grave at an open-necked shirt and sandals.)

In the evening, Alastair and Mary and I went to Chinatown. Part of it was like East Street, Walworth: narrow streets lined on both sides with stalls selling food and household goods. From peeling dilapidated century-old buildings hung multi-coloured flags strung across bamboo poles. This Chinatown is fast disappearing. 'Urban Renewal' is removing it. Its present poverty depressed me. 130,000 people live in its square mile, with half a dozen families to one floor of a shop-house. Small wonder that the children roam the streets till late at night. But many Chinatown residents are unwilling to move out to the new 'vertical receptacles'. They know they will miss its community. The poor and congested housing situation has led to half of the residents eating out every day. It is cheaper and simpler than trying to cook at home. So you can eat at food stalls in the streets, or in a kind of market place. We each had an excellent bowl of steaming noodles and shrimps, and fresh lime juice. What was lovely to see was a crowd of seventy men squatting around an old Chinese story-teller, his face illuminated by a flickering wick light, mounted on a soap box. He had his audience spell-bound - for ten cents. Most of the listeners were old and uneducated men, who preferred to pass the time of night in the open air rather than be cooped up in their airless cubicles. A herbalist sat on the pavement, displaying his bottles of ointment, and manipulating the ankles and wrists and backs of those with aches and pains. We walked down Sago Lane, which had several death houses, century old institutions for the care of the dying and the dead. Many old people prefer to spend their last days waiting for death in these houses rather than get medical attention in hospitals. Relatives and friends were gathered round the houses, playing mahjong, card games, and drinking tea and gossiping. Several priest-like characters were busily engaged with it all, clashing cymbals to ward off evil spirits, playing flutes, flashing lights on and off, burning this and that - curious model houses and dolls. There is nothing that makes one a Christian more quickly than seeing the paraphernalia of primitive pagan religion. We also went into the Sri Marianman Temple, its roof adorned with gods and deities. Firewalkers 'do their thing' here during important Hindu festivals. There was little of beauty about the temple, and much that was crude and barbaric.

May 2nd 1972

I was collected at 6.30 am, and taken to the Cathedral for Holy Communion, followed by breakfast with the English-speaking staff of the Diocese of Singapore; and then their staff meeting, at which I was to speak to them.

Most of the population of Singapore - forty per cent - is Buddhist. The Moslems are fourteen and a half per cent; the Christians, eight and a half per cent; the Hindus, five per cent. The remaining thirty two per cent are either of no religion or of the very many small sects. Half the 160,000 Christians are Roman Catholic. There are 8,500 Methodists, 6,500 Anglicans, 4,300 Presbyterians, 1,500 Baptists. Of course, the Anglican Church is minute (0.3 per cent), in relation to the total population.

I greatly enjoyed meeting Ronald Weller again, the Dean of the Cathedral. (I had last met him when I preached at his Ordination at Birmingham, when Leonard Wilson was Bishop.) I was impressed by the team, who have a difficult task. There is complete freedom of worship in Singapore. There is no 'official' religion. The Government is entirely secular in outlook, and tends to want the churches to deal only with 'spiritual' matters, and keep well out of politics and social affairs.

The Bishop, Ban It Chui, (who was away) had arranged that one of his young priests, Geoffrey Johnson, should take me to look at one of the new estates, in which he is heavily involved.

In 1961 a huge fire broke out in the Bukit Ho Swee slum area. 16,000 people were made homeless. On the morning after the fire, Lee Kuan Yew, the Prime Minister, toured the burnt-out area and promised that all victims would be provided with new houses, on the site of the fire, within nine months. He kept his promise. Now there are 11,426 flats for 80,000 people on the site; 214 shops, 2 primary and 2 secondary schools; a child health and maternity centre; 2 community centres; open spaces; and a market for nearly 100 traders. Each of the flats is ten storeys high.

Before going round the Estate I attended the meeting of three Christian workers who assist with the social work on the Estate. There had been a meeting of tenants the previous evening, and the meeting of the social workers consisted mainly of going through questions that had been raised. Many of the complaints were all too familiar to me from flat dwellers in South London. "The people upstairs put too large things in the rubbish chute, and block it up." "The people on the floor above make too much noise." "The people at the top throw things out which land on our clean washing." (The washing is hung out on bamboo poles projecting at right angles to the balconies. It provides a colourful patchwork display from the street below.) "The flat roof leaks, and the rain comes through the ceiling." Half of the flats are one room; some have two, and some three rooms. Each has a kitchen, bathroom/WC, and balcony. They are therefore still very crowded. The children sleep in bunks. But it is clear from the number of people who want to buy the flats that most people are happy with them.

After visiting the Estate, Geoffrey Johnson took me up Mount Faber, an eminence from which one can survey the whole of the Island - a great panorama of land and sea.

In the evening, Alastair had to give a dinner at the 'Club' for one of the partners of his Civil Engineering firm out from London. Most of the firm's employees were invited - Chinese as well as English - and government people concerned with the dam. Twenty-nine of us sat down to a splendid dinner. It was a great opportunity to meet and talk at length with middle-class Chinese.

May 3rd 1972

I should have left Singapore at 8.30 am; but 'mechanical faults' in the 'plane delayed us five and a half hours. I indulged in a *Sunday Times* and *Observer* for April 30th. They were full of industrial disputes in England - rail, Underground, docks. A curious contrast to this place. Here there is a huge admiration for the Prime Minister, and 'the people have a will to work'. (A not too inapposite quotation, for there is something of the atmosphere here of building the wall with Nehemiah.) Odd, how leadership can mobilise a nation - or a church. Odd, how a nation will have a will to work in one generation, and not in another. (It's too easy to say the Chinese always work.) Odd, this elusive business of corporate and personal goals and ambitions. Even in a couple of days here you catch the thrill of a nation rebuilding.

We were away by 2.00 pm, and by ten to three were coming in to land 200 miles away, in Malaysia, over vivid green plantations on low hills. The roads and tracks often followed the contours of the hills, making deep orange patterns of sand against the green. We stopped only briefly, and were soon traversing the jungle of the Malayan Peninsular, and then leaving the mainland at Kota Bharu and flying out over the South China Sea. We approached Bangkok through the Gulf of Siam. It was difficult to believe we had come a thousand miles, except that now the fields from the air were flat and brown, with long lines of green enclosing a thousand small square or rectangular fields. As we came nearer the land, the lines of green were clearly trees either side of long straight muddy canals, like the Fens at Ely; and the fields were water-logged paddy fields. While we were on the ground in Thailand, the usual group of cleaners came through the 'plane, emptying ashtrays, disinfecting, removing papers. They had a great warmth and friendliness about them, and the faces of the young men and women had a unique beauty. From Bangkok, we made our way due east over Cambodia, and then over Viet Nam. Somehow I had not expected civilian aircraft would fly over Viet Nam. We crossed it not far south of the border between North and South. It was dusk as we travelled across it, and there were thunderstorms about, with lightning every few seconds. For a time we were knocked about a good deal. I thought of Bruce Nickerson, a much-loved Winant Volunteer from the USA, who came to us at St George's, Camberwell, and to whom I wrote fairly regularly after he had left us. Bruce was shot down over Viet Nam. RIP. I found it difficult to think of 'the suffering of Viet Nam'. I found it difficult even to think of the suffering that was going on below, on the ground. It seemed impersonal, meaningless, unreal - until I thought of Bruce. The wound of his death is still tender. I could imagine mothers, fathers, sons, daughters and friends from whom their Bruce has been - is being - wrenched away: of North Viet Nam as well as South, and others besides Bruce from the USA. *Dona nobis pacem.* After Viet Nam, we flew out again over the South China Sea for the last stage of the flight to Hong Kong. It was like escaping from the scene of a huge disaster.

Stage 15: Hong Kong

May 4th 1972

I suppose I have been waiting to see Hong Kong as much as any city on this odd itinerary. I was all but committed to coming here eighteen years ago, to the Cathedral staff. Then the Dean's young son died tragically while having a minor operation. In consequence, the Dean had to return to England for a time, and it was thought better for me not to come out here. But much of my heart was here, and I had read a good deal about it. Several of my friends have served here since - Barry Till as Dean; Timothy Beaumont eventually came instead of me, then Simon Ridley.

So, as the aircraft came down on the landing strip, constructed in the harbour itself, out of reclaimed land, and I looked out from the cabin on to the dazzling lights of Hong Kong at night, I was as excited as a two-year old.

It was not long before Uisdein McInnes, a friend of mine from Trinity College, Cambridge, was driving me through the fascinating streets of Kowloon, ablaze with neon signs in Chinese, to the ferry which takes you to the Hong Kong mainland. The journey at night by ferry is even more thrilling than coming in to land from the air. There are sampans, merchant ships, and other ferries, with their lights on, and floating restaurants, with coloured lights from stem to stern. But you look up to the lights of hundreds of towering hotels, multi-storey office blocks, and flats that have been built not only on the waterfront but further and further up the hillsides. Uisdein drove me to his flat, on the eighth floor of a new block of flats half way up the Peak. All the way up you look out on great panoramic views of the city. Then, from Uisdein's flat, there is a view of the opposite side of the island, of the little harbour of Aberdeen, of the sea beyond, and distant islands.

Uisdein is in the financial and economic side of the Government. He left Zambia, after thirteen years there, only last year. I hadn't seen him or his wife, Dorothy, for fourteen years. I had tried to see them in Zambia, only to find they had moved here just before I started my travels. Uisdein has been in hospital for three months of his short time here having a spinal operation.

The Dean had left a note inviting me to Holy Communion at the Cathedral at 8.30 am, and to breakfast afterwards. It was a marvellous way of getting to know people, for all sorts of people came to the breakfast: clergy and social workers, and anyone whom the Bishop and the Dean discover may be in Hong Kong. I was particularly glad to meet the Revd James Chu, a young Chinese priest, whom the Bishop had asked to show me some of the ways in which the churches are involved in the life, and meeting the needs, of Hong Kong.

It was not long before I was being thrown in at the deep end. I was taken across the Kowloon ferry again to the great industrial complex of Tsuen Tan and Kwai Chung, to look at a roof-top kindergarten, a primary school, and a Workers' Centre; all part of the work of 'Crown of Thorns' Church, amidst vast new towering blocks of workers' flats. I can happily look at children in kindergartens and primary schools for hours! Young children the world over are so marvellous, and these uniformed tiny tots - 900 of them - were specially marvellous. (There are 764,313 in Hong Kong Primary schools at the moment. 1,268,660 pupils were enrolled in 2,861 schools, colleges and education centres last year. There are 34,451 full-time teachers - 8,148 graduates and 15,694 non-graduates qualified for the teaching profession.)

Even in this first drive I was able to see something of what has been done to solve the problem of housing the four million people of Hong Kong by the provision of multi-storey blocks of government or government-aided housing, which at present accommodates 1,749,460 people. For speed and size the building programme has few, if any parallels. No doubt, later on this week, I shall be able to have a closer look at this re-housing.

Only a few hours of walking round schools and housing in the hot and humid climate of this time of the year can be exhausting, and I was glad that James Chu had in mind next a long car ride between 'Crown of Thorns' Church and the Chinese University of Hong Kong, the second university of Hong Kong, in which the principal language of instruction is Chinese. The new campus of the University is a most lovely site on the Tai Po Road near Shan Tin, ten miles from the Kowloon ferry. It overlooks the Tolo Harbour. Already there are over 2,000 students at this new University (in addition to well over 3,000 at the University of Hong Kong, established in 1911). The architecture is superb, and I was delighted to be shown over one of the colleges, provided by the Anglican Church - still in process of construction, and to look at the University Chapel and the other marvellous buildings, some provided by the British Government.

The traffic problem of Hong Kong and Kowloon is already huge (even though car ownership does not yet approach the figures of Europe or America) and I was not 'home' from Kowloon until seven - tired out! It was good to relax with Uisdein and Dorothy over dinner.

What I haven't said is that, during the day, I also met a young Englishman I had never set eyes on before who was in need of personal help. I lunched with him and had a very good talk - from which I personally received a great deal. It was one of those occasions of immediate rapport which makes it impossible to describe the encounter in terms of helper and helped. It is more appropriately described in terms of immediate friendship.

May 5th 1972

I made my way across to Kowloon again by ferry. Dear James Chu was there at 9.45 am waiting for me, and I was taken first of all to Calvary Church in the Wong Tai Sin and Chuk Yuen area to see a primary school, church, youth centre and hostel for young workers, which it was difficult to separate into separate compartments. The actual Church was used as classrooms during the day and as part of the youth centre at night. It was clearly a splendid piece of work.

Then we walked through the very crowded market area, and drove to the Hong Kong Christian Service Handicraft Workshop, in the Wan Tau Hom resettlement Estate. We had to walk up ten flights of stairs and along the narrow balcony of the block of flats, past where people were doing their cooking on the balcony. It gave me a chance to see inside the flats - although I hate looking at other people's houses as though one had a right to look at them. There was one room, ten feet by ten feet, for up to four people, and two hundred square feet for a family of more than four - with communal wash houses and latrines. The latest blocks are being built to a larger specification: thirty-five square feet for each adult, with private lavatories and water taps. I was utterly depressed by all this overcrowding in new premises. The Workshop provides relief and temporary help for many refugees, and it helps them to recover their dignity by earning their own living. But the very busy-ness of the workers - making neckties, smocked dresses, knitted sweaters and crochetted suits, etc. made me depressed. They worked without looking up, as though their life depended on it: which, I imagine was true.

Then we went to Christ Church, Kowloon, where Timothy Beaumont and Simon Ridley had served, to the Mary Rose School for Mentally Handicapped children, named after Lady Mary Rose Beaumont. There are 120 children at the school, six groups in the care of seven teachers and the assistant teachers. There is also a social worker in charge of the welfare affairs of the pupils and their families. The young headmaster and the teachers were simply marvellous. The children, many of them with some spastic condition, were all full of joy at what they were doing - naming vegetables a teacher produced from a bag, painting, making music, etc. I shall never forget the percussion class. As I looked at each child, before they 'struck up', I was feeling that ache in the pit of the stomach you sometimes feel at the sight of handicapped children. Then they began to play and sing together - one little chap banging a drum as big as himself, others with tambourines, cymbals, triangles, etc. And what they sang with gay abandon, and clapped hands to, and crashed, and tinkled, and 'bomped' to, was the wonderful 'Joy' theme at the end of Beethoven's Ninth Symphony. I shall never again hear Beethoven's Ninth without thinking of those little kids. The School, founded by Christ Church, is subsidised by the Hong Kong Education Department. It is another wonderful work, and will enable a good deal of pioneering to be done. (There are 130,000 handicapped children in Hong Kong and there is a great need for more to be done for them.)

James Chu insisted on taking me out to lunch at a Chinese

restaurant in the Ocean Terminal. Our window seats had a magnificent view of the harbour. James, who is married and has three children, spent a year at Westcott House, Cambridge, two years ago. He is a really lovely person, quiet and sensitive. From him I get so much of the feel of things in Hong Kong. He will make little statements, every one of which has weight and substance. "I think in Hong Kong everyone puts the education of their children first. No matter how poor they are, they know that education is important for the future." "I worry about my children. I had very little as a child, in Canton and Macau. They have much. But in Hong Kong we know that the ninety-nine year lease runs out in 1997 and I wonder what will happen to my children then. I shall be nearing retirement then. They will still be young."

Of course, the relationship with Red China is not something that related only to twenty-five years ahead. China is twenty miles away. Last year, about 12,000 illegal immigrants came from China to remain in Hong Kong. Half of Hong Kong's food, and sixteen per cent of other imports, come from China, and could be cut off at China's will. When you make a decision about, say, an underground railway for Hong Kong (currently a matter under discussion) the people who finance it will want to know whether they will be able to get their money back before 1997. And Hong Kong in general will interpret whatever is done (or not done) as an act of faith in the future beyond 1997 - or as an act of no faith. 1997 is a sword of Damocles; a guillotine; the 'eschaton'.

In the afternoon, James and I went to Holy Carpenter Church Hostel and Centre. It is in one of the main industrial areas of Kowloon, close to docks, cement works, and a power station. It is encircled by poor streets of small shops and daily work rooms, squatter shacks and a congested resettlement area. It is a remarkable place. In 1949 the influx of refugees from China to Hong Kong began. (The population had risen from 600,000 to 1,800,000 by 1947, but as the forces of the Chinese Nationalist Government began to face defeat in 1948/9, the influx of refugees started - three quarters of a million during 1949 and in the Spring of 1950. By the end of 1950, the population was 2,360,000. The 1971 census put the population at 3,948,179.) In 1949 Bishop Hall acquired a new site. Fourteen unemployed boys levelled it. Gradually a church and hostel were built. Now it is a place for three hundred workers in carpentry, motor-car repairs, air-conditioning repair and basic electrical instruction. Meals are provided for those who belong to the hostel and to other local workers. There is something of a family atmosphere about the place: the older helping the young.

There are regular evening classes and recreation together for members of the hostel, with discussion, debates and films; a Marriage Savings Scheme and cheap medical treatment. About a thousand 'old boys' of the hostel already come together regularly. They have just acquired a 9,000 square feet site nearby from the Government, so as to expand from 300 to 800 student workers. The Church of the Carpenter itself is a simple rectangular structure, with breeze bricks instead of windows. Frances Yipp, the priest who leads it all (and of whom I have heard a great deal) was in England, but it is no one-man-band and there was a good team of workers.

At 4.00 pm I went to tea at Bishop's House with Miss Cheng Shui Chun. She has recently retired after a lifetime of Social Service in Hong Kong. (It was clear that she had not retired but was now doing whole time, voluntarily, what before she had done in Government service, etc.) She had lived for a time in Lady Margaret Hall Settlement , in Kennington, South London, so we were friends from the start! Recently she and the Bishop's wife had been heavily involved in creating a

Neighbourhood Advice Council which trains volunteers, 192 of them, to staff really local information and counselling centres. Eight such centres now exist.

I learnt a great deal about Government Social Welfare from Miss Cheng - Dame Eileen Younghusband, who I see from time to time in England, had just been out here - but I learnt of its failure as well as its success. There is the same complaint one finds in city after city, of the lack of consultation with people concerning Urban Renewal, and few opportunities for citizens to participate in policy formulation and decision-making on any matter of public concern.

The gap between Government and governed in Hong Kong is particularly acute, because, *as a matter of policy*, there is no *elected* Government, only advisory and consultative committees, of which the Executive and Legislative Councils are the most important. These consist of *ex-officio* and nominated members. The Government is not exposed to criticism as a routine part of political life. There is no government of the people by the people. Opposition is treated as ill-informed or irresponsible. And, although the advisory committees have unofficial as well as official members, it is overwhelmingly clear that the kind of people who are put on these committees are most often elderly, respectable and rich, and there is no means of changing them. The Urban Council - consisting of twenty-six members - six *ex-officio*, ten elected unofficial members, and ten appointed by the Governor, looks as though in 1973 it will get shot of all its official members. But the point is clear: this is the kind of mild amendment which is made, whilst the situation cries out for real participation by the people, and an end to benign paternalism.

During the day I had arranged to see another Cambridge man out here whose marriage is in a mess. It was a very human story. I just cannot understand how some 'religious' people live by the application of simple rules on, for instance, divorce. Almost every 'story' I hear is so 'understandable' and complex. But what is also clear is how few people are willing to consult anyone in this life - priest, or Marriage Guidance counsellor. They will only go to a friend - if he happens to be around. I am conscious of the may people whom I have met up with around the world who would not have consulted anyone had I not *happened* to be around, as someone they knew in the past. But I might so easily *not* have happened to be around. It certainly helps me that I have to swing from thinking about vast subjects like Hong Kong's Social Welfare, with a budget of several million dollars, to a particular individual in need. It's like those television programmes which have photography of vast areas of the earth from the moon and then centre down on one peasant on a boat or a river in that part of the earth. There's no point in this life at all, to my mind, if it isn't primarily concerned with John Smith - or Susie Wong.

May 6th 1972

I spent the morning preparing sermons for tomorrow. I wanted to see a quite different 'slice of life' in Hong Kong, where many of the people enjoy themselves. Uisdein's suggestion, that we should go to the races in the afternoon, seemed a very good one. The Royal Hong Kong Jockey Club is an immensely influential non-profit making organisation, which has its stadium for 35,000 people in the centre of Hong Kong. It has a monopoly of lawful gambling in the Colony and contributes vast sums to Welfare work - £10 million since 1961. It thereby justifies itself, and does not have to make its accounts available to the public. A very small exclusive group decides what shall be done with the profits. It was fun to see half a dozen races in the crowded stadium. There were a few British jockeys, but most of them were Chinese, as were the owners. Needless to say, not knowing the horses, or the trainers, or the owners, or most of the jockeys, I did not 'contribute to charity' - ie bet! But it was fascinating to watch the Chinese engrossed in the betting. I imagine that people who spend so much of their time on Mahjong are well-educated for other forms of gambling.

In the evening, Hamish and Fiona Macleod, (he is an Administrative Officer on the finance side of the Government) invited us to dinner with an American in a container ship company (and his wife) and a lawyer, the son of an Australian bishop (and the lawyer's wife). The conversation at the end of the evening concentrated on this very important subject of whether there *should* be an *elected* Government here.

The last Governor of Hong Kong, Sir David Trench, said, "There is no one brand of policies which is right for all stages of development. And wherever you are, and whenever you are there, you must select the best course of action for that time and place and that set of circumstances, and these become your politics or your policies." I have learnt this to be true in many places on my journey, eg Uganda, New Guinea. But the bland statement of Sir David cannot justify in a *developed* country like Hong Kong the failure to provide the rudimentary provisions of democracy unless there are dire alternatives. The question is: are the alternatives as predictably dire as the Government suggests? There is, in fact, very little population pressure for the vote. This may be through fear, or even through that rather passive attitude to life which many people here assure me characterises Buddhist people. Of course, the fact that so many here are refugees, who have already in their lifetime lost all they had, and have rapidly gathered something together again, a kind of middle-class affluence, makes their fear very understandable.

May 7th 1972
I preached in the Cathedral at 9.00 am. It was odd to feel that

one might so easily have served there for a number of years. How the course of one's life can be altered by accidents! At 11.00 am I preached at St Paul's Church, to an entirely Chinese congregation, with the admirable help as translator of Peter Kwong, the priest who is to be Warden of the College I had visited at the Chinese University. He was so good as an interpreter that I felt something of the unity that I have sometimes experienced when accompanying a singer on the piano. I think the sermon was appreciated more by the Chinese congregation than by the Cathedral congregation, and this was largely due to Peter.

It was a privilege to administer the Holy Communion to Chinese people. The faces of people kneeling at an altar speak eloquently of who they are.

I was taken out to lunch at Kin Kwok's Cantonese restaurant by a very kind layman, Paul Cheng. All his family came and some friends - about a dozen men sitting at one table and a dozen women at the other.

At 3.00 pm I was due to see the Bishop of Hong Kong. I nearly did not see him, as three inches of rain fell between 2.00 pm and 3.00 pm. He is a quiet person, but a man of great resolution and courage. Recently he had ordained Miss Joyce Bennett (whom I shall be seeing on Tuesday) to the priesthood. His Charge to his November Synod is of great dignity and strength. What he had to say to me on Church and Government in Hong Kong underlined what a wise bishop he is for this place at this time.

He told me the news of the rejection by the Church of England of the proposals for Anglican-Methodist Unity. I was not surprised, for part of my disillusionment with the Church of England has been that I judged there was little or no hope of the required majority in the General Synod. What is so astonishing is that the rejection should have followed the Synod's approval of the reunion scheme between the Church of North India and the Church of Pakistan. As someone has said, "The Church of England will unite to the last Indian.". I can testify to the disillusionment with the Church of England that many parts of the Anglican Church outside England now feel. From outside England it looks as though the Church of England is pleading for a diplomatic immunity to change - like an old lady saying, "I'm too old to change now, dear.".

I went to Evensong at the Cathedral, partly to sit quietly, and hear good music, and be refreshed; partly to hear the sermon of the Chaplain to the Cathedral, John Tyrrell, who has been a very special friend to me in my days here.

May 8th 1972
John Chisholm flew in early today on his way from Honiara to England (having been to New Guinea, Australia and New Zealand since I last saw him). It was a very wet day, but John Tyrrell kindly drove us all the way round the Island. It was John Chisholm's only chance of seeing it. He flew out again tonight.

It was a memorable day - of fun, recounting the days together in Melanesia; but also taking in so much of Hong Kong in one drive 'does something to you'. John Chisholm was clearly appalled by the magnitude of the housing resettlement, the size of the buildings, and the density of the population. There certainly is nowhere quite like it. As a matter of statistical fact the population densities in the urban part of the Colony in 1961 were the highest in the world.

What also hits you are the extremes of affluence and of overcrowded poverty. Near to John Chisholm's hotel on Kowloon is a vast new enclosed shopping centre, which for the abundance of beautiful things for sale must rival any other place in he world. (Even in cheap Hong Kong, what is sold there eats up your money.) But within five minutes you can be in the midst of appalling conditions. In comparison with the West, the standard of living is for the majority very low, but after Japan, Hong Kong has the highest average income per head in Asia. It is now probably the greatest trading centre of the under-developed world. The value of its exports exceeds that of India. And all this takes in an area less than the size of Kent - but composed mainly of steep and rugged hillsides from which sites have been blasted, on which the huge blocks of flats have been built.

May 9th 1972

I went this morning with James Chu to look at the new town of Kwun Tong on Kowloon, near the airport: more massive housing, running alive with people. Then I was taken round St Catherine's School for Girls, Kwun Tong, by Joyce Bennett, the Headmistress. There will soon be a thousand girls at the School. I am suspicious that the Church here is as heavily involved in education as it is until I see someone like Joyce Bennett at work, who has produced such a fine school. The Government subsidises the schools, and very much wants the Church to be a partner with them in education, bringing money and manpower, but above all a living pressure towards excellence. There is no doubt that the Church schools are specially admired. Joyce Bennett, as I have said, was one of two women, one Chinese, who the Bishop ordained priest recently. It would be difficult to find a more suitable candidate. It is good she can now be a priest to her own school, instead of having to call in a male priest from outside.

After the morning's exertions, and a little shopping, I was exhausted. (When I went into the Cathedral to rest, there were twenty people sitting there, asleep under the whirring fans!) I went out for an excellent meal with Uisdein and Dorothy, on what is, regrettably, my last evening in Hong Kong.

May 10th 1972

Geoffrey Shrives and his wife came out from Southwark four years ago, from St Michael's, Sydenham, to be in charge of the Missions to Seamen here. He was on the Southwark Ordination Course when I first knew him. I wanted to see him before leaving Hong Kong, so I caught the ferry to Kowloon again. Geoffrey was able to tell me a good deal about shipping in Hong Kong. (I am one of 190 million passengers on the ferry in a year!)

The Missions to Seamen Hostel has only been open five years. It can put up 120 seamen, and its twelve floors really are a very worthwhile amenity for seamen who 'fetch up' here. It contains a bowling alley, a swimming pool, a good restaurant, several bars and lounges, a place for quiet, and a magnificent chapel - which is used by the Roman Catholics as well as the Anglicans. It was very good to hear how the Roman Catholic equivalent of Missions to Seamen, *Stella Maris*, works in complete partnership with Geoffrey.

It was pouring with rain all day, and I was glad to go to a Lunch Hour Recital of music by St Paul's School, in the Cathedral. It was really refreshing to listen to a Beethoven Sonata for Piano and Violin and some excellent singing. I probably ought to have realised how gifted the Chinese are at Western music (eg Fou T'song). The music I have heard from the schools here leaves me in no doubt.

James Chu showed me his own church, school and settlement, St James', in the afternoon. The Church was fully occupied by classes of infants. It was like the Charterhouse Mission in Southwark on a huge scale (2,000 schoolchildren). I adored seeing the children, the old people's club, and the ping-pong playing adolescents. The Church obviously serves the neighbourhood around it, which until recently has been one of the worst slum areas of Hong Kong. Many of the people have now been moved to resettlement areas.

It was still pouring with rain when Uisdein and Dorothy and three-and-a-half year-old Andrew drove me to the airport. Indeed, there was the umpteenth cloudburst that day, with thunder and lightning every few seconds. The rain and the wind whipped the sea as the car ferry took us across to Kowloon, and, when we landed, the streets were flooded. People stood in the open shop fronts unable to move in the streets, like crowds watching a procession. It was the normal crowd of people, but you saw just how thick upon the ground people are. (You don't spend more time than you can help inside a room in this hot sticky atmosphere - not in a room ten feet square.)

"A barren island with hardly a house upon it" was what Lord Palmerston said of Hong Kong in 1841!

There was again a mechanical fault in the 'plane, and we were an hour late leaving for Calcutta. It was a five hour non-stop flight in darkness, traversing again much of the journey I had made last week - over the South China Sea, Viet Nam to Bangkok, and then over Rangoon and the Bay of Bengal - 1,642 miles.

These periods between the various stages of my journey that I have spent encapsulated in an aircraft - a VC10 this time - have assumed a significance of their own. It may be in part that the regret at leaving friends heightens one's self-awareness - and the unknown that lies ahead (especially this time, Calcutta). But I think there is more to it than that. These periods remind me that it is not entirely true that 'all life is meeting'. All life is 'being', and from that being one emerges from time to time into 'meeting', into various degrees and depths of meeting. It may be for transient surface meeting with the chap seated next to you. It may be for the renewal of friendship, like my meeting this last week, with Uisdein and Dorothy - or that meeting of friends for the first time, that, nevertheless, you know has made you friends for life - however often or seldom you see one another again. (James Chu and John Tyrrell here I shall regard as 'friends for life'.)

But 'being' and 'meeting' are not entirely separate. For the Beyond of 'being' - which I was thinking about particularly in New Guinea - includes something of 'meeting'. And 'meeting' is not something which simply starts and stops: it furnishes being with new dimensions. The fellowship of friends remains as part of being. 'No man is an island'. I think it is important to affirm this in a world the pace, mobility and multiplicity of which may seem more and more to make all relationships transient.

Stage 16: Calcutta

May 11th 1972

It was nearly midnight, Calcutta time, when we reached Dum-Dum airport, ten miles outside Calcutta. Even then if was eighty-four degrees Fahrenheit, and had been one hundred and four degrees during the day. There was no note from the Brotherhood of the Epiphany with whom I hoped to stay, and their house at Behala was eight miles the other side of Calcutta. BOAC had advised me to spend the night at a hotel. I had some small trouble with the Immigration authorities. "Missionary?" said the civil servant aggressively, looking at the clerical collar on my passport photograph. Mercifully, I had taken the precaution of obtaining a letter from the High Commissioner for India, in Canberra, stating that I needed no visa for a three-week visit. With some reluctance, the civil servant accepted this explicit statement! The airport 'bus took me to the Oberoi Grand Hotel. It was as depressing a ride as I had feared. All the buildings on the way into the centre, even by lamplight, had a forsaken, uncared-for look about them. The pavements towards the centre were littered with sleeping figures, sleeping anywhere and everywhere on the pavements, the very position underlining the it-doesn't-matter-where abandonment of the homeless. As the airport 'bus drew up at the hotel, figures rushed forward with outstretched hands. At one o'clock it was not too late for a coin. I felt sick as my bags were carried up to my room. (Why should I have had to use a hotel in Calcutta - the first I have needed in five months - and the Grand Hotel at that?)

When the morning came, Ascension Day morning, I 'phoned the Brotherhood of the Epiphany, and was greatly relieved when the 'phone was answered. They had not received my letter. They were coming into the centre an hour later, and could collect me, and would be delighted for me to stay with them. (How blest are they who are neither homeless nor have to live in the Oberoi Grand Hotel!) One night cost me 93.50 Rupees, 6.50 for breakfast, and a tip for the bedroom attendant. ("I'm your boy, sir" he said with a bow, at 65); a tip for the waiter at breakfast, and a tip for the luggage-carrier, twice - 104 rupees: Five Guineas.

The truck duly arrived, carrying Fr Peter Thorman, Fr Chatterjee and a VSO.

We drove past the Maidan, like Clapham Common, and had a look at St Paul's Cathedral. Three thousand refugees from Bangladesh had camped in the Cathedral grounds until February 19th. It was the best utilised Cathedral I have even been in - an impressive Victorian building, with some fine Indian Christian paintings, but evidence all round of the relief work in which the Cathedral has been - and still is - heavily involved. It is trying to raise a million rupees to erect 30,000 mud plaster houses in Bangladesh. It is dispensing £20,000 a week on Bangladesh relief, and the Government had handed over a large proportion of its aid programme to the care of the Cathedral. In the Cathedral, I felt very connected with the Christian past of India as well as the present. There is a memorial to Bishop Heber ("Holy, Holy, Holy" Heber); and another to Bishop Cotton ("O God who has made of one blood all nations of men for to dwell on the face of the earth...."); and on the wall was a memorial to CF Andrews, one of my heroes, with a shining, smiling photograph of his bearded face alongside it. His Centenary last year was celebrated in India with a special stamp. He was Warden of the Pembroke College Mission in Walworth before he went out to India, to become there the friend of Gandhi and Rabindranath Tagore - and of the poor. He is buried in Calcutta's Lower Circular Road Cemetery.

Our drive out to Behala reminded me of one of those car rides in a Buster Keaton silent film of the Twenties. It's 'every man for himself' on the Calcutta roads. They are long strips of licensed 'dodgems'. The crowded pavements overflow on to the roads, and 'right of way' is a joke. You sound your horn (every twenty seconds), and put the nose of your car where you can get it. On the outskirts of Calcutta you press on through unconcerned crowds, rickshaws, wandering cows, trams, bicycles and coaches.

I was in Calcutta because I would have felt guilty if I had avoided it. But I wanted to go to Behala for a reason which has nearly a century behind it. In 1879, the Bishop of Calcutta appealed to the University of Oxford to come and work among the educated people of Calcutta. Ten men met in Bishop Edward King's rooms and founded the Oxford Mission. By 1880, the first men, calling themselves the Brotherhood of the Epiphany, sailed for Calcutta; their rule of life drawn up by Bishop Gore. They were to live and work in the city, close to the university and its colleges.

In 1892 Frederick Wingfield Douglass - Christ Church, Oxford; Cuddesdon; and then curate of St Pancras - joined the Brotherhood. He was soon the leader of the work amongst educated Bengalis. But, at the turn of the century, there was a call for the Brotherhood to work amongst rice-growing villagers in Barisal, east of Calcutta, now in Bangladesh, and for many years Douglass served there.

It was when he was forty-four that Fr Douglass began his work at Behala, near the village of Barisal. He found a site near a bathing place; cleared the jungle; raised the swamped flat Bengal land, by building a second 'tank' - a bathing pool thirty yards by twenty - and then spreading out the earth; built an apprentices' school, a hostel for young men, a church, and a place for the Brothers to live, and for the Sisters of the Epiphany (founded at Barisal in 1902). For forty years Father Douglass was Superior at Behala. The Brotherhood drew all sorts and conditions of men there.

As I look out of my window now - on to the 'tank' in which boys are bathing, with the Church alongside - I think particularly of one young man, an engineer, who came here and helped Fr Douglass - Cecil John Grimes, later Archdeacon of Calcutta and then of Northampton: the father of a friend of mine (and of many in Southwark) Geoffrey Grimes. Fr Douglass wrote of Cecil Grimes: "It is doubtful whether Behala could have come into existence but for Mr Grimes. He not only planned and estimated for every scrap of the buildings, but he measured them out, found their levels, and did all those mysterious things which buildings seem to require. He gilded the altar and built the tower."

The work of the Brotherhood in Calcutta is now all housed at Behala. Here there is an orphanage and three types of school - an industrial School, St Joseph's Primary School, and a school which caters for boys who want to qualify for the industrial course.

As soon as I had settled in, the Superior, Peter Thorman, who has been out here since 1937, took me round the 'compound'. It was marvellous to see all that is going on. A new project, sponsored by several leading businessmen in Calcutta, aims to help young men to become self-employed in various trades, providing them with capital. So there they are, being taught electrical repair, plumbing, cement brick-making, tyre re-treading, paint-spraying, toy-making, light engineering, welding, refrigeration and air-conditioning repair, and poultry keeping.

The rains are long overdue, so everything is dried up by the burning heat. But there are great rain trees giving shade by the 'tanks', which are seldom free from one or two young swimmers. To inspect a bakery, when *outside* it is 'like an oven', is to know what it means to be hot. But the young bakers (who made a thousand loaves a day for the Bangladesh refugees) were wonderfully welcoming, and I enjoyed their hot biscuits.

What amazed me was to discover fifty violins and 'cellos in the Music Room of the School. Fr Douglass was a man with music in his soul. This side of his work has been carried on by Fr Theodore Mathieson, who, when he heard at lunch (hot curry!) that I played the piano, immediately arranged for one of the boys to come over with his 'cello. I shall never, never, forget this Bengali boy, Anup Biswas, playing *Slumber on*, from Bach's Cantata no. 82. He should have a great future as a 'cellist before him, if somehow the money for his training can be found. It was a great privilege to accompany him.

In the evening, I went along to the music room, where the boys were singing Bengali songs. They were enchanting. They are very trusting. They smile, and I smile, and they come up and loosely hold my hand. The young Bengali 'cellist accompanied their singing as though it was an Eastern instrument.

May 12th 1972

I thought I would read myself into Calcutta a little today. I read Malcolm Muggeridge's *Something Beautiful for God*. It is a fine book on 'Mother Teresa of Calcutta'. I was particularly grateful for the lines of William Blake:

"Joy and woe are woven fine,
A clothing for the soul divine;
Under every grief and pine
Runs a joy with silken twine,
It is right it should be so;
Man was made for joy and woe;
And when this we rightly know,
Thro' the world we safely go."

But I think he - and Mother Teresa - are wrong at one point. They so emphasise the need for individuals to help individuals that they attack 'organisation'. This, I think, is naive, romantic and misleading. Mother Teresa would have no drugs but for the organisation of industry. It is true that in the city of Calcutta thousands die, but thousands more would die but for organised medicine. This attitude is part of the reaction to the urban world which I have found all round the globe: the desire to have some of the products of organised technology but to attack it at the same time. It is a very sacred-secular division. To 'deal with people' is sacred and good. To deal through organisations is secular and evil. But it is not from organisation that Calcutta is suffering from but *bad* organisation. It desperately needs more good organisation. Christians ought not to be attacking organisation, but seeing that it is shot through with a true theology, that it serves the sacred, albeit impersonally. I think it was Canon Max Warren who once said in my hearing "The Form of the Servant must often in our age take the form of the civil servant".

This place has been an ideal first place to come in India. With half a million sleeping in the streets at night - out of six and a half million - anyone would be a fool to think he could do much in a week to understand, let alone do anything about, Calcutta's poverty. I do not think it would achieve much for me to pour over statistics, or to try to do what I did in Hong Kong: seek out new housing projects and visit them. (Indeed, I doubt very much if it could be done.) An Englishman in Calcutta is not left alone for five minutes; there is the endless importuning by the poor. But here I can observe; I can look and listen from a lodgement that is inevitably to some extent outside, but is also several steps within the lives of some of the people of Calcutta.

This afternoon, Fr Theodore collected in the library two of the boys who play first violin and two who play second. He and Anup played the 'cello and I played the piano, for the first two movements of Bach's D Minor Piano Concerto. I had never looked at the score in my life, and had to sight-read it; but the thrill of the occasion provided a curious afflatus, and we got through with surprising success. The rest of the Brothers and the Sisters had gathered in the library at the sound, and a crowd had gathered the other side of the open windows, pressing themselves to the iron grill - old men, middle-aged, youths and boys - they come in to the field surrounding the Mission building every evening after work, to play football, or to stroll and gossip. When we ended, the little crowd outside clapped and smiled. This Bengali love of music breaks all barriers down. At least, it breaks some down, and I'm deeply grateful for that. What amazes me is that the lads who play this heavenly music either at the Industrial School or, like one of the first violins, a particularly brilliant fellow, just out at work, and living in the workers hostel. He in fact looks after the machines at a tobacco factory. He only has a job because he has been trained here.

May 13th 1972

I do not think think I shall have much to report during my stay here on things I have done. It is what I see which fully occupies me. I shall never think of India now without thinking of pale white cattle, ambling aimlessly in the fields and the streets.

Across the field there walks at this moment, as gracefully as I have seen anyone walk anywhere in the world, a young man. What gives to people of one part of the world a beauty of bearing which excels that of all the rest? (Is it only Bengalis? Shall I find it in Bangalore?) It is partly the pace of walking (the temperature yesterday was again 104 degrees Fahrenheit). You need to walk without hurry. But there is a gentleness of manner and a majesty of bearing which matches the movement. It is as though all the time a ballet was going on, on a vast stage outside my window.

What I thought at first was swimming - which it is - is also 'bathing'. At the moment there are a dozen boys soaping themselves and then swimming around - gliding through the water. Hindus wash to avoid ritual pollution. They have an almost obsessive concern with cleanliness - not a bad obsession, in a land where the gutters are full of filth.

It is a society from which the girls and the women seem much of the time to have been hidden away. Men and boys come out into the field and the streets - old men were sitting in white on the grass last night, playing bridge on a newspaper - but most of the women and girls live within, so that the sight of a woman in a sari (again, the most graceful of all garments), walking slowly across the fields, catches your attention.

I went this afternoon twenty minutes' walk along the road to the 'Forty-seventh Annual Rally of the Bharat Scouts and Guides Behala Local Association'.

Even twenty minutes walk is a revelation. The steel grey single-decker coaches, crammed tight with people *inside and out* continually push you off the road/pavement - and the bicycles, cars, taxis and rickshaws. I walked past the crowded open shops of the 'bazaar' amidst the noise of bells and horns and shouting. A woman was putting pots of cow dung on a wall, drying them for fuel. I noticed the regular sound of a bell behind me. I turned round to see what it was, and, overtaking me, were a dozen men with the dead body of an old man on a wooden stretcher on their shoulders. They were taking him to the river for burial. I looked at the old man's face as he was carried past me, and the faces of the bearers. They did not look particularly concerned. He just looked asleep. Who will miss him? Anyone? It was not his death which made me shudder, but his anonymity.

I loved the Scout Rally - rather as I had loved the race-track in Hong Kong. There were ordinary mothers and fathers there, proud of their ordinary children, just as they would be at Camberwell or Clapham Common. (There were more women in saris than I had yet seen in public.) I felt more appreciative of the Scout Movement than I have ever felt before. There were twelve groups taking part, and there must have been a thousand onlookers. They did all the normal scout things, like putting up a tent in record time, and climbing through rubber tyres. But there were some events of particular interest to me. There was, for instance, a pageant of Religious festivals, with the Christians doing 'Christmas' and the Hindus doing their thing. The first tableau was the 'Spring Festival' - Doljatra - with boys and girls throwing red powder over all and sundry, imitation aphrodisiacs. The second was of the Goddess Durga. Durga you buy fresh every year from the local image-maker. She is made of bamboo and clay. You decorate her as well as you can (having paid out a good deal on her); you drape her and fit her out with electric lights. The one for the Scout display was, of course, a cub made up as an idol. 'She' looked like a cheap Piccadilly prostitute, with a sword in her hands - plural, because I counted eight arms and hands. Her festival lasts two or three days. (Most feasts only last one day.) A Brahmin priest is hired to say Sanskrit incantations over her, and then she is put on a lorry. At the end, everyone who can gets on to the lorry, and she is driven off to the river, where she is drowned. Durga, of course, dissolves. She is the most popular Bengal Goddess. Most Hindus have her as a household God/Goddess.

Then a phallic symbol was brought in: The Feast of Shiva, worshipped for male fertility.

The last 'feast' was rather nice: a day when sisters greet their brothers - tying a red thread round the right wrist of the brother, wishing him long life and claiming his protection. Bhai-phontra or Rakshabandan. Of course, even this 'nice' festival speaks of male domination. What one learns (as I learnt about Popular Buddhism in Singapore) is that *popular* Hinduism, as distinct from the Hinduism (or Buddhism) I have learnt about in England from Hindu/Christian dialogues, is often not all that 'nice'. While it remains at the level of *fun and games* for popular festivals it is harmless enough, but true religion must cope with the elemental events of life: and in practice this popular Hinduism is often a tissue of superstitions. Of course, Hinduism is not a matter of festivals only; it pervades, for instance, much that one sees of the day-to-day world, on the way to and from and at the Scout Rally - the cattle, the brass pots, the bathing men and women, the saris, the gold bangles, the divisions of society - and the filth about which so little is done.

I felt proud of the Scout Movement this afternoon, because, clearly, it is such an educating force, and an internationally educating force. I simply loved the message in the programme from the Governor of West Bengal - via his secretary. It began:

"I am delighted to refer to your letter No.BSG/191/72-73/F.4, dated 21.4.72, and to say that the Governor of West Bengal...."

The walk home was hazardous. Many cars and cycles do not have any lights on, though they speed along the roads. Presumably the police have given up the unequal struggle. That makes one more struggle that has been given up here.

May 14th 1972

I am conscious of having run out of superlatives in these last five months. I shall need them today, if ever I did.

Mass was 6.20 am. I hadn't realised what was in store for me. It was all in Bengali, liturgy and sermon. But I hadn't expected the orchestra to accompany the service, nor had I expected the Bengali setting of the Mass to be half as beautiful as it was. In the left hand aisle of the Chapel was the orchestra; in the left centre aisle were the older boys and men; in the right centre aisle the small boys; in the right hand aisle the women, in beautiful saris. All either stood, or sat cross-legged on the floor. The orchestra played the Bengali music in parallel movement, a haunting unison with all the voices, whilst the tabla (drums), and the mandira (small cymbals), gave a repetitive ground rhythm to the melody. The sitar joined with the violins and 'cellos. I cannot remember a lovelier act of worship - 'Something Beautiful for God'. And, in the middle of it, during the Communion, a complete change from the Bengali idiom, the strings played very quietly one of my favourite English folk songs, arranged, I think, by Stanford, *My love's an arbutus*.

This Bengali Mass can only have the Congolese Mass (used in *Lord of the Flies*) to compare with it.

Fr Thorman had asked me to preach at St Stephen's Church, Calcutta, at 8.15 am. It was a considerable contrast - an almost entirely Anglo-Indian congregation, about sixty people, half of them children. The Church is closely related to two very large schools, and this was mostly the remnant left in the school holidays. The memorials on the walls of the church (the church and vicarage were built in the time of Warren Hastings) were without exception to Englishmen. The setting of the Communion was Victorian. The hymns were from the early edition - 1750 - of *Hymns Ancient and Modern*. I felt bound to preach on 'What I Owe to Christ - through CF Andrews'. The congregation were kindly folk. One of them told me of his meetings with 'Deenabandhu', as Andrews was called - 'Friend of the Poor'.

After the service, Peter Thorman drove me into the city to see Bishop's College, the Old Cathedral (St John's) and the Roman Catholic Cathedral. I could not bring myself to photograph the crowded squalor and destitution of the streets, though I suspect it must be seen to be believed.

In the afternoon, at 3.00 pm, there was Evensong; again, the orchestra accompanied Bengali settings of the psalms, canticles and responses. It was utterly lovely. And when there was something I could not follow - because of the strangeness of the language - the lessons, the psalms and the sermon - I could always turn my eyes to look out from the church to ten or so local lads diving off the spring-board into the 'tank', twenty yards away.

Over tea with the Brothers, we had an interesting discussion. I had gathered that Fr Theodore had preached at Evensong on the Ascension, and I had heard him say suddenly three English words in the midst of all the Bengali. "Were you preaching on the Ascension?" I asked. "What were you saying was a 'figure of speech'?" "I was saying that to talk of Heaven as 'above the bright blue sky' was just a 'figure of speech'.", replied Fr Theodore. "Then do you believe the Ascension actually happened?" - I asked. (I am unconvinced myself there was literally an Ascension - mainly on grounds of Biblical criticism.)

But there was a 'division among the people' on that. It is one thing to say that 'rising above' is a 'figure of speech' and quite another to relate that statement to the record of Our Lord 'rising above'. It is curious how easy it is to leave the intellect at the door of the church. "Take off your intellect, for the place whereon you stand is holy ground"! Not that I believe intellect alone can take you all that far into the Holy of Holies.

I also had a fascinating chat after tea with Fr Sushil Chatterjee, one of the Indian Brothers. I wanted to find out from him whether what I had so far concluded on popular Hinduism was wide of the mark - he was born a Hindu. I read him what I had written in my journal yesterday. He approved what I had written and added, "You see, the Hindu has no such thing as the corporate worship of the Christian, involving regular weekly instruction. There is no 'church' to define and teach what you must believe. You may think that ordinary Christians are greatly separated from those who confront the intellectual problems of Christian belief, but that separation is far greater in Hinduism. As a Hindu, you are very much an individual who simply picks up what is popularly believed."

In the evening I had the privilege of going to a wedding feast in Calcutta. On the way to the wedding, we passed another little group carrying out of Behala a man who had died. The father of the bride, whose wedding feast we were attending, had been killed by Pakistanis in Bangladesh (the frontier is only a few hours' drive away); the bridegroom's father was also dead, so an uncle of the bridegroom was giving the feast. The bride, with a ring of pearls in her nose, gloriously attired in a red and gold sari, and with many gold bangles, sat in a room with many other ladies, also in beautiful saris. After the men had chatted for an hour and met the bridegroom, clad in white Bengali traditional dress, with a thin gold decoration and gold studs, we were ushered into the presence of the ladies, where we paid our respects and took our leave. Not a word passed the lips of the bride. It was an occasion for looking beautiful and solemn. The feast was the kind of curry and sweets that I am now used to at the Brotherhood. (I imagine I have now had most of the Bengali variations on the original theme of curry, and quite enjoy them.) But this time, there was no alternative but to eat, as Indians do, with their hands, washing them afterwards. I cannot say eating with *my* hands improves my appetite - not curried fish, curried meat, mangoes and yoghurt, all from the same banana leaf.

We had to take Fr Chatterjee to Calcutta Railway Station after the Feast. It is here that words must fail. It really needs a Hogarth to portray it all, or a Doré, who did those frightening pictures of Victorian cities. In words, only a Dickens could begin to describe it with any success. It is significant that I think immediately of the time of Dickens - or earlier - when I think of Calcutta. The approaches to the railway station, the great Howrah bridge over the Hooghli river, were totally congested. As we edged our way forward in the jeep, inch by inch, I could look out on to an unbelievable world, the men standing sweating within the harnesses of their rickshaws, loaded with people - and parcels and trunks - having dragged them over the bridge; and bodies on the pavement lying there like Henry Moore drawings of people asleep in the Underground shelters during the War, body to body. (Imagine the approaches to Waterloo or Liverpool Street stations littered with bodies.) As we stopped at one place, ten yards from where we have stopped before, a child with its back towards me defecated in the gutter. (Where else could it go?) Taxis sounded their horns at ten second intervals (still the horns you squeeze). A coach came at our jeep from one side, a taxi form the other. Besides the rickshaws and the taxis were landaus, and stage-coach-looking affairs, (Hackney carriages?) drawn by horses. Of course, there were cows in the middle of the melee, and, on the pavements, the flames of oil stoves where those that had food were cooking it. The stench of food and excrement, and petrol, was sickening. But it was the sheer numbers of people which was overwhelming - like a Coronation crowd.

To 1971, Mother Teresa's order alone has picked up over 23,000 people from the streets of Calcutta, about fifty per cent of whom have died.

Yet it would be wrong to give the impression that all those sleeping in the streets are dying or starving. Some will prefer to sleep outside rather than in, guarding, perhaps, their little shop. Many will come to Calcutta who, like those who came to minute Honiara, prefer the dream of the city to the reality of the village, and stay there in the hope that it will give them what life in the village has failed to provide. It would also be wrong simply to describe Calcutta as a city of suffering and woe. You do not need to be a Dickens to see the smiles in the light of the oil lamps. When I have said all that is evil about this city, I know that already I have also found it exciting. Already I have a love-hate for Calcutta. Perhaps, as a Londoner, I could never simply loathe such a city; and, as a priest, I could never simply hate a place so pulsating with *people*. The pageant and panorama of its life is enthralling. But I can find it so because I have enough and to spare. As I came back to the Brotherhood in the jeep, jolted from pothole to pothole, I found myself humming the Kyrie from Bach's *B Minor Mass*. The sights and sounds of this city make up a kind of symphony. Somewhere - up, or across, or down; wherever the cries of the human heart are heard - the city of Calcutta may be heard, like the elemental *Kyrie* that opens the B Minor.

In fact, when I reached the Brotherhood, Fr Theodore was in the 'bandroom', taking four violinists and 'cellists through one of Beethoven's last Quartets. Bach or Beethoven, Hogarth,

Dickens - I imagine they were all struggling to understand, interpret and articulate the misery and glory of man that is found in such places as this.

O Calcutta!

May 15th 1972
Fr Theodore drove me in to the Cathedral, with some dustbins full of biscuits from the bakery, which the Cathedral Relief Service would distribute. It was good to find a real team working from the Cathedral - representatives of the Relief Service, the Cathedral Social Service, the Port Chaplaincy, the Samaritans, the Hospital Chaplaincy, the School Chaplaincy and the Chaplaincy to the Cathedral Congregation - all meet fortnightly as a team, under the inspired leadership of Canon Subhir Biswas.

It is clear that, in the 'impossible' situation of Calcutta, the Churches are doing a great job. In such a situation, characterised by 'the paralysis of resignation' - tolerance becoming apathy, then inertia, indifference, carelessness, and then despair - it was good to hear that, out of the general thinking in the last decade in Bengal concerning urban industrial issues, 'Calcutta United Service' started - in July 1970. CUS has acted as a spearhead for the creation of a wider organisation called the Calcutta United Service Consortium - CUSCON. CUS is a Christian body - before the united Church of North India recently came into existence. It started as a co-operative venture of the uniting bodies, with a Roman Catholic 'observer'. CUSCON is a wider body, representative of some twenty-two different voluntary bodies in Calcutta, religious and secular. They had decided that the only way to begin to 'save' Calcutta was to concentrate on one 'bustee' (slum) area at a time; by 'Community Development'; working from the ground up. The Consortium works with the Government and the City

Corporation, and the very local community - trying to attack the problems of poverty, disease, apathy, illiteracy, etc., at their roots; involving the local community itself as fully as possible in a 'pilot' area. The Government and the Planning Organisation allocated a particular area. (The State Government has recently taken over the running of Calcutta from the City authorities.)

I went on from the Cathedral to spend some time with the Senior Development Co-ordinator of CUSCON, Amit Das Gupta. The project is, in fact, now working in several areas, totalling nearly 400,000 people. Of course, it is 'marginal' in terms of the task, but the method of working slowly with the local communities is very important. So much has been lost by plans born and operated from 'on high', with little attempt at really local co-operation. What local clubs and leadership there are have often been completely ignored. The project involves the training of local leadership in the areas concerned, and the recruitment and training of social workers. It also acts as a pressure group upon, for instance, the Welfare Directorate of the State Government, and sees that the local communities are involved in physical planning of their area. They are concerned with everything from nutrition to education, to septic tanks and drains. As a result of their work, various 'clinics' have been opened, distributing, for instance, milk and bread to 1,500 children. There are alarming 'discoveries'. The incidence of leprosy in the Dock area has been found to be way above the national average, itself high. Several organisations are now involved there trying to cope with the 'discovery'.

I could go on about the details of the work - the educational work, for instance. But although the poverty of Calcutta is unique, what needs to be done, and the way it needs to be done, is not all that unique.

What I was particularly interested to hear about was the

problem of getting so many voluntary organisations to work together. I was not surprised to hear that the separate organisations were often reluctant to be subsumed under a 'bridge' organisation and wanted to be known separately as the 'do-ers' of a particular piece of work! But CUSCON undoubtedly has real life and hope. I read through the detailed report on one area of the project, alternately buoyed up by the work that is being done and crushed by the problems - and then buoyed up again. Quote: "Provision of latrines and tap water and a bustee clinic and three slices of bread till the sixth year of a child does not solve anything basically in the bustee problem. So long as the general economy of the bustee people is in a crumbling state the problem remains...." But it is already clear to me that in India there are thousands of educated people - trained engineers, for instance - who have no appropriate employment. The problem of the total economy of India lies not far behind the slums of Calcutta.

Fr Theodore took me from CUSCON to the cemetery in Lower Circular Road, to visit the grave of CF Andrews. The grave, only a few yards away from the traffic, is inscribed with the words: "Known to India as Christ's Faithful Apostle and as Deenabandhu". The House of Mother Teresa's Missionaries of Charity is not far along the same road, No. 54A. We did not go to the House itself, but decided to visit the Home for the Dying Destitutes. It is a disused pilgrims' rest house, the 'dormashalah', attached to the Kali Ghat, a temple dedicated to the cult of the goddess Kali. The main ward is dark, lit by small windows high up in the walls. It reminded me immediately of pictures I had seen of wards full of the wounded at Scutari, and Florence Nightingale visiting the wards - 'the lady with the lamp'. There were three rows of low simple beds - as though in a London ward an extra row had been placed between beds - with a paliasse, a pillow, and a blanket, on each bed. Almost every patient was lying down. Most of them were 'aged'. Those who sat up stared at Fr Theodore and me. The nurses were distributing simple food on plates. I shall remember those stares, but I shall also try to remember the joy of the Sister who received us. In the last few days I have 'bumped into' several of the Sisters about the streets - three were in a taxi which stopped by our jeep at the traffic lights on Sunday. Immediately they were waving joyfully to us - in our while cassocks. It is certainly not the joy of the callous and insensitive. 'Never let anything so fill you with sorrow as to make you forget the joy of Christ Risen' Mother Teresa has written.

We drove back to Behala by the back streets, through the slum districts (if you can separate the slums of Calcutta from the not so slum). Again, part of me was filled with anger that such conditions should exist, and part with admiration at human resilience and vitality. Seldom is a smile not returned to me, a stranger. As a stranger, I cannot give less than a smile to my fellow human being. Thank God it is so rarely rejected.

Theodore had to be back for a rehearsal at 6.30 pm. The orchestra this time had grown to twenty-one boys, ranging from ten to eighteen years old. They were practising a Schubert Rondo. The attention of TV and, significantly, of a journalist, has been given to Mother Teresa's work with those in dramatic need, the dying destitute - and nothing can detract from the magnificence of her work. But I wish that a spotlight could also be turned on a less 'journalistic' subject: those who patiently, over a number of years, try to produce from the material of those in need, in the conditions of this amazing city, human beings who can *survive* in this society, and change it into something nearer the Kingdom. That is what is happening in a very small but marvellous way in this school.

May 16th 1972
Another day of misery and joy. Fr Thorman thought that, since

India is fundamentally her villages, in which eighty per cent of the population live, I ought to see something of the villages surrounding Calcutta. He arranged to drive me out forty miles towards the Bangladesh border, to the home of one of the boys at the school, Samuel Dolman.

But, first, he wanted me to see one of the Leprosy Dispensaries which the Brothers are involved in. We arrived at the clinic in the Acharya Prafulla Chandra Road, and I met the doctors and staff and some of the patients.

I was already beginning to realise that Calcutta must be one of the worst cities in the world for leprosy; but I was astonished to find that the dispensary treats over 8,000 regular patients a year; that there are other organisations which are also treating thousands; but that there are *thousands* who are receiving no treatment.

The treatment is comparatively simple, and the vital drug inexpensive, but it needs careful supervision, and persistence and regularity in treatment, over a long period of time. Amongst the outpatients waiting in the courtyard were several fairly young people.

The Dispensary aims at bringing the best treatment to the poorest, but that inevitably raises problems needing a social worker. Some patients are undernourished, and need milk-powder, and wheat, and oil. Some need their ulcers dealt with, and dead skin removed. Some need physiotherapy. Some need injections. All need diagnosis, and prescription; and often the patients are suffering from more than leprosy. There are considerable administrative problems for a dispensary dealing with so many people, so many of whom are destitute. The Dispensary had dealt with 1,688 new cases during 1971. More than two thirds of the cost of the work came from private funds - not from the Government.

Here I could do little more than give people a smile. I could do what I saw Fr Thorman doing - put my hand on some of them. I could not do less to people whose bodies must seem only a curse to them.

We drove out along the road to Bangladesh, with villages every mile or so, through places where only a few weeks ago nine million refugees were camped. It is an unbelievable immigration and return, unique in history. We stopped on the way, at the house of a former school boy of the Oxford Mission, Prouat Roy. He is much concerned with politics, and had recently returned from seeing Mrs Gandhi. He had helped to oversee the care of 150,000 refugees in the locality, organising local school boys and girls to help with their feeding. He immediately organised care for us too - cool cucumber, and melon, and orange juice. It was very refreshing. (I have stopped recording remarks about the weather, but every day here the temperature is 100 degrees Fahrenheit or over.)

We drove on to Samuel's parents, ten miles from the Bangladesh border. It could not be a fast drive, for often you have to make your way through the village bazaar, and often the village is nearly a town. Samuel's father had just retired from a lifetime as a train driver in Calcutta. Rail fares are cheap in India, and each day, for more than twenty years, he had travelled to and from Calcutta from this village, having bought a little land inexpensively. The trees that were now a tall leafy grove around the house, he had planted. After tea in the shade of the trees, we went into the house, a tiled roof over thick bamboo supports, with plaited bamboo 'walls' - which he had turned into a house church - with candles on the table, and incense burning. This vigorous Gandhi-like old man wanted to give thanks for all the blessings of his life. All his family was gathered round him, the women in beautiful saris, one boy out at work, some still at school. We were a large company. Fr Thorman led the prayers, then the old man. Afterwards we were given lunch under the trees, and then slept for a while on tables under the trees, that had been provided for all, with a cloth and a pillow! The heat was terrific and I needed no encouragement to nod off. No family could have been more courteous, and I felt real affection for them as I took leave of them.

The forty or so miles travelling in the Ganges Delta had taken more than three hours in the morning, but the journey home was quicker. The rice fields, where there was irrigation and the trees lining the road, where there was often a canal or a 'tank', looked a vivid green in the evening light; but much of Bengal is suffering from really serious drought. The bones of the cattle were often only thinly covered with flesh. But the poverty of the village people - so evident when they come into Calcutta - is disguised in the village. In a village, there is nearly always *something* to eat and someone who will feel some obligation to you in the hierarchy of caste and custom. The 'outing' was a happy occasion, not least because Fr Thorman had invited two of the other Brothers to come, Fr Leonard Whitcombe, who is one of the liveliest eighty-six year-olds I have ever met, and Fr Biren Rai Chandhuri. It has been of huge benefit to be able to share the life of this family of Brothers, and to profit from their experience. Fr Whitcombe has been out here since 1921 - four years before I was born! None of the European Brothers has been here less than twenty five years. They have 'stayed with it'.

In the evening, a last evening of music-making. How I have loved it!

May 17th 1972
I was privileged to celebrate the Holy Communion this morning in the Brothers' Chapel. It means something to have

one's feet on Indian soil as one celebrates; and the liturgy says much that is in one's heart about this place which is too deep for words. Before I left Behala, the Secretary of the CF Andrews Centenary Committee, Shri Bansal, came to see me with several gifts of literature produced by the Committee. I am glad I came to India with a real 'attraction' to and strong links with CFA: 'Christ's Faithful Apostle'. It is a real 'point of contact' with Indians, and not simply with Indian Christians. Bansal told me a lot about what it meant as an Indian to be taught by Andrews.

In one of the books, the Visvabharati Quarterly, there is a hitherto unpublished letter of CF Andrews to 'Gurudev', Rabindranath Tagore, on his birthday. It covers twenty pages of print. It is, quite simply, a love letter, gathering up all that Tagore means to him. Tagore, in an address at the time of Andrews' funeral, says "Such a rare companionship of soul existed between Andrews and me. Coming unsought, it was a gift of God beyond price." But not only Tagore, Gandhi himself, and Sushil Rudra, would also have put their friendship with Andrews as central to their life. Gandhi wrote to Andrews one day: "I have missed you every moment today; O your love!" And, after Andrews' death, he wrote: "He was love incarnate."

It has helped, as one has wandered about this multitudinous world of Calcutta, to know one has been walking in the steps of 'Charlie' Andrews, who, though he was often surrounded by the multitudes, and dealt with matters which would make for or against the life and liberty of the many, remained essentially a friend of individuals, one to one.

If I leave this frightening yet fascinating city wanting to return to it, it is not least because, amongst others, Andrews has taught me just a little to think of what lies within the rags on the pavement.

Outside the place in Calcutta where you get the coach to the airport, several bundles of humanity lay stretched out on the pavement in the sweltering heat, at half-past three in the afternoon. I wondered what Andrews would have thought - would have done. I remembered my favourite lines of his:

> "There he crouched,
> Back and arms scarred, like a hunted thing,
> Terror-stricken.
> All within me surged towards him,
> While the tears rushed.
> Then, a change.
> Through his eyes I saw Thy glorious face -
> Ah, the wonder!
> Calm, unveiled in deathless beauty,
> Lord of sorrow."

But I'm no Andrews. Like most people, I can only feel appalled, helpless, and want to do something, somehow. God knows how.

Stage 17: Delhi

May 18th 1972

A wall of heat met us as the door of the aircraft was opened on landing at Delhi. It was half past eight, and dark - with a crescent moon in the sky. I took the coach from the airport to the centre of Delhi. Even in the darkness, the contrast with Calcutta was astounding. I suddenly realised that in Calcutta I had seen very little stone, except the marble of the Victoria memorial and the National Library; but when Delhi was changed by royal proclamation into the Imperial capital, at the great Durbar in 1911, a site two and a half miles to the south of the southern wall of the old city was selected for a new city, and Sir Edwin Lutyens and Sir Herbert Baker were commissioned to plan it. It was built in stone. As the coach swung along wide roads, we looked out on to the neat detached houses of civil servants; on small blocks of apartments, new hotels; on stone, new brick, concrete, glass, chromium, multi-storied buildings, modern sculpture, imaginatively designed and illuminated fountains, buildings of grandeur and simplicity - on New Delhi. Ian Weathrall, with whom I had been a student at King's College, London, had given me clear instructions how to get to the Brotherhood House of the Cambridge Mission to Delhi, where he is in charge. "Tell the driver that Court Lane runs off Court Road, opposite the old Police Lines, near Mori Gate, in Old Delhi" he had said. I did: and the taxi driver soon had me safely delivered.

The Brotherhood House is of stone - a chapel, a library, a refectory, rooms for the Brothers and a guest house. I was glad now to be with 'the Cambridge Brotherhood'. It had been founded in 1877, when two members of the University came to Delhi, shortly to be followed by four more. One of them founded St Stephen's College; some of them ministered in parishes; others engaged in dialogue with men of other faiths. It was to the Brotherhood, and to teach at St Stephen's College, that CF Andrews had come in 1904.

The Diocesan Council was meeting that evening - the Diocese of Delhi, (bringing together, since November 1970, Anglicans, Baptists, the United Church of North India, Methodists, Brethren, and Disciples of Christ) - so the house was full of guests. I retired almost immediately, but it was a very hot night indeed, and the day that followed was burning hot - 119 degrees Fahrenheit. In the days of the British Raj, the Government spent the summer in Simla; nowadays the Government stays here, where the people have always had to stay; but the heat certainly is unbearable. I decided to stay in all day, reading. I whipped through *Political Prospects in India* by Saral K Chatterji and *The Indian Church* by Mathai Zachariah; and, in the cool (?) of the evening, Ian took me for a walk round Old Delhi, full of crowded bazaars, much more like Calcutta, and revealing Delhi to be one of the most ancient and historic cities of India.

At 8.00 pm, I was collected for dinner with the Principal of St Stephen's College and his wife. He had been at Trinity Hall, Cambridge, and Westcott House. He had some fascinating guests, some of the staff at the College, and a doctor and his wife involved in Family Planning here through the World Health Organisation. I fastened on to the head of the Central Institute of Education, Delhi University, Dr Roy, who told me a good deal about Education in India.

It is a remarkable fact that under Christian management there are in India over 90 first grade colleges for men and women, 800 high schools, 1,500 middle schools, and thousands of primary and elementary schools. If it had not been for the Missions, one wonders what would have been done about the education of women until very recently - not that much is done now. Christians in India still are in charge of 400 hospitals and about 800 dispensaries - besides the Christian Medical College at Vellore. Hinduism has tended to hold up the development of social work - which would interfere with people's 'ordained' condition. It is this which has made the social enterprises of the Christians of particular importance - the foundation of orphanages, houses for the aged and the incapacitated, sanatoria and dispensaries for lepers and for tuberculosis patients, and now, social casework and Community Development. Under the present 'secular government' there is considerably more secularly based social work.

May 19th 1972

It was as hot as ever, but Ian and I spent three fascinating hours in the city this morning, which left me half dead. There is a separate lamp shade bazaar, another for furniture, and another for 'scrap' - metal, tyres etc. Indeed, Delhi is, amongst other things, a collection of different bazaars. Ian has been in Delhi for twenty one years, as a priest, besides his time in India in the army, and has a fund of experience which I draw on heavily. He is able to suggest a dozen books on every aspect of Indian life, and the sweltering hours are good for reading - behind drawn blinds, with all the fans on. For example, today: Arthur Koestler's The Lotus and the Robot.

In the evening, I had a marvellous walk with Amos Rajomoney, a young Indian priest, another member of the Cambridge Brotherhood. He took me, first, to a Buddhist temple on the banks of the Jamuna river. It was utterly silent; one American student sitting cross-legged, meditating. It is to this temple in Delhi, more than any other place, that people who come from the West, seeking, have tended to come. There is a hostel where people can stay. The tapestries on the wall, complex embroidery pictures of scenes in the life of Buddha, were rich in evocative detail. It was the first place of worship, Hindu or Buddhist, that I have yet discovered in the East which has suggested that in the religion of the East there is a way of sanctity. In the Hindu and Buddhist temples, I have seen that there has been noise and little or no reverence. But is this 'place by the river', a source of world-transformation or simply of escape? I cannot have much respect for a religion in India which evades the slums; as much of it seems to have done.

This afternoon I came across an intriguing passage in *The Continent of Circe* by Nirad C Chaudhuri: 'Occidentals come from a clean and tidy material world, in which dirt, squalor, and disorder are sins. But I declare every day that a man who cannot endure dirt, dust, stench, noise, ugliness, disorder, heat, and cold has no right to live in India until he has conquered squeamishness to the point of being indifferent to the presence of fifty lepers in various stages of decomposition within a hundred yards, or not minding the sight of ubiquitous human excretion everywhere, even in a big city."

It is an eloquent plea for indifference, and though it says something important - and there is an element of humour in it - it is directly opposed to what I believe as a Christian.

He goes on to say: "I at least can claim that I have not run away from any of these. For the last twenty years I have lived in a part of old Delhi where none of the makers of new India ever visit me, not only because that would be physically unpleasant to them, but also for the reason that it would be socially derogatory. Yet I have not moved out, nor will."

Some of the makers of new India, against whom the shaft is aimed, have, of course, been upper middle and upper class English Christians, who preached involvement but practised indifference.

Amos and I walked further along the river bank as dusk descended. It has recently been made a series of rather beautiful public gardens. The city has spilled across the wide Jamuna, but from the city side the far side appears to be one flat plain. We walked along the river bank until we came to a 'ghat' by the river where three dead bodies were still burning in the open.

May 20th 1972

It has been another scorching day. I went into the city - old Delhi and New Delhi - for a couple of hours, but I felt weak with the heat. I am getting the feel of the place by travelling around in the new form of rickshaw, odd open three-wheel taxis, more like chauffeur-driven mobile invalid chairs! These great Indian cities must be nightmares to the authorities. Delhi is now four million people. Thirty years ago it was less than a million.. Four years ago it was estimated the population would be five million by 1981 but that estimate has just been revised to 6,724,000. Think of the difference that makes in terms of housing, sanitation, water, electricity, transport, hospitals, schools, social services. As I went round this morning, and came up against the language barrier, I thought of the Indians who do not speak Hindi here - there are fourteen major languages to the 547 million people of India. So many of the people who are coming into Delhi, come from places in India many miles from Delhi.

I have to preach in the Cathedral tomorrow, Whitsunday. I count this a very great privilege, and I have spent most of the day working on the sermon. I have decided to preach on the text which has been in my mind ever since New Year's Eve in Nigeria: "Can a man be born when he is old? Can he enter a second time into his mother's womb and be born?" I want to preach on Rebirth (a) for individuals (b) for the Church (c) for the nation.

I walked to the river again this evening with one of the Brothers here, Kenneth Clark. We went into the Buddhist temple again, which I find a very powerful place. I thought tonight of Leonard Cohen's song,

> "Suzanne takes you down to a place by the river
> You can see the boats go by...."

for beside the statue of Buddha tonight there were 'Tea and Oranges that come all the way from China'. We walked back through some very lovely gardens. The dust made the setting sun a pale white ball in a yellow grey haze, I read today, 'To find the One in the Many is the eternal quest of the *East*'. I was told many years ago by Eric Abbott: "You will spend your life learning how to find the One in the Many", but I had never particularly associated that quest with the East, and I have yet to discover what special light Hinduism or Buddhism have to shed on what is a fundamental subject for me. So far, I have found that what looks at first sight in the East to be about 'finding' turns out to be more about 'losing' - loss of one's identity - though, as Jesus made plain, there is a paradox here. "He who would lose his life for my sake shall find it...." Travelling around these five months has introduced me to so many - to so many more: to the problem of 'the One and the Many' in an acute form. It could have been an agonising experience, though it has had its agony, it has not been primarily agonising. It could also have been an experience of too easy meeting and departing, surface meeting only, avoiding the agony, by 'indifference'. I do not think it has been that either.

Hammarskjøld talks of 'the *freedom* of the continual farewell', received in 'unconditional obedience', hourly surrender, to the demands of the situation. I have begun to understand a little what he means.

Before I turn in I shall go and have my fourth shower of the day. Perhaps the Hindu's bathing may not be quite as 'obsessive' as I first thought. Kipling (how he knew this place and the Englishman in India!) wrote,

> 'Wash daily from nose-tip to tail-tip; drink deeply but never too deep;
> And remember the night is for hunting, and forget not the day is for sleep.

May 21st 1972 – Whitsunday

It was a great joy to preach in the Cathedral. I had seen a good deal of the plans and drawing of it twenty years ago. When I was a curate, one of the congregation of St Stephen's, Westminster, was the architect, H.A.N. Medd. He won the prize in the competition of architects for the new Cathedral in 1925. The main selector was Sir Edwin Lutyens, and it is very much in his style, and so fits in with the rest of New Delhi. (The Lutyens-Baker style of New Delhi both pleases and embarrasses Indians today, I find. On the one hand they are proud of its dignity; on the other, it could not signify more clearly the domination of an Imperial power. It is quite alien to any Indian style.) The Cathedral meant much to Lord Halifax when he was Viceroy, 1926/31, (then Lord Irwin), and it is interesting to find that he is the Viceroy whom today people still think of as giving a *spiritual* lead. (He and Gandhi were on terms of personal friendship.) He used to walk to daily Communion at the Cathedral. It was Lord Irwin who chiefly saw to it that the Cathedral was built.

Michael Wimshurst, now at St Peter's, Battersea, and recently for a short spell at Southwark Cathedral, served at the Cathedral during his time in India, and was well remembered by many of the congregation. I found the service most moving. (The hymn to the Holy Spirit, *Veni, Sancte Spiritus*, seemed to be specially topical when it referred to 'grateful coolness in the heat', but later, I noticed, we were employing the contradictory symbol of Fire with reference to the same Person of the Trinity. Very paradoxical!) I think this Whitsunday service meant much to me not least because I am beginning to feel that the time has come to 'gather up the fragments' of this journey, and I was able to employ Dag Hammarskjøld's Whitsunday 1961 entry in his journal in my sermon with a heartfelt conviction. He had written on that day: "I don't know Who - or what - put the question, I don't know when it was put. I don't even remember answering. But at some moment I did answer *Yes* to Someone - or Something - and from that hour I was certain that existence is meaningful, and that, therefore, my life, in self-surrender, had a goal. From that moment I have known what it means 'not to look back', and 'to take no thought for the morrow'.

I went from the Cathedral to St Stephen's College, to see Dan O'Connor (a Cuddesdon friend and contemporary of Patrick Miller). He has recently edited an Andrews Centenary Number of the College Magazine, which I am glad to possess. In it there is a photograph of the Games Committee of 1913, which has CF Andrews (Cricket) sitting next to FA Cockin (Hockey). The latter was eventually Bishop of Bristol.

On this memorable Whitsunday evening, Fr Amos took me out of Delhi about eight miles across the Jamuna river, to a village which was entirely composed of lepers - about 300 of them. We first walked around their little houses to greet them. They were of all ages, and the leprosy had attacked them in different places. Some had stubs for arms; others, no fingers; others, a stub of a leg, or no legs, or no toes; some were affected in their eyes, with not much left for eyes at all; some had the leprosy on their flesh. Some hopped, some dragged themselves along the ground to where we were talking. The leprosy was in most cases no longer active. We held a Communion Service in their minute church. It was full and overflowing. The sweat was pouring off me in pints, and I was very touched when one of the lepers passed his fan to me - he was sweating just as much as I was. Amos celebrated the Communion. I spoke to the people and Amos translated. I couldn't say much, except that we were brothers, and that although they spoke Tamil and I spoke English, the language of God's love in us - on that Whitsunday evening - made us understand each other, and was a bond between us. I had the hope that somehow one's smile and the look in one's eyes might convey to people the greetings in one's heart, telling them, unknown to each other as we were, and meeting by a strange chance, that they were not just strangers but recognised, and loved as valuable, and that we belonged to one another in some odd way. Certainly they responded marvellously - the little boys and girls, the teenagers, the grown-up men and women. It was a huge privilege to be with them, and to be allowed to say to them what one was trying to say, whilst at the same time feeling it was a huge impertinence too. How could I meaningfully say that I valued them? And yet that's what that Holy Communion was all about.

And their history alone made me long to say something like that to them. They were all from the Madras area in the South of India. Until a short while before, they had earned some kind of existence by begging in the streets of Delhi. Then begging was banned in Delhi, and their livelihood was taken away. Fr Ian Weathrall, the Superior of the Brotherhood, had discovered them - through a funeral of one of their number which they had asked him to take - living then on the banks of the Jamuna.

The Delhi authorities eventually transported them to the village I was visiting, and provided some kind of basic grant-aid on which they could just about survive. But their leprosy meant they were either cut off from or by their relatives. Often, the Hindu community at large thinks the leper is someone who, for reasons best known to the gods, is rejected by them. Alternatively, leprosy is assumed to be tertiary syphilis. All of this was good reason to try and say in any language available "You are very valuable." I was deeply thankful for this great privilege this Whitsunday. It was an unforgettable Holy Communion. As we got into the car, the people stood and waved and smiled. Amos and I could only grip each other's hands.

May 22nd 1972

I am a very bad 'tourist'. Mercifully I have not needed to make many special sight-seeing expeditions in the last months. But everyone here, Indian and European, has said "You simply must go to Agra to see the Taj Mahal". I wondered very much, especially with the terrific heat. But I have no doubt now they were right.

There is a special tourist train, 'The Taj Express', which connects Agra and Delhi. A luxury air-conditioned express, it leaves Delhi in the morning, returns at night, and has a dining car attached. So, after the hottest night so far - never less than 91 degrees Fahrenheit (I got up and had a shower in the middle of the night!) - I left the Brotherhood House at 6.30 am for New Delhi Station. The sky was overcast, but it was still frightfully hot, for a dust storm was threatening. (The hot wind was blowing from the deserts of Rajasthan - like the Harmattan in Nigeria.)

I was glad to be travelling by rail, for I had not yet had an opportunity of travelling on India's railways. At 6.45 am New

Delhi Station was as crowded as London Bridge Station at 8.45 am. From the cool seclusion of my compartment in the luxury express, I looked out onto packed trains, with people literally clinging to the outsides of them. We travelled through a world which was quite different from any I had set eyes on. The Indian Government is doing a good deal to irrigate the land, but the overall impression of the country between Delhi and Agra is still one of arid waste, interspersed with green, where there is a canal or a dyke. The farming you look out on is primitive - people in the fields bending over their hoes. The rural villages are usually mud and straw hovels, in varying states of collapse. There is the pitiless sky above. Life here is utterly dependent on the coming of the monsoon. Immediately outside Delhi you see the urban slums, and around each station at which you stop there is usually a fragmentary, poverty-stricken world. But for most of the way it is oxen, cows, a well, a shrine, scrub-like trees and barren land from which only a bare and meagre existence can possibly be gained. Vultures, which render great service by speedily disposing of the carcasses of domestic animals, are very common, but today I saw, from the train, herons, storks and kestrels and a host of birds my bird-watching friends would have enjoyed spotting.

At Agra, we got into an Uttar Pradesh Department of Tourism coach, and were driven twenty-two miles to the South West to Fatehpur Sikri, now a deserted city, a collection of mosques and palaces. Sikri is India's Pompeii. The building of it was begun in 1569 during the time of Akbar. He lived in it only sixteen years - probably because of the shortage of water. There seems to have been no shortage of stonecutters, red sandstone, white marble, mother-of-pearl - and concubines! It is a place of superb craftsmanship, and all very 'Arabian Nights'.

I had met up with a British lad in the coach, Charles Mynors, teaching in India for a year, who had finished at Eton and was just going to Corpus Christi College, Cambridge. He had dysentery, and could only watch me eat my lunch in the restaurant at Agra. However, to those with a disturbed stomach in India, a good restaurant may also provide a much desired convenience that is not the purgatory to use that some Indian lavatories are. His luck was in, as well as out.

After lunch, we went round the Red Fort - similar to the Red Fort in Delhi. More exquisite marble and red sandstone, with breathtaking views of the Taj Mahal - through the stone tracery - a couple of miles away along the Jamuna.

Finally, the Taj Mahal itself. It is really the mausoleum of the wife of the Emperor Shah Jahan (1627-1658), who died in childbirth. I have never seen any building more beautiful. The central mausoleum is surrounded by beautifully laid out gardens - thanks to Lord Curzon, who did a great deal when he was Viceroy to see that India preserved its historic buildings, which were falling into disrepair. It is all white, and, set against the surrounding buildings, two red mosque-like structures to the east and to the west, with the sun blazing upon it from clear skies, it looked like a symbol in stone of utter purity.

But we were back at the station at 6.30 pm with the Delhi train awaiting us. Wandering around stone buildings, and treading on burning hot stone pavements - it was 113 degrees Fahrenheit - had been exhausting. India's various tourist departments could not have done better. As we drove into Delhi you could see the shadows of a city bedding down for the night in the open. I was back at the Brotherhood by 10.30 pm, having set eyes on what is without doubt one of the Wonders of the World.

May 23rd 1972
I have had rather a 'top people' last day in Delhi today. I lunched with the Moderator of the Church of North India, Eric Nasir,

who is also Bishop of Delhi, and went on to see Professor A Kisku, who is the Deputy Minister of Health in the Indian Government. The Bishop could not have been more kind, gentle and gracious. I gather he makes an excellent Chairman in this important period in the Church's life, when people of different traditions have to be helped to work together in the newly united church. I have only been in Delhi a matter of days - and the intense heat has prevented my seeing as much as I would liked to have done; so firm conclusions would be unwise; but I have to confess to a certain disappointment. Perhaps a church which has just united is bound to be considerably absorbed in its own affairs. One would hope it was also a time for imagination and adventure. I have seen few signs in Delhi of a Church abreast of the times - or ahead of them. I have been told often enough that what is required is patience: 'Festina Lente', the quiet on-going ministry, not too many specialist ministries etc. And one must remember there are only 30,000 Christians in Delhi. But I can only contrast this with Professor Kisku's approach. It is true, he gave very high praise to the Church - he is a Christian himself - for what it does *in India as whole*, efficiently, without corruption, and in close touch with the ground level of society. He said that the Christian community was an intelligent and compassionate body, the greatness of whose influence is out of all proportion to its numbers. But there was a dynamism and urgency about Professor Kisku which I had not met in the Church in Delhi. He talked about the necessity for Community Development work, especially in rural India, and about Family Planning, to be treated as one aspect of work with the family in community. The difficulties of promoting family planning amongst illiterate peoples are huge, and particularly amongst Moslems and Hindus. The Hindu , for instance, thinks it very important to have a son - to bury his father. Until a son is born, no family planning; and probably until a second son is born (for insurance purposes). Professor Kisku impressed me very greatly. He talked much of the quite new society which is arising in India, one aware of its rights. He reminded me of Nkambo. He had the light of battle with a nation's social problems in his eyes.

Whether Mrs Gandhi and the Indian form of democracy will win the battle remains to be seen. In the India I have already seen - Calcutta, Delhi and some rural areas - the problems are mountainous. If, with her new majority, Mrs Gandhi does not give real evidence of surmounting some of the problems, a more radical and totalitarian government is almost bound to arise - though there are few signs of any effective alternative at the moment. It is the Gandhi - Nehru - Shastri - Gandhi dynasty's last chance.

May 24th 1972

I went to bed at 9.00 pm last night, immediately after supper and a final walk and talk with Amos. In spite of the heat, I slept until 3.00 am. I got up and said my farewells to Ian, who has been a meticulously kind host; and a taxi had deposited me at the Indian Airways office in New Delhi by 4.30 am. The flight to Bangalore was mainly over the baked and arid wastes of the Deccan, across which silver winding rivers ran, the Narmada, the Godavari and the Krishna. Clouds intermittently obscured our view, heralding the approach of the monsoon, and the end of the punishing heat. The *Times of India* today reports 360 deaths from the heat in the last fortnight, in North India alone.

We came in to land at Hyderabad, over villages isolated in a patchwork of fields of red parched earth, and then flew on to Bangalore. In England, we live for the sun. In India, they live for - and by - the rain.

Stage 18: Bangalore

May 25th 1972

To be in Bangalore after Delhi and Calcutta is like being in Provence after being in Manchester and Birmingham. The houses are mostly red tiled, with thick white walls. The surrounding villages and compounds look neat and compact from the air. There is not that terrible density of population. The taxi drivers have some respect for each other and for pedestrians. It is altogether more civilised and spacious. It strikes you as a pleasant place in the sun. (One brochure described it as 'the Garden City of India'!) Of course, the slums are not too difficult to find. India's poverty is ubiquitous. But it is a relief for a while to be out of the grinding poverty, and the gruelling sun and the bewildering chaos of the great cities. Bangalore is 3,000 feet above sea level, and the climate is all one could wish. We are down to a cool 93 degrees Fahrenheit. But the place is deceptive. Delhi is a relief after Calcutta, but turns out to be concealing its disorders. There is no hiding Calcutta's ills. Bangalore, too, has many more problems than appear on the surface. As late as 1940 it could not be called an Industrial City, though a few textile mills and Mysore Government Industries existed at that time. It was known as a 'pensioner's paradise', where residential facilities and cheapness of vegetables contributed to comfortable living at low cost. That is still its top surface, in the centre of the town - wide avenues off a main street; flowering trees - flame, jacaranda, cassia, laburnum, tamarisk, etc; large separate houses; parks the size of Hyde Park. Then you discover Hindustan Aircraft Ltd., 18,000 employees; Indian Telephone Industries, 13,000; Hindustan Machine Tools, 7,400; Bharat Electronics Ltd., 9,000; Bharat Earth Movers, 4,700 - all established since 1940, when there were 15,000 workers out of a total population of 50,000. Now the total population is 1,648,232 (thirty to thirty-five percent Kannaren, thirty to thirty-five per cent Tamil, and the rest a mixture of other groups). The sudden growth after 1940 has made it difficult for the State Government and the Corporation to tackle several problems, eg transport, housing. Most of the industries are on the fringe of the city and have provided their own transport, and their own housing 'colonies'. But the rate of growth of the industrial population is greater than the rate of construction of houses, and many new workers coming to Bangalore have very great difficulty finding accommodation.

I wanted to come to Bangalore for several reasons. I wanted to visit a city in South India which I had heard was so different from the North. I wanted to see a city whose rate of expansion rivalled Delhi's. I wanted to visit the place where the Christian Institute for the Study of Religion and Society has been based since it was established in 1960, and also where, from all reports, there was as good an Industrial 'Mission', (though they have avoided the term) based on St Mark's Cathedral, as anywhere in the world. Bangalore is in many ways the Rome of Christian India. (There are six Roman Catholic seminaries alone.) But I doubt whether I would have come had I not had a good friend to stay with. Alan Batchelor has been a member of the Industrial Team for eight years. I first knew him when he lived in Westminster, when I was a curate. He was a student at Bristol University then, before going to Lincoln Theological College. In his curacy at Hull he did a thesis on ST Coleridge, FD Maurice and Westcott, on Christian Social Theology.

When I arrived, Alan was away for the day at Neyveli, 200 miles away, setting up a programme for a big company which has problems in both labour relations and management. But he had arranged for Francis, who cooks for him, and Leon, a twenty year-old Singalese (who has absconded from college after a row with his father, and has no job, no income and no accommodation!) to collect me and look after me. (Alan's wife, an Indian, was out at work with the Public Transport Corporation. They have been married for only two years.)

I again decided to spend the day 'reading myself in', but Leon took me first to the Museum of Industry, and walked me around the centre of town. Then I got down to *Human Problems of Industry in Bangalore, The Pace of Modern Change - The Changing Family and Social Life of Immigrants to an Industrial Housing Colony in Bangalore* and - a third joint publication of the Christian Institute and the Industrial Team - *Leaders and Leadership in the Trade Unions in Bangalore* by Julian Reindorp. You could have 'knocked me down with a feather' when I saw the author's name attached to the third book. George Reindorp, Julian's father, now Bishop of Guildford, was my vicar when I was a curate. Julian I have therefore known for more than twenty years (ie since he was about six). I have watched him go from school to school, and then to Trinity College, Cambridge, to India for a year, and then to be ordained to a curacy in Poplar. But *Leaders and Leadership in the Trade Unions in Bangalore* !! I chuckled to myself, and read on. It is, in fact, a first rate and fascinating piece of work from any angle, that makes me a valid judge - and shows just what can be done with a year abroad. (I have also read three reviews from the Indian Press which give it a warm welcome.) The lack of education of most of the workers gives a far greater importance to the educated leaders of Trades Unions here than in more developed countries. The eleven leaders interviewed were Communists, Christians (Roman Catholics and Protestants), and Hindus.

In the late afternoon I went for a walk with Leon to the Town Hall to get population figures, etc. The enquiry resulted in an hour and a half's fascinating walk round the back streets of Bangalore, trying to track down the appropriate department, which was not housed in the Town Hall. Having got up at 3.15 am I decided to go to bed early.

Alan returned in the morning and set me some homework (a) 'India's Fourth Five Year Plan 1969-74'. The mind reels at the population problem. India has to reckon that her population will be 890 million in the year 2,000. Of course, there are many variables, (b) 'India's Urban Future'. (Did you realise that our word 'bungalow' came from the Bengali 'bangla' - eg Bangla Desh, and 'verandah' from the Hindi 'baranda'?) The split between the westernised elite and the mass of the people in India's urban areas is even greater than the class split in England. Not only has one to take note of the population increase in India but also the particular increase of population in urban areas, of which Bangalore is a good example. It is this which makes the prospects for the big cities daunting - though India is trying to locate her new industries away from the present big cities. In the afternoon I went for a walk to the Mysore State Library, in the middle of one of the beautiful parks, ablaze with blossoming trees. The Library was crammed with Indians at work. It is difficult for English people to realise how lucky we are to have houses in which it is easy to study.

This evening, when Alan was out, a priest from Bangladesh called. He was looking for a house which he could not find. While we were waiting for Alan we talked about Bangladesh now - the rising prices; the disorder - people using the guns they had in the war; the profiteers. We talked of his experience as a refugee, having to bring his family out of Bangladesh and return. (It is amazing what human beings can survive.) And then, as a ridiculously long shot, I mentioned the only person from Bangladesh I knew something about - a boy of Mohammedan parents, who had had an enlarged head as a child. His superstitious parents had taken this as a sign of evil and had rejected the child after terribly ill-treating it. The boy had virtually been in the care of the Oxford Mission to Calcutta. He had just gone back to Bangladesh, to Dacca. I asked the priest whether by any chance he knew of the lad. "Yes, I know him well. He stayed with me and my family his first night in Dacca. He is alright. His parents have now accepted him again. They see he is a good boy." It is so odd that in this multitudinous world, of such vast distances - Dacca must be well over a thousand miles as the crow flies from Bangalore - a casual meeting can make a small world in which people know one another. Of course, wherever you have a minority movement, like the Christians in India, you have a kind of close-knit club within that area.

May 26th 1972

I spent this morning with Alan at the Indian Social Institute, a Roman Catholic establishment. Just under twenty professors from their Catholic seminaries all over India, more than half of them Indians, had gathered to discuss how they could relate the training of ordinands in India more closely to the urban world. I felt very privileged to be 'let loose' on such a highly qualified group. They responded very well, and I received a lot from them. I learnt, for instance, of Roman Catholic training in Brazil, where ordinands are sent out to work in groups of six in the cities, earning their living. They do their theology on the basis of this experience. The prophets of gloom had said they would lose the ordinands this way. They did - for the first four years - eighty per cent of them. But now the 'image' of the training is so good that it attracts more ordinands than before, and loses fewer. A different kind of ordinand is, of course, attracted.

It was good to hear Alan speaking, too. I realise that (as with Theodore Woods) my mental picture of him was of an undergraduate twenty years ago, and that a lot of development had taken place which I hadn't anticipated.

One of the Indians pressed the question: "Hasn't the Bangalese Industrial Team become almost exclusively concerned with leaders and managers in industry rather than with 'the masses'?" I did not think Alan was able to answer this satisfactorily. It is sad, but true, that not only the parochial ministry fails to reach 'the masses', but when Industrial 'Mission' is set up, all too often it, too, only manages to get alongside the 'principalities and powers' - though that is an achievement.

I had another 'small world' experience this afternoon. I went to the National and Grindlays Bank in Bangalore at 2.45 pm to cash a Traveller's cheque. The bank was closed at 2.30 pm, but they took pity on this ignorant Englishman and said I was to go and see the Manager. He gave one look at my passport, with Date and Place of Birth, and said, "We were born within a year of each other in Chadwell Heath. Where did you go to school?" I told him I went first to the little two-form primary school, Ford's Endowed School, in Whalebone Lane. He said "So did I". He lived in Whalebone Grove until his parents moved when he was seven. He, John Watts, and I must have been at the school at the same time, under Miss Jenkinson and Miss Chipperfield! We were able to reel off names we both remembered in these infant's classes - Graham Catterall, Ernest Trayler, etc. He had just been transferred to Bangalore from Colombo. I suppose a mathematician could very easily account for this coincidence. I still find such events unnerving - we could so easily *not* have met. (Though, as far as I know, there was no particular 'point' to the meeting.)

In the evening, I met with a group of Christians in middle

management in Bangalore - all Indians, with the exception of two Germans. It was an interesting group. In the morning session, someone had said, "Indians have a great capacity to keep in separate worlds work and religion" - meaning Hindus. I tried to investigate whether these Christian managers did likewise. At one point, one of the Indians protested "Oh, but family planning is very *personal*. I don't see what that has to do with holiness."!! I said, of course, that just because it is so personal it has a great deal to do with holiness, and also because it is not simply personal but social. I learnt later than this particular man, a senior civil servant, is a Roman Catholic. It was a very profitable evening. I learnt a lot about Indian attitudes.

Alan has been driving me around the town on the back of his scooter. It is a very good way of getting about this place, very free and refreshing. At 9.30 pm we drove to one of the local cinemas to see *Waterloo*. I would have preferred to see an Indian film - like those of Satya Jit Ray, but the only Indian films that were showing were rubbish. India has a huge popular film industry - cinemas are still growing in number; but a film of quality, like a Satya Jit Ray, is a rarity. There is, of course, the language difficulty. There are no great Tamil film producers. Most of the films here are 'escapist' - palaces etc., plus a few songs and dances in idyllic surroundings. Kissing is forbidden on the screen, but that doesn't mean you can't be 'suggestive' in other ways.

The conflict between a very structured and authoritarian top surface and all sorts of explosive psychological and social forces not far below the surface - which is fast cracking - is most marked. It came out in the discussion with the managers this evening, though it has cropped up again and again since I've been here.

For instance, in sexual matters there is this 'no kissing on the screen' attitude, whilst the temple decorations are notorious for their voluptuousness, and the people themselves are undoubtedly of a highly emotional and erotic nature. There is often extraordinary ignorance of the 'facts of life', because one does not talk about such things. (Yet this is Karma Sutra country!) There is a great prurience and sexual guilt. Sex is a regrettable necessity. Abstinence is virtue (which makes women second-rate, as the fundamental seducers). In the traditional world there is segregation of the sexes in the home - the men are distinctly uncomfortable in the company of women, and *vice versa*. The unmarried woman - who is not a 'bad' girl - is chaperoned. The film is therefore one way in which you can sample the non-traditional relationship between opposite sexes vicariously. There is very little 'friendship' between husband and wife, with relaxed conversation and communication - as distinct from general family life together - and with a large family in a small house there is not a great deal to encourage it. This itself creates difficulties for Family Planning, in which there needs to be at least some minimal discussion and consultation between husband and wife. The film, college life, urban life and other factors are breaking down this pattern. Father-son relationships are basically authoritarian in the old tradition - a barrage of prohibitions and threats - which (the managers averred tonight) in no way imply rejection by the parent or lack of affection. The traditional family is, in fact, very close-knit. (Gandhi is an interesting example here. He issued orders, often very bad ones, to his sons, and they left him.) It is both the close-knit-ness of the family and the authoritarian father which the son may want to escape from to the anonymity of the city. But he has not been trained to stand on his own feet and is often lost in the city. (In this, India may not be particularly different from the English working-class family set-up. Alf Garnett and Gandhi have a lot in common.) The effects of urbanisation on the traditional pattern are probably slower in India than in England because there is a curious overlap between the urban and the rural. Parts of Calcutta and Delhi - and to some extent Bangalore - look like places into which the village and the villagers have moved, retaining their way of life. They often migrate in large groups. It is not that the villagers are just what they were - urbanisation is changing them - or that the towns are 'rural towns'. The effects of urbanisation are great, and the pace of the changes they effect accelerates, but people hold on to their rural patterns with a very considerable tenacity.

May 27th 1972

Alan and I went today to the last day of a management course for representatives of technical training institutes for socially deprived people which he has helped to initiate. There were about twenty Indians there, and I was glad to be with them now that I have quite a wide 'nodding' experience of such institutions in Nigeria, Uganda, the Solomons, Hong Kong and Calcutta etc. The course was geared to helping people responsible for such institutions to sort out and achieve their objectives. But this raised important questions. Can the objective of such an institution be purely technical? The psy-chological damage to deprived students will often be great. Who copes with that? And how? If the objective is not only to provide technical skills but to enable orphans, people of low caste, etc. to survive, and, indeed, to thrive in the world, this involves the question of placements in employment (or capital to run their own businesses). It will mean training for life in the world (hence, for instance, the orchestra at Barisha). It will mean giving administrative experience, and preparing a person to survive in the world without the protection of the institution. All sorts of questions came up, like 'student partici-pation' in setting the goals of such institutions, ie the community's participation in plans for its own development.

Just those twenty people represented a great many young Indian boys and girls whose lives are being salvaged. I was glad to have the opportunity to sit in on and briefly to address the gathering.

I spent the remainder of the day working on a sermon for the ordination in the Cathedral tomorrow. I am particularly privileged to be able to preach at an ordination in the Church of South India. It is twenty-five years now since it became a united church of Methodists, Congregationalists, Presbyterians and Anglicans. (The inauguration of the Church of South India almost synchronised with the inauguration of Independent India.) Basel Mission churches have also now joined the union, and Lutherans are likely to join soon. The experience of being in the *united* churches of North India and South India makes the Church of England's refusal to join with the Methodists in England seem even more ludicrous to me - tragically so - than it would have done in England, and I have felt moved to pen a letter to the *Church Times* from here. I just cannot see how the Church of England can approve the North India scheme of union and vote against union in its own country. People are saying here "English Christians will unite to the last Indian".

May 28th 1972
I helped at the Holy Communion in the Cathedral at 8.00 am. It was well attended. I felt again that immense feeling of privilege to administer the chalice in a strange land. To go from one person to another with the chalice, in a congregation of five hundred people, is an undeniable privilege anywhere. The faces of people at the close range of the communion rail and at that particular moment - often of sincere commitment, penitence, thanksgiving, aspiration, intercession, devotion - say something unique about what it means to exist as human beings. But in a strange land that feeling is heightened. The beauty of the faces of the Indian women, young and old, the

beauty of the saris, the beauty of the faces of Indian men, has something to do with it. But there was a devotion in the faces this morning which was memorable.

After lunch I was taken to three Hindu temples in Bangalore. They were the complete antithesis of this morning's experience. Where we had to take off our shoes there were masses of flies. The three temples were sordid. One was a vast black granite monkey, crowned with gold. Another was an equally vast black elephant carved out of rock, with gold tusks - Ganesha, the God of good luck and prosperity. The third was a great black bull carved in stone, a symbol of procreation, associated also with the fertility God, Shiva. These huge objects of worship were behind iron grills, though the grill was opened for us at one temple. I always come away from these places sickened. My liberal spirit has been taught to look for points of co-operation and in these places I can find little or none.

The theme for my sermon for the Ordination, at which I was preaching in the Cathedral that evening had been suggested by the day, Trinity Sunday, and by the familiar hymn that is often sung on Trinity Sunday, *Holy, Holy, Holy*, written by the remarkable young Bishop of Calcutta, Reginald Heber, who was drowned in India when he was only forty three. But at these temples another hymn of Heber's came to mind, which before I have always laughed at:

> "From Greenland's icy mountains
> From India's coral strand."

which has in one of its verses lines which are now usually sneered at by liberals like me:

> "The heathen in his blindness
> Bows down to wood and stone."

I felt that some of my liberal mentors may have misled me. Could Heber be more right than they? 'Dialogue' can never be on the basis of pretence. Why is it not more often made clear that the Hindu-Christian dialogue can only be with a minute group of so-called *reformed* Hindus?

Dialogue is like dominoes. If a man puts down a six you see if you have a six to put alongside his six. But though it is sometimes diplomatic to ignore what you have *not* got in common, it is dishonest to pretend you have more in common than you have. As I look at the people who come to the temples, I do not find myself arrogantly superior. The alternative to saying "we're all going the same way really" is not simply arrogance, as often the *liberal* seems these days to suggest. You do not feel *arrogant* when you watch people who have come to a temple at the death of a loved one, or to pray for a blessing on their marriage, or, desperately, for the gift of a child, and so on. You are at one with people in your common precarious and vulnerable humanity. But just as any ounce of compassion in you cries out for people to be delivered from slum housing, or from physical blindness, or from the ignorance of illiteracy, so that compassion in you cries out for them to be delivered from these helpless gods. And if some sight has been given you, you are desperate to share it with the 'heathen in his blindness'. There is a failure of nerve, to say the very least, and certainly a failure of faith, when people feel that they can give other people silver and gold from some international monetary fund, or can give them housing units if they are, for instance, refugees, or can teach them a language, but that to offer what we believe is presumptuous. (Do we feel this about teaching Shakespeare?)

> "From many an ancient river,
>   From many a palmy plain,
> They call us to deliver
>   Their land from error's chain."

I must read some of Bishop Heber's published diaries. To stand at the door of a temple - with the hands of many beggars stretched up to you, kept in their beggary by Hinduism - is to know that Heber is writing from his heart and his experience. Of course, as Rabindranath Tagore said to CF Andrews on one occasion, the British would be in a terrible state if they had not had Christianity preached to them! It is not *whether* you preach Christ to the Indian that I see as the question, but *how* you preach Christ. (But that is a central problem in England, too.) There is an arrogance with which the Gospel can be proclaimed which is not of the Gospel. A western self-righteousness in the proclamation of the Gospel here has done much to close the doors now to western 'missionaries'. But it is not western self-righteousness *alone* which is closing the doors.

It is a tragedy that Christianity is still largely associated with western imperialism. And it is not the association in people's minds alone which is tragic. It is tragic that, in reality, the evil of imperial government, (which had much in it that was good), and the gift of the Gospel, went together. And it is not only the evil of imperial government. The superiority and racialism of the white churchgoer out here as a tea planter, or as a man on the railways, or in the army, as well as the civil service, have left a deep and indelible mark. Then there is the tragedy of a cultural imperialism which has made so little attempt to 'indigenise' the Gospel, so that it still looks and sounds western. The tragedy of the proclamation of a Gospel, which has often been the exchange of one set of legends for another, cannot be ignored. It is the insensitivity of the missionary to questions of intellectual integrity which also betrays an underlying arrogance.

The ferment in my mind which the visit to the temples had produced was not altogether conducive to good preaching. I have little doubt I preached this evening for too long, and probably too passionately. I had too much to say! I tried to suggest how *Holy, Holy, Holy,* which belongs to the God who is 'above all, and through all, and in all' is, through the Gospel, related not *primarily* to holy men, like priests; and holy days - like Sunday; and holy places - like temples, and churches, with altars, and sanctuaries, and chancels, and naves; but to the raw material of the situations and decisions of our day to day life, where one works, lives and spends one's leisure. The sermon was well received. But the afternoon's experience made it a rather unwieldy product!

After the service I had supper with the 'Dean' of the Cathedral, Alexander John, and his wife and family; with the Bishop who conducted the ordination, Anandaro Samuel, and his wife and family. (He is Bishop of Krisna-Godavari and is the Deputy Moderator of the Church of South India.) An American (with his wife and family)engaged in work on Colleges of Education, with a Fulbright grant, was also there.

Alexander John, a very gifted Indian, had worked in Sheffield and with the World Council of Churches at Geneva. He is undoubtedly making a very good job of leading the Cathedral. (The Bishop has just retired so he is virtually acting bishop as well.) The programme of the Cathedral for the year 1972/3, in addition to the work of the 'Dean', involves five other full-time staff:

I   One person who will have the task of education of the members of the Cathedral congregation about the situation of the people in the industrial and urban areas of Bangalore, challenging them to be involved in the lives of the people in these areas and making the challenge concrete by initiating a 'programme' that relates to these areas.

2 One person who will do specific 'Community Development' (on the lines of Saul Alinsky's work in the USA).

3 One person who will be involved in Group Dynamics and 'Sensitivity training' in relation to people in Bangalore, particularly through their work situations.

4 One person who will be involved in industrial relations - with management and the unions, but especially with unorganised labour, ie workers for whom as yet there are no trades unions.

5 One person who will work in close contact with the 'Free University'. This is a group of people who, appalled with the fact that there are 386 million illiterate people in India in 1971 (seventy per cent), and equally appalled that there are so many unemployed who have been through higher education, have themselves opted out of the educational system to commit themselves to a local area. They are buying one and a half acres of land, and will make further decisions as they go, for instance, whether to establish a spinning industry, or to provide local adult education, or a clinic, and so on.

This is, of course, in addition to the normal programme of worship and preaching at the Cathedral, (which depends heavily on part-time help from ministers working in the various Christian institutes in Bangalore). Plain 'missionary' work is forbidden in India. Much of the work of the present Industrial Team spreads far beyond Bangalore. Their services are called upon in other parts of India and beyond. Alan has just had to produce for an International Management magazine an article on 'International Industrial Relations in the Seventies', which reveals his very expert knowledge in this field.

May 29th 1972

I went today to Deena Seva Sangha, a settlement founded in 1930 for educational work, welfare services, and cultural and recreational activities. It is in the middle of the slum area of Seshadripuram. Ordinary amenities like water, light and sanitation were clearly inadequate, and the children ill-housed, ill-clothed and ill-fed. The settlement deals with 173 children in its nursery school, 2,956 in its primary school, 906 in its Middle school and 890 in its High School - nearly 5,000 children. It was a kind of Indian Toynbee Hall, with Literary activities, and Scouting, Sports, Crafts, Music and Dance, and Outings. There is a students' hostel, and a boys' home, and medical service, and a meals service. I greatly enjoyed being shown round it all. At the heart of the work is a community of twenty-five full-time workers committed to the work for life. They meet as a team each Friday and on Sundays they meet for worship. They work with great dedication in the surrounding community.

I also rather enjoyed the Board Meeting. It was much like Cambridge House Executive Committee in Camberwell - although Indians talking animatedly together remind one of Wales. It is not simply intonation, but never less than three people seem to speak at once in committee. The conversation was often anti-Government in that harmless way that people working 'on the ground' always 'beef' about the bureaucracy above them. Most of the men in committee were in immaculate white dhotis, with a white stole over their shoulder, very much the dress of Gandhi; and the lady on the chairman's left (who, just as in English social work committees, knew, or spoke as if she knew, all there was to be known about the locality) was in an equally immaculate white sari. A great blown-up photograph of Gandhi, almost from floor to ceiling, dominated the room.

Later in the day, Alan took me to a meeting of Rotarians. (Rotarians and Free Masonry are numerically strong in India.)

He as acting in a skit they had produced as a self-study. It was particularly interesting to me, for it was about subjects which clearly 'rang bells' for those who watched - a father who was proud to be local president of Rotarians, but who hadn't a clue about his 'Hippie' son; the generation gap; the authority problem; the rather trite morality that can sometimes typify the Rotarian approach to life, a middle-class morality coupled with an overweening middle-class pride, especially in good works. It was a tribute to the audience that they laughed heartily at the whole thing; and the young Indian businessman 'in oil', sitting next to me, thought it was 'spot on'.

May 30th 1972

I began to repack my belongings in preparation for leaving tomorrow, and discovered that the silk ties I had bought in Hong Kong as presents had been stolen from my suiitcase in the course of the week. It was bound to happen sometime. I have been lucky so far. It's an opportunity not only for me to practise detachment, but, I fear, for those for whom I bought them to do likewise; for I can't afford more, not Thai silk! It's horrid, because I hate *not* giving presents. (That requires real detachment - and trust.) But it's more horrid still, because it is fairly clear who took them, and he has become a friend whom I had trusted with access to my room. But if I had no job, and no money, and no prospects of either; if there was no real tradition of honesty, and if most of the pressures were the other way, and I saw a travelling Englishman with what looks to me like money and possessions, what would I have done? Any capacity I might have for dealing with his guilt is largely destroyed by my guilt at being who I am. If I accuse him, he's bound to deny it. If I don't accuse him.....Or do I take refuge in the fact that I leave tomorrow anyway? But he is a good friend, 'my own familiar friend, whom I trusted'. That's what hurts. Was I imagining friendship? Is *he* hurt? Will it hurt more to accuse, given that I may just conceivably be wrong? Taking what you can is so much part of the way of life here, for obvious reasons, that my instinct is simply to forget it, or, rather, 'make light of it', lighter than I would in England. The ties are gone for good.

While I was still turning over in my mind what to do, or not to do, David Hawkey and Francis, and four children turned up. He was living at Cambridge House when I was at St George's, Camberwell. He is now Headmaster of a church technical school for a thousand in Bombay. It was a joyful reunion.

After rice and curds - a yoghurt-like substance - and mangoes, I went off to the Christian Institute for the Study of Religion and Society, to see GR Karat, the Associate Director. CISRS ('Scissors') is one of the very best Christian things in India. For instance, its 'Study Project on National Legislation and Political Life' studies, in Delhi, Bills coming to Parliament and crucial issues in politics. This study has real influence in Government circles in Delhi. The Institute also promotes Hindu/Christian dialogue, and is responsible for a good many very valuable studies and publications. (My one reservation about Christians in Bangalore is that there is so much *talk* about problems. CF Andrews managed to combine talk and theory with living it all out.)

I went to see Mr Karat with a specific question in mind, though I wanted to hear more about the Institute's work in general. I was aware that I have seen little or nothing of 'reformed Hinduism' since I have been here, and wanted an accurate assessment of its power in Indian society. Karat thought a long while before replying, and said, "The simple fact is that Reformed Hinduism has not caught on. It is the approach and interest of a few. One the other hand, those Hindus who have concerned themselves with politics and social reform are almost by definition reformed Hindus. The influence of reformed Hinduism has been very considerable. But, of course, it will not do simply to credit social reform in India to reformed Hinduism. A great deal of social reform is secular - the work of people who have consciously - but probably not vocally - rejected the Hinduism of their birth, and have a humanist approach. Then there is the very considerable Christian contribution which has also greatly influenced those who would claim to be 'secular'." It was a very helpful discussion. It reminded me of an anecdote someone had told me a few days ago. I was talking about CF Andrews to an elderly Indian of some standing, who had known Andrews and Gandhi. He said, "I once asked Charlie Andrews why Gandhi did not become a Christian. Andrews was silent. I interrupted his silence and said, 'Is it because if Gandhi became a Christian, he would lose most of his votes?' Andrews smiled, and I could see by his smile that there in was something in what I said." "But", the elderly gentleman went on, "It is sad that Gandhi had to choose between being a Christian so Western in form and being a Reformed Hindu. His decision might have been different if he could really have been an *Indian* Christian - who knows?"

I went on from CISRS to the United Theological College to see EC John. This year he is Acting Principal, Professor of Old Testament, and Head of the Department of Biblical Studies - and now BSc., BD., MA., Dr Theol. I so well remember him when he was at Westcott House, coming to see me in my rooms at Trinity. He is one of the most lovable Indians I know - and has now a German wife and four attractive children. He had the Bishop of Dornakal to tea as well, and it was good to be with them for a couple of hours. We took up the friendship established in brief meetings in Cambridge where we had left off.

Alan had another of his managers' groups in the evening, addressed by a suave and plausible consultant who skillfully purveyed platitudes. He talked of the evils of the authoritarian approach, in a more authoritarian and hostile-raising manner than I have heard employed anywhere in the last months. However, the company Alan had collected did not take what he had to offer 'lying down'. They were in fact a very impressive group, mostly of young Indians in training in the industries of Bangalore. Alan has an extraordinary gift for collecting top and middle management together, who clearly have many other priorities, yet make a high priority of Alan's gatherings.

May 31st 1972

I woke up this morning to my last hours in India. Three weeks is no time at all to get any understanding of so vast and diverse a continent. (It is really a united states of India.) I have seen nothing of 'the Hills of the North'; nothing of Bombay; today I shall only touch down at Madras, and, of the 700,000 villages of India, I have passed through hardly more than a score. I should like to have set eyes on a model steel town such as Durgapur or Rourkela; and, as I have said, I should like to have had more contact with reformed Hinduism. Yet I can only feel grateful that I have seen all that I have seen, and that I have been allowed to see it, in the time, at such depth. My admiration for what India has achieved in twenty-five years is great. What she must yet achieve cannot blind one to that.

I said goodbye to the Hawkeys and to those that help in Alan's house (his wife has been away for a holiday most of the time since I arrived). I shook hands with 'the suspect'. (On reflection, if the pressures on stealing are so great it seemed important to suggest that yielding to the pressures could not break the bond of friendship.) Alan saw me off at the airport at midday, and we were soon flying over parched fields that looked from the air like a pavement of pink granite chips that had turned sometimes to grey, with a vast crack, the course of a wide muddy river, across it.

We came down at Madras to the savage heat again, with only

half an hour before the 'plane to Colombo departed, I anxiously awaited my luggage, then rushed, sweating, through Immigration and Customs, and soon the lovely city of Madras was beneath us, and then the sea.

I am sad to be leaving India. I have seen why even those who came to exploit it have often left loving it; and why others were willing to stay and serve it, to give it internal security, and railways, and save something of what could be saved from famine and fever, and give it the semblance of an educational system. We have received so much from India. We should, of course, have done so much more, and done what we did do differently. But there are still surviving signs of selfless love and sacrifice expended even in the Imperial era.

It was seeing EC John yesterday that made me think of Kipling's lines that are so often shamelessly and so significantly half quoted, and thus totally misquoted:

> "Oh, East is East, and West is West, and never the twain
> shall meet,
> Till Earth and Sky stand presently at God's great
> Judgment Seat;
> But there is neither East nor West, Border, nor Breed,
> nor Birth,
> When two strong men stand face to face, though
> they come from the ends of the earth."

I am not strong with the kind of strength I think Kipling probably had in mind, the courage of soldiers. But I can't help having strong love for people. And when I shook hands with 'EC' yesterday, and stood 'face to face' as I said farewell, I knew there was neither East nor West, though we 'came from the ends of the earth'. And, as usual, I am sad not primarily at leaving the streets, or the soil of a place, but because Time is the Border, not place or breed or birth: Time which means I shall not set eyes on this Indian friend and that again for a very long time, if ever. But, in a country whose second city is Calcutta, one dare not harbour self-centred sorrow. And, granted Calcutta, there's so much to be grateful for. As I say, above all, friends.

Stage 19: Ceylon

May 31st 1972

The channel between South India and Ceylon is a matter of only twenty-eight miles. You are, therefore, totally unprepared for the astonishing change of scenery, which gets more and more surprising as the 'plane takes you further south to Colombo, seven degrees Longitude, north of the Equator, 240 miles south of the extreme north of Ceylon, the Jaffna peninsula. Ceylon is lush green. The Jaffna peninsula, from the air, is simply more bleak in its beauty. As you land at Bandaranaike Airport at Katunayake, it is clear that it is not only the terrain that marks off Ceylon from the Indian mainland; the saffron robes of the Buddhist monks, signifying the survival and dominance of Buddhism, colour the waiting crowd.

At the airport, it was a great joy to see the youthful figure of the white-robed Bishop of Kurunagala, Lakshman Wickremesinghe, who had come to meet me. I had seen something of him when he was last in London for the Lambeth Conference, in 1968. (After Keble College, Oxford, and Ely Theological College, he had served a curacy for three years in Poplar before returning to Ceylon.) He seemed to me then to have a spiritual and personal quality that singled him out - the 'light and fire of love'. But he is far from solemn; he is an attractive amalgam of priest, pastor, prophet and politician - a difficult combination, but one which Isaiah achieved! He is a prince among men. Lakshman had planned that we should spend three days in Colombo. (His diocese of Kurunagala is in the central hill country.) We therefore drove from the airport to where he had been brought up as a boy, to the Colombo home of his seventy-two year old mother, who lives with his sister and brother-in-law and their family. Lakshman's father, dead now many years, was an eminent Ceylon Civil Servant; his brother-in-law, Sam Wijesinha, is now Clerk to the House of Parliament. It was a delight to meet Lakshman's mother - clearly a woman of great sensibility and grace - and to be refreshed for an hour in their most lovely home.

At 5.30 pm we drove out of Colombo to Moratuwa. We were going to the Council Meeting of Sarvodaya Shramadana - 'Welfare for All' and 'Sharing of energy'. It is a movement led by one of the most remarkable men I have met, Ahangamaga Tudor Ariyaratne, who in 1969 was awarded the Ramon Magsaysay Award, for service to the community, one of Asia's most coveted prizes.

Sarvodaya has become a popular movement, the largest voluntary movement in Ceylon, drawing into it tens of thousands of volunteers of all classes. In 1967 Ari decided to launch his 'Hundred Villages Development Scheme', a plan to attack the economic and social ills of a hundred very poor villages. But the movement has been such a phenomenal success that the target is now a thousand villages. Ari is in many ways a young Gandhi. The movement is based on community participation, personal sacrifice and non-violent personal and social action. Ari's volunteers join with the villagers themselves to 'develop' a village, through literacy classes, new farming techniques, providing the essentials for sanitation, health, hygiene and nutrition. The volunteers may be called in to build several miles of road, or a drain, etc. They enable a village to have a transfusion, but something that has more than a momentary effect. They work *with* the villagers rather than *for* them.

More than eighty per cent of Ceylon's twelve million people live in villages, and it is the towns, predominantly Colombo, to which social advance has come. One way of preventing (or delaying) Colombo becoming yet another 'megalopolis' - it has a population of over a million already - is to do what can be done for the villagers.

The Council meeting was fascinating. The President of the Senate (Ceylon's House of Lords) recently abolished, was there, alongside two Buddhist monks. Lakshman was sitting next to the Professor of Education of Vidyodaya University. But the 'top people' were mingled with young students and very ordinary people. £30,000 has been raised throughout the world for the movement, but the bulk of the money expended comes from the volunteers and supporters in Ceylon.

The centre of the movement is now an ancestral home given to the movement, not far out of Colombo. The forty permanent residents have formed themselves into a community which sets aside an hour each day for spiritual training. The movement looks to the great religious teachers, 'such as Lord Buddha, Hindu Saints, the Lord Jesus Christ and Prophet Mohammed', believing in the one-ness of all mankind.

The Community House has visual aids to its spirituality around its walls - not religious *objects d'art* so much as illustrations of the educational process they encourage through the eight traditional Buddhist virtues of:

Metta - loving kindness, friendship between individuals.
Karuna - compassionate social action.
Muditha - the joy of selfless service.
Upekkha - equanimity in the face of gain or loss, praise or
      blame, success or failure.
Dana - sharing.

Priya Vachana - pleasant speech.
Artha charya - constructive activities.
Samanathmatha - equality.

Sarvodaya is not only a social movement, it is also a religious revival of a very realistic kind, with its roots in Buddhism; but its branches spread out to welcome Hindus, Muslims and Christians. It is not only at the Centre where there is this emphasis, but at the Work Camps related to the villages. It is a kind of non-political political movement, for it aims to put back power where it belongs - not primarily with the government, and the government bureaucracy, and the elites, primarily urban-centred, but, as Gandhi said, in a "commonwealth of village republics". The resurrection and transformation of the *village* is an important contribution to the urban/rural development problem. I was suddenly asked to address the meeting for ten minutes on 'Non-violent revolutionary action'. I remembered William Temple had said that the way of Christ is the Way of 'Power in subordination to Love' and I spoke on that, illustrating it from CF Andrews, Martin Luther King, Dietrich Bonhoeffer and Julia de Beausobre (Lady Namier) - 'The Woman Who Could Not Die', whose published lecture on 'Creative Suffering' has remained very much in my memory.

The Bishop had to talk, too. It was odd to be wanted, and to be eagerly listened to, in a basically Buddhist situation. As Lakshman said afterwards: "Wasn't it good to be there not as the Establishment, but as the 'jokers'?".

We came back for dinner with Lakshman's family, and I began to pick up a little knowledge of the complexities of Ceylon's politics!

June 1st 1972
I am to give two addresses to clergy and laity in Colombo, the first, this evening, so I spent the morning preparing them.

I lunched with Brian Bradley and his wife, the Chaplain to the Missions to Seamen here. I met Brian on a Southampton / Waterloo train in 1953. We had not met since, though we had corresponded. It had been one of those conversations one remembers all one's life. I have always counted him as a friend, though life has taken him to Africa, Canada and all around the world. Partly as a result of that conversation in 1953, he eventually decided to be ordained. He still looks exactly like the young man who came into the restaurant car of the train nineteen years ago. It was a very happy lunch.

The talk to the clergy and laity was, I suppose, profitable. I did my expected stuff; but I was aware that although what I was saying was 'strong meat' for some who were there - a fairly conservative group of Anglicans - what I had to say was really needed to be talked about. The form the Church should take in this new religious and political situation in Ceylon should really have been the subject; but this could only be tackled by someone from within the situation - the situation the Sarvodaya movement is speaking to. After the talk, I had to go out to dinner with a priest and one of the leading laymen who is opposing in court the Ceylon scheme of Reunion of the Churches. It was a polite and pleasant meal. But I cannot conceive how anyone who thinks Anglicanism here should have a continued separate existence can have a heart and mind related to the realities of existence.

June 2nd 1972
I worked a little on the second lecture, for this evening, and played a game of 'Scrabble' with Lakshman's mother. She is a very intelligent old lady indeed.

Lakshman then took me off to the House of Parliament, where Sam Wijesinha, his brother-in-law, the Clerk to the Parliament, was giving me lunch. It was a marvellous occasion. We had lunch in his rooms. He had gathered a fine company of his friends. One was the Secretary for Constitutional Affairs in the Government; another had been in Parliamentary affairs, but was working now as a consultant on development through banking circles. He was a Hindu, a deeply religious person. Another bright young man, Army and Tea, added a kind of 'go-getting' sparkle to the Civil Servants - Sam's own assistant was also there, and, of course, Lakshman himself.

The photographs in the corridors of Parliament are enough to show what a tradition of Parliamentary service here has been in Ceylon. There was a universal franchise there as long ago as 1931, when Ceylonese Ministers were placed in charge of Government departments. The people I lunched with are all in that tradition, loyally serving their country, when there are great temptations to get out, which they might easily have yielded to. Ceylon - I should say Sri Lanka - is virtually a totalitarian state at the moment. (Last year there was an insurrection, and for six days the gutters flowed with blood. Well over a thousand young men died.) None of those I lunched with were sympathetic to a totalitarian approach. Ceylon has never yet changed its Government except by due electoral process, but there has been continuing political instability since some time before the assassination of the Prime Minister, SWRD Bandaranaike, in 1959 - whose widow is Prime Minister now. Such a long period of political instability cannot but encourage economic instability. Certainly Ceylon is economically at a low ebb just now.

The Bishop of Colombo chaired my second lecture. It was a happier occasion than yesterday: more relaxed, more honest exchange, less ecclesiasticism.

After the meeting, I was taken off to a meeting of the Christian Workers Fellowship at Ratmalana, seven or so miles out of Colombo. It is a very 'Leftist' group, and I enjoyed it very much. They sang me some of the Tamil and Singhalese melodies of the 'Workers' Mass'. Their liturgy is based on, but is a considerable improvement on the St Mark's-in-the-Bowerie Liturgy, which WH Auden had a hand in producing. A Buddhist monk had spent a lot of time on the words and the music!

I'm a good deal clearer on the complex Ceylon political situation now. Briefly, it is this. During the first eight years of Independence, the United National Party (UNP) - Right Wing - dominated the scene. It was essentially the party of the English-educated affluent middle-class, and by 1956 it had lost whatever touch it had with the working-class. In 1956, the UNP was decisively defeated by the Mahajana Eksath Peraumna (MEP), Bandaranaike's coalition composed of:

the SLFP, the Sri Lanka Freedom Party (nationalist and Buddhist) the VLSSP, the more extreme of Ceylon's two Trotskyite parties, and NLSSP, the other Trotskyite party, and the Communists.

There were communal disturbances in 1956 and 1958 and the MEP coalition broke up in 1959. Bandaranaike was assassinated that year. In April 1960, the UNP came back to power, but only for three months. There was an attempted coup by police and military in 1962. Mrs Bandaranaike was defeated in 1964, and UNP was back again with Tamil (Indian) support. There was a second attempted coup in 1966 and in 1970 Mrs Bandaranaike was back yet again with overwhelming support.

The Christian Workers Group I was with tonight were Christians and extreme Leftists, a refreshing combination! Mrs Bandaranaike has a good deal of this 'Trotskyite' within her Buddhist/Nationalist Government at the moment, oddly enough. It is not the 'Leftist' tendencies which the group I was with tonight are questioning but the dictatorial nature of the Government.

June 3rd 1972

Sam, his wife, and his eldest son, Lakshman and his mother and I, all drove to Galle, about eighty miles to the south of Colombo, to a family wedding. The drive was along the coast road, much of it like the coast of Guadalcanal, but sometimes more built up. It was fascinating to pass fishermen carrying on the backs of their bicycles sharks the size of the bicycles! Their outrigger canoes were drawn up on the beaches. Ceylon has fallen successively under Portuguese, Dutch and British rule during the last 450 years. Galle is a quaint old fortified Dutch town. The wedding we were attending was in the Roman Catholic Cathedral. Roman Catholicism was implanted in the Portuguese period.

I much enjoyed the wedding. In spite of the saris, it was very Western - even to the hymns - 'The voice that breathed o'er Eden', 'The King of Love', and 'O Perfect Love' - and Mendelssohn's Wedding March. Although it was Roman Catholic, it was a model of congregational participation. The procession was led by a well-rehearsed little Indian boy, carrying the ring on a cushion, who did very well indeed at a slow march, until his over-loving mother in the pews at the altar end of the procession, started over-fussing, as mothers do! Only then did he begin to lose his nerve. If only she had left him alone! The Indian woman singing in the pew behind me reminded me of my mother. She sang very well, but with a rather embarrassing volume, and a slight vibrato. I wanted quietly to move away - as I did forty years ago! The reception was held in what had been a British East India Company house, overlooking the sea. It was white and lovely in the sun. I have immensely enjoyed these days with Lakshman's family.

When I got back to Colombo, I went to a meeting, in a private house, of a small group of people concerned with Civil Rights, mostly top lawyers, a QC, and so on. The Government has passed 'emergency regulations' which will allow them to do almost anything. There are 14,000 political prisoners. People are arrested and disappear without trace.

Lakshman and I drove out fifty miles to Kurunagala after supper. It was our first real opportunity to talk at length to each other. He is what can only be called a 'man of God'. God is a reality for him, and prayer. He has sympathy for things for which I have little sympathy, eg Pentecostalism. But he is also sympathetic to Buddhists (and has just written the article on 'Buddhists and Christians' for the Buddhist Encyclopaedia). He is sympathetic to my radical approach, too. It is not that he is 'syncretistic', but his security in God enables him to be generous. He has a harsher idea of God's judgment than I think God has, and I do not think he takes quite seriously enough the intellectual problems these days. When I raise what I regard as genuine intellectual problems he tends to write them off as "'you Westerners making religion too cerebral", nor does he, in his belief, for instance, in spiritual healing, take into account the full impact of his personal authority here as a high-born man of God, of considerable personal power and magnetism, who is a bishop. But when all this is said as reservation, I know that he has something as a man of God which, if more of us in the Church had, the people would be queuing up at our doors. I emphasise that he is a lovable human being too. In the car we laughed and laughed at his recollection of his Poplar days when he was very fond of the nurses at Poplar Hospital!

When we arrived at Kurunagala in darkness, at his lovely house, adjacent to the new Cathedral, I knew we were at one of nature's holy places. In the darkness it was clear that the house and the Cathedral lay under a huge sheer rock, a hill that stretched up to the starlit skies. The scudding clouds were bright enough to silhouette faintly the outline of the rock against the sky. We sat in the garden till midnight, rejoicing in the silence, the gentle breeze, and the scent of flowers on the night air. A Buddhist temple crowns this great rock, Kurunagala, Elephant Rock.

June 4th 1972

I preached at the Cathedral at an early hour this morning. It's a marvellous place. (It is the brainchild of, and largely financed by the former Bishop of the Diocese and Metropolitan of the Church, Lakdesa de Mel.) It is very much in keeping with the architecture of this part of the world, a tiled vaulted roof with pillared supports. The Bishop celebrated the Communion with very great reverence. Before the Communion of the people, the ordained ministers lay prostrate upon the floor in silence for a while.

The hill overhanging the Cathedral - topped by a Buddhist temple - loses nothing of its awesome majesty by daylight. I have never seen any hill in any part of the world which has quite this numinous quality. Later in the morning the monkeys were scampering about on it, and swinging from the trees, which sprout at right angles from its walls. Lakshman had arranged that we should lunch with a Buddhist monk at the Diocese's farm school. The discussion was somewhat frustrating. I was intent on learning, but the Buddhist monk - a PhD of London University - seemed to play a kind of avoiding game. We did not really communicate. The discussion went like this:

EAJ   It is a privilege to meet you and a great kindness of you to be willing to instruct me. Will you please assume that, as yet. I know very little about your religion.

Buddhist monk (smiling) Buddhism is not a religion.

EAJ Well....you have temples, presumably for worship in some way.

Buddhist monk (smiling) Buddhists are not interested in God. They are interested in man.

EAJ The ordination we are coming to tonight, is it not in any way to the service of what you will understand to call God?

Buddhist monk (smiling still) No. It is a dedication to a way of life; a way of education.

EAJ Then how do you conceive of man? Is there not an element of mystery in his origin and destiny?

Buddhist monk (continuing to smile) Why do you speak of 'mystery'? Buddhists are not interested in how men arise on the earth or where they will go. We are interested in man now.

EAJ Yes....but....to educate someone presumes you know what you want to educate them *for*, presumes you understand who they are. How do you think of 'persons'?

Buddhist monk (smiling still) We have a scientific knowledge of the individual.

EAJ But what does your 'science' tell you about the man?

I was very surprised at some of the replies. They were so unlike what I had expected, that I could not believe they were typical. But he was a very high-up Buddhist monk. Bishop Lakshman had told me that there were many divisions in Buddhism. He works with this monk a great deal on the problems of development of this under-developed part of Ceylon. I still haven't recovered from the puzzlement of the conversation. I rather escaped from it eventually by being taken round the farm school. A very nice young Singhalese priest was looking after fifteen boys from impossible homes and teaching them to farm.

When I got back, I shared my puzzlement over the Buddhist monk with Lakshman. He said he thought I might have pushed my questions too hard - 'with an aggressive humility' - so that the man was put off trying to communicate. Oh dear!

We set out in the afternoon for Kandy, twenty-five miles away. It is a drive of peculiar loveliness, virtually a pass through the hills all the way. Green paddy fields, terraced and contoured on either side of the road, look like green carpeted stairs. There are plantations of palms and of tea - I have never seen such a variety of vivid shades of green - and everywhere flowering shrubs and trees. We made our way first to the University beyond Kandy, where I shall be spending twenty-four hours later this week - no university ever had a more lovely setting. We than came back to the ancient capital itself.

In the middle of Kandy is a huge artificial lake that gives it a stillness at its heart. Abutting on to one side of the lake is a large monastic establishment to accommodate Buddhist monks from temples of royal foundation. We first sought our host for the evening in this inner city, teeming with saffron-robed monks with shaven heads, one of the most senior monks. He assigned us to the care of a young monk, who would stay at our side all through the Ordination for which we had come. An Ordination is one of the greatest occasions of the whole year. The young monk first guided us in our car to the other side of the lake, to the Temple of the Sacred Tooth, a Relic of the Buddha, the Dalada Maligawa. The great moated Temple, beside the palace of the last King of Kandy, was floodlit for the night. We stood outside in the warm night air, waiting the arrival of the procession of those to be ordained. It was a procession of mediaeval splendour never to be forgotten. We first caught sight of those bearing torches of flame who flanked the moving procession. Then came the band of drummers, pounding urgently, and those who rang small cymbal-like bells; then came the trumpeters, their sound not like our triumphal trumpets, but more reed-like, plaintive and mysterious. Then followed the dancers, whirling and twirling ecstatically; and all, musicians and dancers, in glorious regalia. Finally, elephants, caparisoned in gold and in other fine coverings, bearing on top of them, clothed like Kings for their one day of bright glory and riding in majesty, those to be ordained, seated solemn and still.

When the procession had passed on its way, our guide led us across the moat, into the great towered building that houses the Shrine, and, by many stairs, we were taken in bare feet to the Shrine itself - like the house of the Crown Jewels in the Tower of London. The Tooth, an object of immense popular devotion, was enshrined in seven womb-like cases of gold inlaid with jewels and precious stones - royal gifts of earlier times. Before the Shrine lay bowls of the most lovely lotus flowers. The Tooth had been brought to Ceylon in the fourth century AD.

For me, and I thought for our guide, this episode in our evening was an interlude, a courtesy and great privilege to visitors, but betraying the embarrassment popular religion often gives to the intellectual, revealing how far it has changed from the time and the teaching of the Buddha.

We were escorted back to the far side of the lake, to the monastery, to await the end of the procession. It was now clear that the Bishop and I were being treated as very privileged guests indeed. We were brought to the doorway, where we could watch the final ecstatic dance of the dancers, and stand by the entrance as the elephants, only a few feet away, allowed their 'royal' cargo to dismount. We were then escorted into the Chapter House, where the Ordination would take place, and given two cushions of honour, not six feet from where the senior monk would preside over the ordination. The Chapter House is a long hall with rows of pillars forming an inner space. The ceiling was highly decorated. The hall was lit with lamps of oil. At the end, beyond the President's throne, was a statue of the seated Buddha towering from floor to ceiling.

The hall filled with about fifty monks and with the relatives of those to be ordained. First, those to be ordained were ceremoniously stripped of their 'royal' robes (just as the royal Siddartha had stripped to become the Buddha). Then each candidate, dressed now as a layman, but having the saffron robes of a monk in his arms, and accompanied by his tutor, prostrated himself before one of the elders. Then he arose and said: "Grant me leave to speak, lord", and kneeling down, said "I pray, lord, to be admitted again as a Novice. In compassion for me, lord, take these yellow robes, and let me be ordained, to destroy all sorrow and to attain Nirvana." This was repeated three times. The elder then gave the bundle of robes to the candidate, tying a band of it round the candidate's neck, reciting a meditation on the perishableness of the body. The monk, while he changed from the dress of a layman, recited a prayer which described how and why he should wear the clothes - "as protection....not for ornament or show". When he had put on the saffron robes he returned to the side of his tutor, asked for forgiveness for all his faults, and that his tutor might share in whatever merit he had gained, and prayed to be given the Three

Refuges and the Ten Precepts - which he received kneeling - repeating then three times:

"I go for refuge to the Buddha (The Teacher)
I go for refuge to the Dhamma (The Teaching)
I go for refuge to the Sangha." (The Taught - the Fellowship)

When all this was completed, the candidates were restored to the novitiate they had temporarily laid aside, and were ready for Ordination. The monks who had been standing around informally in groups, like roman senators, in saffron togas, began to take their places in order of precedence. The first candidate went with his tutor to the President, prostrating himself, and asking that he might receive the permission and the support of the President. The President said, "It is well." The candidate replied, "I am content. I am content, I am content,", and three times repeated his vow: "From this day forth I am responsible to my lord: My lord is responsible for me." After another obeisance, the candidate retired to the 'chancel step', as it were, where his alms bowl was strapped on him. The tutor then went down and took the candidate's hand, and brought him to the President, and with another monk on the other side of the candidate, the two monks examined him. The examination, though it was a most down-to-earth interrogation, was a most beautiful chanted dialogue. (Much of the questioning in the service was in this lovely chant.) "Have you boils, itch, epilepsy? Are you a human being? Male? A free man? Free from debt?" Eventually, one of the tutors reported on the result of the examination. The President asked if anyone knew any impediment to the ordination. And, after the silence, he announced that, because the assembly had kept silence, it had shown it approved the ordination, and he declared the candidate had received ordination.

After the ordination of the first candidate it was signified to us that we could withdraw. It was completed at this stage entirely for our benefit. The ceremonies so far had taken about three hours, and the ordination of the other monks would go on into the night. The alternating of standing up and sitting on cushions, and the atmosphere of formal informality, made the evening without strain. But permission to withdraw at that time was welcome. Our senior host and the guide came out with us, and the host provided us with food and drink in his room. It had been an interesting evening of memorable kindness and courtesy as well as of intense fascination. Above all, it was moving to witness the self-dedication of the monks 'to a way of liberation' accompanied by ceremony and symbolism that had such clear meaning.

We made our way back to Kurunagala, dropping our guide at his monastery on the way.

June 5th 1972
Yesterday's experience was wonderful. The courtesy of the monks to us was so great that my mind had little room for negative thoughts. But, for the honest record, I ought to set down one or two further observations. The courtesy to us - to a bishop, ie a top person in the Church, and to a guest of his from a far country - did not always extend to the simple folk from nearby. A peasant was given short shrift, and even junior monks were told in no uncertain terms to 'get out', as part of making room for us, part of their exceptional courtesy to us. Secondly therefore, it is the feudal hierarchy I must 'observe'. I suspect that Buddhism, like the Church, is in for a few shocks from its own lands, and from this generation of its own people, if it goes on touching its cap to 'top people' and to feudal hierarchy. This revolution against a feudal Buddhism has to some extent already begun.

With these thoughts in mind, I could not have gone to a better place today than 'Devasaramaya' to see Yohan Devananda, a very fine priest in his early forties, who went to Selwyn College, Cambridge, and Cuddesdon, Oxford, and who founded in 1967 an 'Ashram', a Franciscan-like Community, with the express aim of 'dialogue' between Christians and Buddhists. The ashram is about six miles from Kurunagala. Yohan, and what he is up to, is in many ways a kind of 'happening'. But it is interesting that though there has been a lot of contact between him and Buddhists over the years, he would say that progress has really come through taking seriously the needs of young and old in the Buddhist community around the ashram, the needs and rights of the villagers. This political and social involvement with one sort of Buddhist could lead to trouble with another sort, the older, more feudal, generation of Buddhists. What began as primarily a life of corporate prayer has become more recently rather more a life of corporate action - a co-operative farm and political involvement. This may well be a right development. But when a person of education and intelligence from a 'good family' settles down in a poor area, urban or rural, and makes contact with what he calls 'the people', I have often found that he is not in contact with what others would recognise as 'the people', but with a group of more articulate people who have found a sympathetic ear and a voice in him, as he has in them. It could be that 'Devasaramaya' is not much more than the latter, but I doubt it. For Yohan has at least 'stayed with it' for fifteen years. His type usually 'up and off' after a while. But Yohan struck me as a prophet with his 'calling' and with such people as he *can* get close to. He is already something of a 'guru'.

June 6th 1972

I was up at the crack of dawn and was driven fifty miles with a young priest, Udeni de Silva, to, first of all, the ancient rock fortress and palace of Sigiriya. It is a strange isolated mass of granite, 600 feet high, ovoid in shape, with a flat surface on the top. From afar it looked like a massive petrified monster. The area at the front of the huge rock mass is strewn with boulders. The main formation was made the abode of King Kassapa I (AD 478-496) who built a fabulous palace on the summit, to which he could escape from his brother. For eighteen years it was the royal capital of Ceylon.

We climbed nearly to the top before the sun had reached its height, with a wonderful view of the Matale hills. The entrance to the fortress is across a most lovely moat, full of pink and white lotus; then you walk through the ruined precincts outside the city walls, passing caves which have been the ancient cells of Buddhist monks, and the remains of an audience hall. The ascent begins with a fairly modern flight of steps. At a height of 150 feet above the plain, there is an ancient gallery pinned to the western face of the rock. About fifty feet above the gallery, there is a long cave, which contains marvellous frescoes, portraits of jewelled women with flowers, probably the only secular Indian paintings that survive from before Mohammedan times. A modern narrow iron staircase - open to the world below - leads to the northern terrace. From this terrace, the remains of the immense Lion Staircase, with the paws of an enormous beast either side of its stairs, lead to more exposed iron ladders, which take you to the top. The ladders did not take me to the top! There was a strong wind blowing, and swarms of bees in the near vicinity, and I had ascended up on high quite far enough.

From Sigiriya we went on to Dambulla, to a cave temple founded in the first century BC high up in the rocks. The caves were filled not only with a colossal reclining Buddha image, but with dozens of images of the Buddha seated and standing. The walls and ceilings were covered with frescoes depicting various events and deities. In spite of their two thousand years of history, passing from one image to another, the guide providing us with vital statistics - "This image is forty-seven feet long, cut out of solid rock....", what I saw left me unmoved. I was more moved simply by the young Buddhist monk who hovered into our vicinity - we could not converse, but we could smile - and by the ordinary men and women in the rice-fields, the buffaloes who slowly turned and gazed, and the elephants padding along the road, as though there was nothing for it but silently to endure a weary existence.

In the evening, Lakshman took me with him to visit one or two villages and their clergy. The paddy-fields were of surpassing beauty as the sun set across them, gold on green. Lakshman is so much part of this country, He is not 'of the people' but it was clear that the people feel he is part of them.

June 7th 1972

The Communion this morning in the Cathedral was sung to haunting Singhalese chants. Lakshman generously gave me his car and driver for two days, and at eleven I was driven over to Kandy. I lunched with the wife of the Professor of Geography at the University with whom I was to stay the night, George and Vijeyadevi Thambyapillay, and, in the late afternoon, I addressed a group of clergy in Kandy. It was a happy and profitable time, followed by a meal with some of them. They were good and genial company. Then I went back to the University with the Chaplain to talk to a group on a subject of their choosing: 'How can the Church be protected from the Establishment?' They were an interesting group of different Christian denominations, Roman Catholic to Pentecostalist, and were mostly senior staff, lecturers and professors, with one or two really first-class minds among them. I felt that the occasion would be most profitably used if I gave them maximum time for discussion, and I simply commented on what they had to say, though I gave a very brief introduction. The discussion was characteristically diffuse for a university discussion, but there was an urgency about it which revealed that the subject was of considerable important to those there. We covered much ground. "In founding the Church, did Christ intend to found the kind of institution which has a hierarchy?" "Is an 'establishment' inevitable in any large institution?" "How can self-criticism be built into an institution - self-criticism which releases rather than stifles leadership?" "What are the insights and principles that Christ gives to the Church for its self-criticism?" It was generally felt that there would be little loss if the whole institutional fabric - for instance, in England, 15,000 full-time priests, with all that that implies for the 'employing agency', eg the power of the employer, the raising of money, the possession of property, and the dominance of central authority and of the full-time workers - were to come to an end, and the Church be a loose federation of groups of people trying to follow the way of Christ in this situation and that!

As I have travelled through various lands since I left the Solomons, reading literature that gives me a rudimentary appreciation of the land I am in at the time, I have been more busy than I had hoped. I have not been able to read many novels. But today I have read a great novel: *Siddhartha* by Herman Hesse. For some years I have had it in the corner of my eye, but almost consciously refrained from reading it. I read Hesse's *Narziss and Goldmund* a year or so ago, and realised then why he had become almost a passion with hippies. It was the story of the friendship of two mediaeval priests, one contented with his religion, the other wandering endlessly in search of peace and salvation. *Siddhartha* is about a young man who leaves his family for a contemplative life, then, restless, discards it for one of the world and the flesh. His mistress conceives a son, but bored and sickened by the world and the flesh, Siddhartha moves on again. Near despair, he comes to a river. It is as he looks into the river that 'from a remote part of his soul, from the past of his tired life, he heard a sound......' This sound signals the true beginning of his life, by way of more suffering and rejection he arrives at peace and wisdom. "Within Siddhartha there slowly grew and ripened the knowledge of what wisdom really was and the goal of his long seeking. It was nothing but a preparation of the soul, a capacity, a secret art of thinking, feeling and breathing thoughts of unity at every moment of life...."

Siddhartha is a very great book. I know only a little about Hesse's life. I know that he was brought up in the home of a missionary. At one time he was going to be ordained. He left the seminary before ordination and attempted suicide. 'Spiritual healing' did not help him greatly. He underwent analysis with Carl Jung. Certainly *Siddhartha* is a book of a man who has travelled far and painfully in search of himself. It is not only about seeking but about finding - finding the One.

June 8th 1972

I spent an hour or so with a professor and his wife who were torn in their heart and mind as to whether they should leave Ceylon. They told me of the many academics who have got out in recent months, on the surface for academic reasons, but really because the Government has removed academic freedom. Examination marks are interfered with by the Government - Tamils have to get twenty-five per cent more marks than Singhalese. Admissions to the University are also interfered with. Appointments to staff are often political. Student power has taken ugly forms, putting intense pressure upon the Tamil minorities. It is a sick situation.

Later, with James, the University Chaplain, I visited Trinity College, Kandy, one of the great schools of Ceylon, where 'Fraser of Kandy and Achimota' had been Headmaster, and the United Seminary. I also visited Lakdasa de Mel and his wife, the former Bishop of Kurunagala and Metropolitan of the Church of India and Ceylon. He is a great characterful prelate who has been responsible amongst other things for the indigenisation of the music and architecture of the Church here. Before I was driven back to Kurunagala James took me to the very lovely Botanical Gardens.

In the evening, Lakshman and I went for dinner to his family home in Kurunagala, where his cousin now lives alone. It was like visiting another world. Around the room were the sepia family photographs going back a hundred years and more, and Victorian prints like GF Watt's 'Hope'. In the corner of the lofty main room was a piano, and a music cabinet full of Victorian ballads, which we enjoyed singing, eg 'Love's Old Sweet Song'. It is difficult for most English people to realise how English and how educated such a Ceylon family was a century ago.

June 9th 1972

I caught an early train to Paranthan, about 150 miles North of Kurunagala, forty miles south of Jaffna. It is always interesting simply to watch from a train window another world go by. When we were seventy-five miles north of Kurunagala we caught a glimpse of the dome-shaped shrines of the ancient Buddhist capital Anuradhapura, founded in the fifth century BC. Beyond Anuradhapura the country began to change from a wet tropical scenery to a land that was dry and flat.

I was met at Paranthan Station by the Revd AC Thambirajah, who drove me the four miles to Navajeenam Farm. There he and his wife and his eight sons, with Sister Elizabeth Baker, a devout and redoubtable Yorkshire Methodist, form a small Christian community which cares for about eighty homeless boys, some of whom are on probation, and prepares them for a useful existence in the world, by teaching them farming. It is a place of simplicity, doing a very valuable piece of work.

Thambirajah is a kind of Tamil Conrad Noel. We went over to tea to a neighbouring young priest for his small daughter's birthday party. The young priest I thought a specially fine person. He has a share in the farm project and helps the boys with their studies. It was time for evening service when we got back, and I enjoyed giving a talk to the whole community, boys and all. They sang Tamil lyrics very beautifully. After supper I went to bed early, by hurricane lamp, glad to have shared in another humble Christian attempt to live out a community life, closely related to a local community's needs. There is a real power to such projects, if they are 'close to the ground', however small they may be, and however far from the great centres of population. In this very remote area, with rudimentary 'facilities', it was difficult to believe that I would be back in London in only five days.

June 10th 1972
Thambirajah drove me in the Land Rover forty miles across the isthmus to Jaffna itself. It was along a straight road through coconut plantations almost all the way. There were also long stretches of salt flats and inland sea. He delivered me to the Christa Seva Ashram where I was to lead a seminar in the morning and afternoon for clergy and laity. It was a lively meeting of about thirty people. For me, the most interesting part was a discussion which developed on what is the essential difference between Buddhist, Hindu and Christian spirituality. It was claimed that a decade or so ago Christians tended to join in dialogue with Buddhists and Hindus by emphasising what was held in common and playing down the differences, but that this had the opposite effect of what was intended. It upset the Buddhists and the Hindus, who felt that Christians were pretending there were no significant differences. They were happier when Christians stated the differences as clearly and as charitably as possible. The difficulty for me was that even intelligent people who had been Hindus and Buddhists

disagreed as to what Hinduism and Buddhism stands for. (If *they* are confused, I felt forgiven for myself feeling some confusion!) It seemed undeniable that by and large both Buddhism and Hinduism stand for a way of holiness the summit of which is the individual giving himself to asceticism and prayer, whereas Christian holiness always includes love of God in 'friend and stranger'. I liked this dialogue which Sevak Selvaratnam, the leader of the Ashram, produced to exemplify the Christian way of holiness:

"Lord, I would be one with Thee."
"Is thy brother there?"
"He will not come with me."
"Go thou, and bring him here."
"And if he will not come?"
"Then come not thou to me.
We shall be three in One -
Yourself, and he, in Me."

After the meeting I spent two hours with the young Church of South India Bishop in Jaffna, who a few years ago was a student at King's College, London. Then after supper with Selvaratnam and his niece - after a very beautiful drive along the coast road (except for the palm trees very much like the coast near Aldeburgh) - I went early to bed.

June 11th 1972

At 7.00 am I preached my last sermon of these months away from England, at St John's Church, Jaffna. It was St Barnabas' Day, and I preached on 'But Barnabas took him' - Barnabas welcoming St Paul. It was a kind of personal and public thanksgiving for all those many friends - and strangers - who have stood at airports and railway stations, and so on, holding out their hands to me in greeting. I had breakfast with a very fine doctor and his family, and went round the Dutch fort in

Jaffna (where now there are many political prisoners) and, finally, after lunch with the Archdeacon, JJ Gnanapara Gsam, and his family, I caught the 1.40 pm train back to Kurunagala.

As I got on the train I felt I was beginning the long journey home. I had decided to read in the train something which would begin to transfer my mind again to the West: Albert Speer's autobiography *Inside the Third Reich*. It is an astonishing book, which gripped me for all the six hours of the hot train journey. It almost makes Hitler a credible human being! Indeed, some of the relations between the Nazi hierarchy were not all that dissimilar from relationships I have sometimes known within the Church of England! It could hardly be a more engrossing study of how human beings behave towards one another.

June 12th 1972

I got up early to have a last chat with Yohan Devananda at his ashram six miles away. I was with him by seven. There were several things I wanted to talk to him about. He is a man of God, miles away from England. I wanted his objective advice on how to work out forgiveness in a situation in which I had been involved in England. (Not that he could be entirely objective for he would have to depend on my description of the situation.) I had recently been struck by two more sayings of Dag Hammarsjkøld:

"You can only hope to find a lasting solution to a conflict if you have learned to see the other objectively, at the same time, to experience his difficulties subjectively."

"Forgiveness breaks the chain of causality because he who 'forgives' you - out of love - takes upon himself the responsibility for the consequences of what *you* have done. Forgiveness, therefore, always entails a sacrifice."

Yohan helped a great deal.

I wanted also to talk to him a little more about the nature of 'dialogue'. He said: "Remember that dialogue can never be a matter of words alone. Dialogue is primarily a matter of life together, not words together. Buddhists and Christians need to share life together, not just meetings with the exchange of words. But life together takes time, perhaps years."

"I rarely say 'This is what Christians believe. What do Buddhists believe?' I look for what I believe as a Christian in Buddhists and Buddhist writings and say 'Look: this is how you act. This is what you believe. So do we!'"

He was unconvinced that many Christians in Ceylon had spent the necessary time in 'living' dialogue with Buddhists. I also wanted to speak to Yohan about the political trials beginning this very day in Ceylon - several of his friends are in prison and will be tried. He did not think they would get a just trial. Yohan is one of the people most concerned with justice that I have met.

After two hours with him I said an affectionate farewell to him, and, soon after, to Lakshman, who has been a perfect host. Without him I could not have seen a tenth of what I have seen in Ceylon. He has made this last stage of my 'exploring' one of the most memorable.

Bishop de Mel and his wife had kindly come over from Kandy to drive me to Colombo. The Bishop, knowing I have become very interested in Asian music (I wanted to try and get the Bengali, the Tamil and the Singhalese music for the liturgy recorded) wanted to take me to have lunch with his cousin, Devar Surya Sena, OBE, the 'Cecil Sharp' of Ceylon. He has collected folk music for thirty years - and folk music instruments. Bishop de Mel has had words written to the folk tunes so that they can be used as hymns. Devar Surya Sena gave me a marvellous display on his collection of drums, and had fascinating stories to tell, just like those of Cecil Sharp and Ralph Vaughan Williams, about collecting the folk tunes. Bishop de Mel drove me then to Lakshman's mother, with whom I was specially glad to stay my last night in Colombo. It was good to sit and chat with her, and then to go and fulfil my last speaking engagement. I had dinner with Celestine Fernando and his wife and then talked with a group of clergy and laity. Celestine is the very sensitive and perceptive chairman of the Committee for Social Study and Action of the Colombo Diocese, the wise friend and counsellor of many of his fellow clergy and laity here. I was glad to have such a person with whom I could discuss my impressions of Church and State in Ceylon.

I wish I could feel that Ceylon is not at the moment primarily a land of tragedy. It is in the unhappy position of having to depend on foreign sources for the basic requirements of food, clothing and shelter. She pays for these with foreign exchange - ninety per cent of which comes from the export of tea, rubber and coconut. Although her production of these has increased considerably, foreign exchange has not increased proportionately - and the cost of imports has risen steeply. I wonder if many in England realise what it is like for so many developing countries to be so much at the mercy of the 'developed' nations. It ministers to a kind of corporate despair. All your best achievements often seem doomed.

In recent years Ceylon has achieved a great deal. The expectation of life, which was about thirty five years in the mid 1930's, has risen to around sixty seven. The population has therefore been growing fast. About forty per cent of total government expenditure is on health and education. But there is much unemployment amongst the educated, though there is a shortage of skilled craftsmen and technicians. Last year the population increased by 2 per cent but the economic growth rate was 0.9 per cent. In other words, Ceylon, economically, went backwards. But the economic depression is as nothing compared with the depression of spirit abroad in the country. I have spoken to no one of any class, in any part of the country, who is hopeful. The Emergency Regulations restricting personal freedom, the currency regulations making travel abroad virtually impossible for the moment give people a sense of imprisonment and doom.

June 13th 1972

I woke up early and stretched out my hand for *Markings*, by the bedside lamp, to read my daily passage of Dag Hammarsjkøld, and see what he would serve up for this last day out of England. It was a particularly fine passage:

> "Give us
> A pure heart
> That we may see Thee,
> A humble heart
> That we may hear Thee,
> A heart of love
> That we may serve Thee,
> A heart of faith
> That we may live Thee.
> Thou whom I do not know
> But Whose I am.
> Thou whom I do not comprehend
> But who hast dedicated me
> To my fate,
> Thou - "

Lakshman's mother came with me to the Colombo Museum which I had not yet visited. I shall remember it always for one great and marvellous statue of the seated Buddha, the very image of serenity. It greets you in the doorway of the Museum. Everything else is secondary to it. I am glad to have seen that statue, stood still before its stillness at the end of my 'exploring'. Mrs. Wickremesinghe and I then did some last minute shopping, using up my remaining currency. It was good to be with her.

Sam Wijesinha had gone to enormous trouble and kindness to make my last lunch in his country memorable. He had invited me to meet over lunch in the Speaker's Rooms in Parliament Felix Bandaranaike, the Minister of Home Affairs, Public Administration and Justice; and JP Obeysekera (a Trinity man, as his father and grandfather had been).

He had been a Senator (until the Second Chamber was abolished). His wife, Siva, who was with him, is the Deputy Minister of Health in the Government. He had also invited Sir Angus Mackintosh, the British High Commissioner, and his wife; Mrs Edmund Wickremesinghe, Lakshman's sister-in-law, who is a Director of Associated Newspapers of Ceylon, and a Mr and Mrs Barlow, seconded from the BBC to work on a British Council assignment with Ceylon Radio. It would have been discourteous to my host, I felt, to press some of the questions in my mind. It wasn't the place, and in fact there wasn't the time. Mrs Obeysekera, sitting next to me, dilated with some passion on the problems the virtual ban on foreign travel raises for education - the education of teachers as well as students. There was no sign here of simply a 'party line' or a closed mind. I talked to Mrs Wickremesinghe about censorship. Her newspapers are allowed eight pages of newsprint (which may be cut down) and are under heavy censorship. Again, there was no mere submission here. As it turned out, most of those who were at the table were Christians. It would be easy for some of the 'radicals' I have been with to add 'top-draw establishment Christians out of touch with the masses'. You can't accurately gauge people's 'contact with the masses' at such a lunch. I would not be surprised if the contact was small, but the lunch at least gave me opportunity to assure myself that there is a good deal of Christian integrity at the heart of Ceylon's Government. Sam made a good remark later. He said: "While you still have good judges, who will not hesitate to judge regardless of what the Government wants, you have a great deal for which to be thankful. And we have that." He, of course, knows the judges of the political trials personally, and thinks they are first rate as judges.

The Buddha this morning seemed to me to be saying that he will be sitting still silently, wisely, when all the judges and statesmen and politicians - and 'radicals' - have gone into the dark. He spoke of an Eternal Patience. I have been immensely privileged, thanks to Lakshman and his family, to have seen such a wide spectrum, of the life of Ceylon. It is so complex, I think I leave it with more open questions in my mind than any other country I have visited. Just after the passage I have already quoted from Hammarsjkøld, he simply sets down the verses from Psalm LX, "Thou hast moved the land, and divided it; heal the sores thereof, for it shaketh."

I said goodbye to Lakshman's family with heartfelt gratitude for their special kindness. The airline 'phoned to say my Qantas Boeing 707 was delayed an hour *en route* from Sydney. I therefore went out by coach to the airport, gazing on my last glimpse of the Indian Ocean in the warm night air and Colombo's crowded street. We began the fifteen hour flight home to London at 10.00 pm

June 14th 1972

I slept from Colombo to Bahrain; breakfasted from Bahrain to Damascus, (golden fields, ready to harvest, with small compact towns in the midst of them looking as if they were built of

'Lego'); and dozed intermittently from Damascus to Rome, waking up to see through gaps in the clouds glimpses of Nicosia, Rhodes and Corfu. The long leg of Italy was mostly surrounded in cloud, and the Appenines had a grey phantom-like appearance. Italians, returning from Australia, stood up and smiled and looked thankfully and eagerly at their homeland as the country around Rome emerged from the grey gloom. The Eternal City seemed to be the appropriate place for lustrations and a quick shave.

I had had no desire to read between Colombo and Rome but, while we were on the ground at Rome, almost for old times' sake I took out the *Four Quartets*, which, with *Markings*, have kept me company all these 45,000 miles. I had expected *East Coker* to 'speak' (I read Eliot and Hammarsjkøld rather as some people read their Bibles, with a sense of their literal inspiration.) *East Coker* always has something to say. I am already looking forward now to evenings 'under the lamplight', - the evening with the photograph album - for I have taken a thousand photographs since I set out. It was, of course, *East Coker* which had produced "Old Men Ought to be Explorers" and it ends, significantly, with "In my end is my beginning". But today it was, in fact, *Little Gidding* which 'spoke'.

As the Boeing was thrusting forward over the coast of France to the end of the journey, I read:

> "Here, the intersection of the timeless moment
> Is England and nowhere. Never and always."

And as we crossed further into England, I read the passage where Eliot virtually says again what he had said in *East Coker*:

> "And to make an end is to make a beginning.
> The end is where we start from."

Eric James

As we drew near to London I read:

> "With the drawing of this Love and the voice of this
>   Calling
> We shall not cease from exploration
> And the end of all our exploring
> Will be to arrive where we started
> And know the place for the first time."

In the last five lines of *Little Gidding* Eliot includes the words of the Lady Julian of Norwich, which are equally the words of Christ and of the Buddha: "And all shall be well and all manner of things shall be well."

I read them above the white clouds just as we were breaking through them into the outskirts of London. It was easy to say them above the clouds, unclouded blue above and brilliant fluffy white clouds below. I think I could say them in Windsor Great Park, (in view from the air now), English green trees and grass, with flashes of gold from the sun. The Sister in Mother Teresa's Order seemed to be saying them with her smile when she received us into her Dormashalah in Calcutta. No one could say they were an escape from reality there. I must see if I can say them in Southwark; and go on saying them.

Coming in to land now.

> "Old men ought to be explorers
> Here or there does not matter
> We must be still and still moving
> Into another intensity
> For a further union....a deeper communion....
> .....In my end is my beginning."

EPILOGUE

A letter to my sixteen year-old great-nephew, Charlie Rowland, on his return from three weeks in China, with the Yorkshire Schools' Exploring Society.

My dear Charlie,
November 3rd 2005

It was lovely of you to make a special journey from Yorkshire to London, to come and see me - and to borrow your father's laptop, so as to show me your marvellous photographs of China.

What struck me most of all was the huge contrast between the teeming population of a city like Beijing and the rural areas, where you were travelling into the mountains, by horseback and camel and 'bus and train and, of course, on foot.

You reminded me of Walt Whitman's lines - which Vaughan Williams set to music (and which I first heard in Southwark Cathedral, before I was ordained - indeed, when I was just a year or two older than you are now):

Darest thou now, O Soul,
Walk out with me toward the Unknown Region

In fact, your journey reminded me of my own six-month journey, in 1972 - to Nigeria, Uganda, Zambia, South Africa, Australia, New Zealand, Fiji, the Solomon Islands, Vanuatu, New Guinea, Australia, Singapore, Hong Kong, India and Sri Lanka. All the countries I visited were then for me 'unknown regions'. Recently, I've been reading again the journal I kept of my journey. (I called it *Old Men Ought to be Explorers* - quoting T S Eliot's *East Coker*.)

What hit me is how changed each country I visited is from what it was like thirty or so years ago - South Africa, for instance. (Each country now deserves a separate essay *Thirty Years On*.......; but not by *me*!)

People have changed, too - and so have I. Jan Mugerwa - whom I baptised as a child, in the Chapel of Makerere University, Uganda - is now a solicitor in London! I conducted his marriage to Amal, and, alas, buried their first child, Alexander. Mercifully they have two more children, Louis and Gabriel. They now live not far from me in Dulwich, South London, and we see each other quite often.

I'm also very aware of the number of friends I made - or met - on my journey, who are now dead. Of course, I myself am in my eighties - and, as you will have observed - am now somewhat frail.

The death of friends - and my own age - give another meaning to:

Darest thou now, O Soul,
Walk out with me toward the Unknown Region.

Your coming to see me has given yet another meaning to the phrase.

When a sixteen-year-old journeys to meet an eighty year-old whom he has hardly ever met before, it takes a good deal of courage and daring. It was, I think, very brave of you to journey towards the 'Unknown Region' of your great-uncle.

Friendship, I think, always involves a sort of journey towards the Unknown Region. (But, of course, so does playing the violin, as you do - and getting 'inside' Shakespeare - as you do; and getting alongside the people with whom you work in the restaurant on a Saturday evening.) And going on a 'gap year' will involve other 'Unknown Regions'.

I'm so glad you say you hope you will be able to get down to see me again after Christmas. Au revoir!

Lots of Love
from
Eric

PS Forgive me if this letter has become a kind of sermon. Your turn next!

Postscript after my Fall

Two sermons preached by Eric James

Sermon preached by Canon Eric James
at St Botolph's, Aldgate
August 27th 2006

Some of the best sermons are the shortest - like the parable of the Good Samaritan! I want to preach you a very short sermon this morning, for Bank Holiday!

It is now six months since a stroke - most probably - caused me to fall to the bottom of the stairs in my home and be taken off to hospital and, in due course, to have twenty-seven stitches put in my head. I had been preaching that morning at St Paul's, Covent Garden. It was Chris Eldridge, from here, who drove me to St Paul's, Covent Garden, and who drove me after the service to lunch and then drove me home, and it was he who called the ambulance which took me to St Thomas's Hospital, and who stayed with me there awhile.

Since then I have received much care and kindness in four different hospitals or infirmaries. I cannot pretend the experience has been pleasant, although I have been supported and surrounded by a wonderful collection of friends.

I have learnt a lot in these months, not least about old age and old people. (I was myself eighty-one last Good Friday when I was in St Thomas's Hospital.)

I do not think of myself as particularly devout, but when a friend, a fellow priest - a good deal younger than I - suggested some words of scripture to assist my recovery, I knew he had spoken to my condition, and indeed to my soul. That verse was John 21 verse 18: "When you were young, you girded yourself and walked where you would; but when you are old you will stretch out your hands and another will gird you and carry you where you do not wish to go."

In the last six months, and in four hospitals, I have encountered many old people who are no longer "where they want to be". Some illness of old age prevents their being where they want to be - for example, arthritis, diabetes, Alzheimer's, or some other illness may prevent them getting up and down stairs in their own home.

We are, most of us, living longer now than we used to, but often old age brings us some new infirmity.

It is not always easy to get help - especially at home - but that is what old people often need. Indeed help *when and where you require it* is a growing need for many. People talk about *young* people and *their* needs but I believe we now need to think of the needs of the elderly as much as of the young.

Fifty years ago, when I was a vicar in South London, I opened an old people's club in the large end room of my vicarage in Camberwell. I can still remember seeing on the first day Mr Buckler, an old man with a white stick, at the vicarage door. "Goodness" I said to him "How many more of you?" "Didn't you expect so many?" he said. "No", I continued, "I expected a few on the first day and that numbers would then slowly increase." "Then you can't know how lonely we are", he rasped.

I told that story many years later to an old people's club in a church in Chelsea. A woman got up when I'd finished speaking and said, "Just because we here have *money*, it does not mean that *we're* not lonely - this afternoon is the most important one of the week for most of us." People called out their agreement.

Loneliness is a particular feature of old age. I should rather like every Christian congregation, including this one, to address itself to the question of the elderly and to examine what it has to offer - indeed, not least what each member of the congregation has to offer to the other - and to acknowledge the experience the elderly have to offer.

To end, I commend my text to you - John 21 verse 18:

"When you were young, you girded yourself and walked where you would; but when you are old you will stretch out your hands and another will gird and carry you where you do not wish to go."

Sermon preached by Canon Eric James at the Wedding of Stuart and Susie Owen

St Mary's, Hendon
September 30th 2006

Words fail when I come to thank Susie and Stuart for inviting me not only to come to their wedding, but to preach at it. But I'm not really going to preach: I'm going to gather my thoughts under one heading - one word - and that word is the single word 'Mystery'.

I choose that word for two quite different reasons.

First: St Paul in his letter to the Ephesians refers to marriage as a 'great mystery' - with which, of course, some of you - who happen to be married - will solidly agree!

But the main reason that I want to talk about 'Mystery' is because Susie - when she came to see me on Saturday, a month ago - told me with great enthusiasm that she had suddenly come to the conclusion - had suddenly discovered - that Stuart was the person she wanted to marry: the person with whom she wanted to share the rest of her life. It was a sudden and overwhelming discovery.

We are here today to celebrate Stuart's discovery of Susie and Susie's discovery of Stuart.

That was the first 'Mystery' revealed. But Shakespeare, in the very last lines of his play *King Lear*, tells us to "Take upon us the mystery of things as if we were God's spies". Stuart and Susie have been God's spies - that's why we're here today! - and I think they would encourage every one of us to take upon us the 'mystery of things'.

Marriage is a mystery not least because it means working out who other people are, and who we are ourselves. But there are at least a dozen mysteries involved n marriage. Let me name just a few:

The Mystery of Time: it takes time to discover who people are.

The Mystery of Place: places change us - Stuart is wearing a kilt today!

The Mystery of Persons: everyone is a mystery.

The Mystery of Music, Art and Literature: it's amazing what beauty comes through sound and sight - and can I just say how wonderful it is to come into this church, with its choir and its music.

And the Mystery of Love itself, and of Forgiveness - both hugely important in marriage.

But I think that for all of us who are gathered at a wedding, that wedding is a kind of invitation to be one of 'God's spies'. To look profoundly at one of the most important events in human life, and to pray - not only for the two who are getting married, Susie and Stuart, but to pray for all who will come into being as a result of the wedding, or who may be influenced or affected by it. We pray, for instance, that Stuart and Susie will have their own children, each of them a mystery. We pray that all of us invited to the wedding will see ourselves as 'God's spies'.

Susie is doing her own responsible and demanding secular job. Stuart will be doing the job of a parish priest. Both of them, in their own jobs, as well as together, will have opportunity to be 'God's spies' - will encounter the 'mystery of things'.

There is one more and great mystery - a very important one - which involves us all, not least those who marry.

When I last preached for you, Stuart, it was here at your first Mass in July 2001. Only a year had passed since you had pushed Archbishop Robert Runcie round the garden of Cuddesdon Theological College, Oxford, in a wheelchair. But it wasn't long before he died. I wonder what Robert Runcie is doing now? That's the Mystery. I wouldn't be surprised if he were praying for you and Susie.

The life beyond this life is a great mystery for us all. But we need to think, and pray, as if we were 'God's spies'. Please God, Stuart and Susie, you have a long life together, and much joy: but it is important to be alive to the mystery of things, from the very beginning.

God bless you both, and us all, till we come to his everlasting kingdom.

Printed in the United Kingdom
by Lightning Source UK Ltd.
120031UK00002B/115-144